C000186547

Operation Aleppo
Russia's War in Syria

The Inside Story of Putin's Military Intervention in the Syrian War

By

Tim Ripley

Telic-Herrick Publications, 5 St Andrews Close, Lancaster, LA1 3RL, United Kingdom
www.timripley.co.uk

ISBN 978-0-9929458-2-4
Cover Design: Graham Baines, John Freeman

Operation Aleppo
Russia's War in Syria
The Inside Story of Putin's Military Intervention in the Syrian War
By Tim Ripley

Russia's intervention in Syria in September 2015 caught the world by surprise. Since then Russian bombers, warships and special forces troops have helped turn the tide of the brutal Syria civil war in favour Bashar al-Assad's government in Damascus.

As the war enters its endgame, this book looks at how the Russian intervention unfolded, and its implications in the Middle East and further afield.

Drawing on a wide array of sources - including satellite imagery of Russian forces in Syria, as well as live online monitoring of Russian, Syrian and Iranian aircraft and ship movements – Operation Aleppo gives an unprecedented insight into the most ambitious Russian military campaign since the Soviet intervention in Afghanistan in the 1980s.

About the Author

Tim Ripley has reported on the Russian intervention in Syria for The Sunday Times, The Scotsman, Jane's Defence Weekly and Jane's Intelligence Review since its start in 2015. He has travelled extensively across the Middle East, reporting on conflicts in the region for more than 25 years

Table of Contents

With Thanks

Several individuals have helped in my research during the writing of Operation Aleppo but any errors and omissions are mine alone.

Dr Makram Khoury Machool of the Cambridge-based Centre for the Study of Extremism kindly invited me to speak at the Syria- Six Years On: From Destruction to Reconstruction conference in London in April 2017. This and other events organised by the Centre allowed me to meet many Syrians, of all political viewpoints, and gain invaluable insights into their country. It also allowed me to road test many of my ideas and gather evidence from Syrians who had experienced the war in their country first hand.

My old journalistic colleague Andrew Gilligan was very kind in sharing many insights after his visit to Syria in 2011 to interview President Bashar al-Assad

Vanessa Beeley and the Reverend Andrew Ashdown were also very kind in sharing their experience of visiting Aleppo during the height of the fighting to capture the rebel enclave in 2016, including their meetings with many senior Syrian and Russian military officers. Vanessa is a controversial figure in the Syrian crisis and is regularly verbally and rhetorically attacked by opponents of the Damascus government. She, however, is one of the few non-Syrians to have viewed many key events in the conflict from ground zero so is a valuable first hand witness who deserves to be heard.

Professor Colin Boxall of Lancaster University played a major role in the genesis of this book by giving me access to his amazing collection of photographs of the ancient ruins of Palmyra taken during a visit the site in the 1990s. These proved crucial in the geolocation of many of the images taken during the battles around the iconic city in 2016 and 2017.

Jamie Hunter of Combat Aircraft Magazine and Thomas Newdick of Air Forces Magazine provided important information about the Russian air force order of battle.

A number of individuals helped with the physical production of this book. Angus Batey did sterling work proof-reading. Dave Reynolds helped with the imagery. John Freeman and his colleague Graham Baines put together the book jacket.

The staff at Lancaster University's Sports Centre also provided much hospitality and assistance as I worked on this book in their foyer during my frequent visits to deliver and collect my young sons, Fergus and Joe, from tennis, swimming and climbing lessons over the past three years.

Final thanks must go to my wife, Dr Amanda Cahill-Ripley, for her understanding and perseverance during the writing of Operation Aleppo.

Map
Syria - Geography, Urban Areas and Neighbours

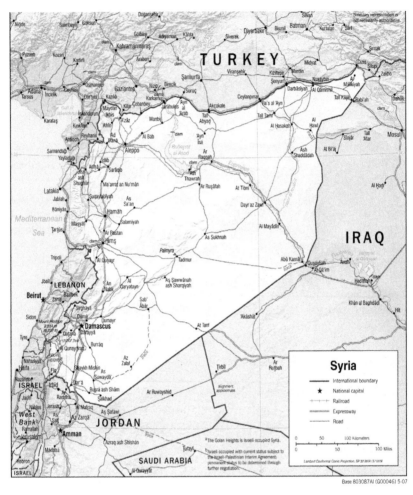

(US Central Intelligence Agency)

Language and Names

Syria has a diverse and ancient cultural, ethnic and linguistic history. This has created a great of confusion over the names of cities, towns, rivers and regions of the country. Specific locations often have different Arabic, Kurdish, Turkish and Iranian/Farsi names. These in turn are often translated into English, Russian and French, adding additional layers of confusion.

As in many civil wars, language has become central to the Syrian conflict and many sides weaponise how they assign names to locations.

For the purposes of this book, I have deferred to using the most widespread English version of names. This is solely for easy of understanding, rather than signifying any political judgement on the status of the location.

Photographs and Maps

The author has attempted to trace and credit all the maps to their originators. If any updates or corrections to these credits are needed they will be incorporated in future editions.

Researching and Writing Operation Aleppo

On a quiet morning in February 2014 I was in my office. Nothing much seemed to be happening in the world and I was getting on trying to finish a couple of long overdue feature articles for defence magazines. I had BBC Radio 5 Live on in the background and was scrolling through some news websites when reports started to emerge about strange events at the main airport on the Crimea peninsula. Unidentified armed men were reported to have taken control of the airport. Soon more reports came in about other sites in the Ukrainian territory being blocked by heavily armed men in green uniforms. They would forever be known as Putin's "little green men". Then the first video clips started to appear online. They were obviously Russian special forces - the famous Spetsnaz - and regular naval infantrymen. All my experience – 30 years of military service and work in the specialist defence media - told me they were Russian troops. Their uniforms, weapons, equipment and the insignia on their vehicles just said "RUSSIANS" in the very big capital letters.

Then something strange happened. Broadcast news media began to ask me for comments. For hours during that day, the main news networks refused to come out and describe the men in Crimea as Russian soldiers. I was told: "The Kremlin is denying they are Russian troops"; "How can you be sure"; or, "We are told they are just disgruntled locals". Western governments were equally confused and were not able or willing to make the call that the Russian military had invaded Crimea. By the time, later in the day, that western governments and news media were willing to name and shame the Russians, it was all over. Thousands of Ukrainian troops on Crimea were blockaded in their bases, the regional parliament was in Russian hands and scores of Russian helicopters were flying in reinforcements. By the end of March 2014, the remaining loyal Ukrainian troops had pulled out of Crimea with their tails between their legs. This was an exercise in the use of strategic surprise on a massive scale. Nothing like this had been seen since the end of the Cold War in 1989. Western governments and the news media were just not able to get their minds around the idea that the Russian President Vladimir Putin would be so audacious as to carry out such a brazen act in the heart of Europe. The "herd mentality" and "group think" of western politicians, diplomats, intelligence analysts, military chiefs, editors, media commentators and journalists just made them unable to believe what was happening. The world had changed.

One of my old friends who worked in the Ministry of Defence in London later provided an important insight that explained much of what happened on that fateful day. The American and British governments have become accustomed to receiving almost real-time intelligence reports on their adversaries and nominal allies from the routine harvesting of global internet traffic by the US National Security Agency and Britain's GCHQ.

"Putin is rightly paranoid about the West's control of the internet and never uses it," said my friend. "On top of that all the old Cold War-era monitoring of Soviet – now Russian – military communications, as well as satellite surveillance of troop, ship and air movements stopped years ago. We were not looking for or expecting trouble from Russia. As a result, we were caught with our pants down in Crimea – the first we knew about the Russian operation was when we saw it on television like everyone else."

Fast forward to the summer of 2015 and the same dynamic was in play in the Middle East. Again, out of the blue, the Russians launched an audacious surprise intervention, this time in Syria. While the Crimea crisis had woken up many western governments and journalists to Putin's modus operandi, there were still many who could not make the leap and get their mind around exactly what the Russians were doing in Syria.

The first indications of Moscow's intervention came from social-media tracking of Russian soldiers by pro-Ukrainian online activists in the late summer of 2015. The Ukrainians had long tried to monitor Russian military operations against their country by tracking the social-media accounts of Moscow's servicemen on Russia's equivalents of Facebook - VKontakte or InContact. Increasing numbers of Russian sailors and naval infantrymen seemed to be in Syria and were posting pictures of their time in the sun. Then Turkish ship-spotters in Istanbul also began to report a surge in Russian transport ships heading south through the Bosphorus into the Mediterranean. By mid-September 2015, construction work was well under way at Hmeinyan airbase to the south of Latakia city in preparation for the arrival of dozens of Russian combat aircraft a few days later.

The strategic surprise was complete again. When Barack Obama met Putin at the United Nations General Assembly in New York at the end of September, the US President warned his Russian counterpart that he would be making a grave mistake if he ordered his air force into action on the side of Syrian President Bashar al-Assad. Russia would be sucked into a quagmire that it would not be able to escape from, said Obama.

Western media commentators joined the chorus. The Russian intervention was "doomed to failure"; "it was a just a ploy to allow the Russian to persuade the Syrian army to launch a coup d'etat against Assad," or "the Russians were just going to secure their naval base in Tartus and let the rest of the country fall to rebel fighters."

It seemed like the Crimea all over again. "Group think" kicked in and seemed to reject any assessments that did not fit the narrative coming from the White House and 10 Downing Street, or major news organisations. The idea that the Russians were actually going to help Assad win the Syrian civil war just did not gain any traction until it was too late. Again I reached out to my friends in the British and American militaries who were perplexed at the unwillingness of their political masters to appreciate that the world had changed. "Our politicians just can't think like the Russians," said a senior British officer. "We had channelled all our intelligence resources in the Middle East – satellites, signals intelligence, cyber, drones - into watching Islamic State so we largely ignored the Syrians and the Russians. All our masters wanted to hear about was; have we found Jihadi John or some other top Islamic State bad guy yet? It was just not considered a priority to track Syrian troop movements or construction activity at their airbases. Our thinking, and that of our politicians, was conditioned by the media view - who in turn got all their information from the rebels - that Assad was doomed and we did not have to worry about him. We discounted anything that he or the Russians could do as having any impact."

It was against this background that I began following the Russian intervention in Syria. The western media, because of its strong affinity and links with the Syrian rebels, had largely ignored any sources linked to the Damascus government. There were few journalists or academic experts who knew anything up-to-date about the Syrian government and military. I soon realised that I would have to start from scratch if I was going to get to the bottom about what the Russians were up to in Syria. This book aims to tell the story of how Russia's armed forces by the end of 2017 delivered their president – and Syria's president – a major military success and transformed the Middle East. It is not a definitive history of the Syrian civil war, just an examination of an important part of the conflict up to December 2017. The Syrian civil war was not over at end of 2017 but its direction of travel was clearly set thanks to the Russian intervention. In early 2018, Syrian troops resumed offensives to clear out the last opposition enclaves in the suburbs of Damascus and elsewhere. US, British and French air forces attacked three targets in the capital and near Homs in April in response to an alleged chemical weapons attack but there was no further Western intervention to change to course of the war.

There is a tidal wave of information coming out Syria - Twitter and Facebook posts; Instagram images; You Tube video clips; news agency reports; non-government organisation assessments; announcements and commentary from armed groups and political parties in Syria; ministers and spokesmen for the US, British, French, Russian and Turkish governments, as well as others, talk daily about events in Syria.

All of this needs to be treated with a hefty dose of scepticism. Everyone involved in the Syria crisis has an axe to grind, to spin their view or to discredit their opponents. This has always been the case in time of war but the "fog of war" hanging over Syria has been magnified by the near impossibility of independent journalists, analysts or aid workers to get anywhere near to the front-lines in Syria, except in rare circumstances on the government side. Foreign journalists and aid workers have long not even been able to visit rebel-held territory because of the very real risk of being kidnapped and sold to Islamic State radicals for beheading. So, finding out what is happening in Syria requires new ideas and methods, many of which in the fairly recent past would have only been available to the intelligence agencies and armed forces of major military powers. This being the 21st Century, there are now some tools that can allow the relatively "unfiltered" or "uncensored" monitoring of aircraft and naval movement. To get to Syria, Russian and Iranian ships and aircraft have to move through internationally controlled airspace and shipping lanes, which means they have to switch on GPS tracking transponders - that in turn can be monitored in real-time on the internet. Sometimes these are switched off but for much of the period of the build-up of Russian forces in the summer and autumn of 2015 these transponders were active, allowing an unprecedented view of Moscow's military deployments.

High resolution satellite imagery of Syria is also available on the open market and this has allowed an unprecedented view of what is happening inside the country. Although there is some time-lag on imagery being posted on line, the imagery available allows the Russian deployment in Syria to be exposed in great detail. Much of this satellite imagery is now hosted on websites, such as Google Earth, Terraserver and Wikimapia, and it allows the provenance of other still and video imagery to be verified. This is a powerful tool to confirm the authenticity of images coming out of Syria. It is a base-line of truth that is very useful to have in your back pocket. The on-line investigative sites www.bellingcat.com and https://informnapalm.org have led the way in this field with their work on the investigation into the shooting down of the Malaysian Airlines aircraft over Ukraine in 2014. However, these organisations have their own agenda; the Ukrainian-based Inform Napalm which is heavily involved in on-line research into the Russian military, calls its contributors "soldiers of the information front" against Moscow.

The Russian government has mounted a high-octane propaganda campaign to back up its military deployments in Syria which has also exposed much of what its troops are doing. Although slavishly pro-Moscow in tone, the imagery put out by TASS, Sputnik News and RT.com is hugely revealing in terms of the exact equipment Russia has sent to Syria, how its troops are operating and where they are based - particularly if compared to satellite imagery.

The western news media make extensive use of pro-rebel blogs, Twitter, Facebook pages and other social media but the Syrian, Iranian and

Russian military also have their own social-media supporters who pump out a torrent of pictures, video clips, troop deployment maps and commentary about the activities of their own forces. Again, this material is imbued with heavy doses of propaganda but it also provides a window on their world to a degree that has never been known before in a major conflict.

When all this material is pulled together it allows a picture to be built up of who is doing what and where on the Russian, Iranian and Syrian side, with a degree of confidence. This is not definitive all the time but there are clearly periods when it is possible to have a high-level confidence in this information.

All this on-line information could be termed the "documents of the digital age". In the wars of the pre-digital age, participants and observers of conflict would record what they saw in letters, diaries or official paper documents. For the wars of the 21st Century new means of communications – cell phones, social media posts, blogs and email – mean there are often no paper records. History has to be sourced in new ways.

Overlying this long-term collection of digital material, I have reached out to my contacts in western armed forces and intelligence organisations to add further information and context. Often their lack of information about Russian and Syrian operations is as telling as what they do know. My contacts in the Russian and Eastern European defence industries have also added further to my understanding of what is happening in Syria and the real capabilities of Moscow's military hardware.

The final piece of the jigsaw has been contacts with diplomatic sources in Europe linked to the Syrian government in Damascus and some of the few western journalists, clergymen and aid workers who have travelled to Syria and, in some cases, met President Assad and his close confidantes in recent years.

This book is the result of this work. It looks at the Syrian war from the view point of Moscow, Damascus and Tehran. Hopefully this will provide new insights and understanding of "the way the world is," not the "way we want the world to be".

Tim Ripley
April 2018

Chapter 1
In the Ruins of Aleppo

The T-72 tank moved cautiously down a narrow street in central Aleppo. A gaggle of Syrian soldiers were waiting in side streets for the tank to silence a rebel sniper who had holed up in a building down the street. When the tank opened fire the street was engulfed by a cloud of dust.

Minutes later a senior Syrian officer walked out into the street from cover and beckoned the soldiers to move forward. He was talking on a radio handset and gesticulating to the soldiers to break cover and continue the advance. Soon the officer and his radio operator joined the advance down the street, while he continued to talk over the radio.

This scene was repeated time and again during the Battle for Aleppo in November and December 2016 as the Syrian army moved to capture the rebel-held enclave in the east of the city.

A few days later, a Russian blogger posted a set of pictures purportedly taken inside the Aleppo headquarters of the Syrian Arab Army's Tiger Force – the unit that was then spearheading the offensive into eastern Aleppo. The pictures showed that Syrian government troops advancing in Aleppo received direct video feeds into their headquarters from Russian Forpost unmanned aerial vehicles (UAVs), or drones, orbiting over the city.

The presence of the Israeli-designed but Russian assembled Forpost system was first confirmed in January 2016 on commercial satellite imagery of the main Russian airbase at Hmeinyan in the coastal province of Latakia. The drones had participated in numerous operations around Syria since then.

The Forpost was the only operational-level UAV system in service with the Russian military in Syria. The procurement of the systems stemmed from a 2009 agreement between the Russian and Israeli governments to allow local production of the IAI Searcher 2 UAV system in Russia. OPK Oboronprom and IAI subsequently established a UAV partnership which led to the JSC "Ural Works of Civil Aviation" in Ekaterinburg setting up an assembly line to put them together for the Russian military.

The layout of the Syrian Army's Tiger Force so-called "special operations room" confirmed that Russian had set up a real-time downlink of imagery from a Forpost operating over Aleppo. A senior Syrian officer, who used the radio callsign "Tiger's Sword", was pictured talking on multiple radios while monitoring the drone imagery of Aleppo's narrow streets.

By western standards the Tiger Force's special operations room appeared to be rather primitive. The quality of the Forpost UAV imagery video displays were nowhere near as sharp or clear as those used with western UAV systems, such as the famous Predator, and there appeared to be limited means to manipulate video feeds. Given that the Russians were late to the drone operations game, this was not really surprising.

The rapid advance by the Syrian army through Aleppo was possible because the rudimentary distribution of UAV video imagery was enough to give the Tiger Force a huge combat advantage. Its commanders had the confidence to advance small units of troops boldly into the opposition held enclave with minimal flank support. Thanks to their Russian eyes in the sky, the Syrian troops could be confident that there was little risk of being attacked unexpectedly.

The presence of a theatre-wide computer display, showing the position of aircraft across Syria and neighbouring countries, in the Tiger Force command post was also a new development. US-led forces have created so-called "recognised air pictures", or RAPs, for more than 20 years and they have become an important tool for the real-time command and control of airpower. This suggested the Russians had established a Syria-wide means to distribute their version of a RAP to front-line land commanders, so they could know when Russian bombers were heading to help them.

Out on the streets of Aleppo, the battle for the city was coming to a bloody climax. The Tiger Force made the first major breakthrough in the rebel lines after a brief series of artillery, rocket and air strikes on the northern fringes of the Hanano Housing Project. Huge columns of smoke and dust could be seen rising over the brutalist 1970s concrete apartment blocks. Columns of Tiger Force infantry, backed by a couple of T-72 tanks and BMP armoured troop carriers, moved forward across open farm fields to enter to the housing project. There can't have been more than 400 troops in the assault force. They met no resistance until they were inside the built-up area. Occasional snipers tried to engage the assault columns. Within a few hours, more than half of the housing project had been cleared.

After halting for the night, the Tiger Force, with its Russian eyes in the sky telling them there were no rebels massing to counter-attack, just kept advancing. On the second day of their advance they completely cleared the housing project and pushed into the old part of the city, with its signature narrow streets and back alleys. The Tiger Force had captured a key district of the rebel enclave without facing any serious resistance – and, by some accounts, not losing any soldiers to enemy fire. The rapid advance of the Tiger Force meant they were just over a kilometre from Syrian lines on the western edge of the rebel enclave. Thousands of rebel fighters were threatened with being encircled in a mini-pocket if the Tiger Force could close the noose. During the coming night the rebel fighters abandoned their positions and fled southwards.

It is a gruesome ritual of the Syrian civil war that victorious soldiers – from all sides – take mobile phone camera "selfie" photographs of their dead enemies and share them on social media. The lack of battlefield body pictures from this period in the battle is evidence of the relatively bloodless nature of this fighting.

Social media was soon full of pictures and videos of thousands of civilians coming out of their homes to greet the advancing Syrian troops. The vast majority of the population of this part of the city did not flee with the retreating rebels. A significant chunk – maybe 8,000 - opted to head into a nearby Kurdish neighbourhood; but the vast majority appeared to decide to stay put in the territory newly controlled by the Damascus government's troops.

The next phase of the battle then unfolded, with small assault units of the Tiger Force being repositioned to attack the Halwaniyah Youth Housing Project a few hundred metres south of the Hanano project. In a heavy rain shower, a column of half a dozen BMP troop carriers delivered the assault troops to the doors of a string of large apartment blocks, while a T-72 tank and an anti-aircraft gun-truck took pot shots at the upper floors of the buildings. Again resistance was minimal; but, for the first time in the battle, the Tiger Force soldiers took the time to pose for selfies with a couple of bodies of their dead enemies.

After a three-day pause to bring up reinforcements and ammunition, the Tiger Force columns began the next phase of their advance, pushing directly west towards the government-held citadel on the western edge of the rebel enclave. This took them to the historic centre of the city, and again, the rapid advance prompted another rebel retreat. There were more dead fighters to be found in the streets but this was still only the occasional body. These were unfortunate fighters who could not find a way to escape. Pictures also emerged of Syrian soldiers guarding groups of cold and sullen-looking young men. Then a torrent of more civilians began to emerge from their houses. This looked like tens of thousands of people, who were carrying all their worldly possessions. They began to walk out of the city in huge columns towards government- and Russian Army-run refugee shelters. They looked shell-shocked and exhausted but seemed happy to be alive.

The rebel fighters were now penned in to a small enclave covering only a few square kilometres in the south of the city. Temperatures were dropping. It was raining constantly. Syrian troops with tanks in support had captured the hills and high-rise buildings overlooking the last rebel enclave. The situation was hopeless and the rebels knew it.

Russian and Turkish diplomats patched together a ceasefire and a plan to evacuate the last rebels and their supporters from the enclave. The world now watched live on television or online as the bedraggled survivors boarded the green-painted buses of the Syrian State Bus Company for the short journey to rebel lines on the western edge of Aleppo. Hundreds of pro-government supporters from two besieged enclaves near Idlib city were moved the other way into Aleppo. Russian soldiers, backed by monitors from the International Committee of Red Cross (ICRC) and the Syrian Red Crescent, co-ordinated the evacuations.

So ended the biggest battle of the Syrian civil war. President Bashar al-Assad's army controlled the country's second city for the first time in four years. Russian President Vladimir Putin also basked in the glory, and - probably justifiably - claimed credit for the victory. For Syria's president, it was a dual victory. Not only had the rebel fighters been driven from the city but the vast majority of the population of the enclave had opted to stay with the government troops. According to ICRC monitors, some 34,000 civilians and rebel fighters had boarded the green buses for the journey to rebel territory around Idlib. Yet in January 2017, the United Nations was reporting that 110,000 civilians from the enclave had gone over to the government side. President Assad also won the battle for the hearts and minds of Aleppo's citizens. In the longer term, this is perhaps the bigger prize and the most important indicator that he will be able to remain in control of Syria when the war ends.

Chapter 2
Syrian War Summer 2015

On an online mapping tool created by the defence-information company, IHS Jane's, Syria's front-lines looked unbelievably complex and confused. This computer generated "map of control" is updated on a near-continuous basis from the online tracking of social-media reports from Syria of territorial gains. Multiple colours representing the territory controlled by the various factions are intertwined and mixed up. For much of the war, the front-lines weaved back and forth across Syria. There were numerous pockets of territory that were besieged by rival forces - and in some cases there were sieges within sieges.

While maps of Syria's battlefields told much of the complexity of the conflict they were not able to portray the unimaginable human suffering that took place across the country. UN statistics from September 2015 painted an apocalyptic picture of a blighted country with some five million people out of its 22 million population now refugees in neighbouring countries or Europe. Of the remainder, some seven million had fled their homes to other parts of Syria. More than 250,000 people – including some 80,000 civilians - were estimated by aid agencies to have been killed in fighting or died from famine and disease. Not surprisingly, many of the survivors were living in primitive conditions and were dependent on international humanitarian aid.

Amid this carnage, a succession of international diplomats had attempted to broker peace deals, ceasefires and access for humanitarian aid. After arriving with good intentions, most gave up and left Syria bitterly disappointed that all the warring sides still seemed determined to settle things on the battlefield.

In mid-2015 rebel commanders – a mix of pro-democracy protesters, defectors from the Syrian army and Jihadi fighters – were vowing to fight on until they over threw Syrian President Bashar al Assad's government in Damascus. The Syrian regime was declaring it would fight on to final victory and the re-establishment of control over all of the country. Kurdish groups wanted to keep control of their enclaves. Out in the eastern desert regions, radical Jihadi fighters from the self-styled Islamic State were proclaiming they would soon march on Rome to overthrow "Crusader Christian" rule of the Middle East and Europe. In the mean-time, the Jihadis set about beheading and burning prisoners alive, as well as trashing the ruins of the ancient city of Palmyra, in a bid to terrorise the population of the towns and cities they controlled across eastern Syria and Iraq.

Every party to the war seemed to have outside backers who bankrolled them with cash, aid and, in some cases weapons. Various rebel groups, were backed by rival outsiders – the United States, Britain, Turkey, Jordan, Saudi Arabia, Qatar, Israel, and the United Arab Emirates. These outside powers all had very different motivations. In the case of the US government, different branches of US President Barack Obama's administration appeared to be backing their own rival groups of Syrian rebels. This confused and fragmented situation seemed to shift over time, and every couple of months the rival Syrian factions would switch their allegiance.

The Syrian government also had the active backing of outside powers - Russia, Iran and Lebanon's Hizbullah movement. For the first four years of the war, Russia kept a trickle of arms flowing to help the Syrian army keep fighting. Iran and Hizbullah sent military advisors and small units of fighters to help bolster the front-lines in key sectors.

That complex and confused IHS Jane's "map of control" did not really provide any kind of flavour of the experience of Syria's war in the summer of 2015 for the country's people. The population and their rulers had become "conditioned" to the state of war and had organised their lives and societies to fight the war. The top-level rhetoric of Syrian leaders, armed factions and political groups was often far divorced from the daily reality of war.

The brutality of the Syrian war was well known to the outside world from daily new and social-media reports of apparently indiscriminate shelling, so-called "barrel bombing" from helicopters, refugees fleeing their homes and chlorine gas attacks. These gave only a partial picture of the Syrian war.

By 2015, the conflict had become a war of survival for all the participants. There was a daily struggle to provide food, water, heat, shelter, work, electricity, telephone and internet connections. While much is made of the dictatorial nature of the Assad regime and the brutal rule of Jihadi fighters, they all needed the support of their populations. To keep their populations fighting they needed to be fed and their homes and lives protected. Leaders who could do this got the loyalty and support of their people. Those that did not soon found their populations would flee or not fight for them. This was "wining hearts and minds" at its most basic.

The Syrian war had increasingly became focused on the control of the things that allowed normal life to continue – food, water, gas, electricity, telephone and internet services. But the psychology of war also meant that on many occasions all the warring factions would find in their interests to co-operate, do deals or trade.

For most of the war, it suited every faction – including Islamic State - to allow the Syrian State Water Company to maintain and operate the country's water resources, dams, pumping stations, water-treatment plants and pipelines. Syria's front-lines never neatly aligned with the water network so it was in everyone's interest to make sure it kept working.

Shutting the water supply down in one location could easily be countered with an enemy shutting it down somewhere else - so for long periods every side saw the benefit of treating the water supply as "neutral". Syria's oil and gas resources were also predominately in the east under the control of Islamic State, so every faction – including the Damascus government – had to do deals with the Jihadis if they wanted to have oil and gas. Up to the summer of 2015 no side could see total victory on the horizon - so trading with the enemy was a logical compromise, if it kept the lights and heaters on. Swaps and ransoms of prisoners and dead bodies were also a routine feature of this wartime trade that kept populations happy and boosted morale at dark moments.

The daily experience of war for most Syrians was not prolonged fighting, 24/7, but short periods of intense violence and then the war would move somewhere else. The vast majority of Syrian front-lines rarely moved. A grim form of siege warfare was being played out.

Front-lines were delineated in cities and towns by large barriers of concrete blocks, barricaded buildings and ramparts made out of scrap vehicles. In the countryside, huge earth barriers called berms weaved between villages to signify the line of control. Bored, poorly paid and ill-equipped militiamen and fighters manned all these lines of control for days on end. These were predominately local men - in some cases women – who pulled shifts to protect their communities. They also helped to stop any outsiders who might fancy looting property, cattle or crops. Not surprisingly, these local fighters often took to levying unofficial taxes or bribes from travellers or trade to supplement their almost non-existent incomes. In areas controlled or dominated by Jihadis the kidnapping, ransoming or sale of foreign aid workers and journalists to Islamic State was profitable business until foreigners decided to keep out of most rebel-held areas of Syria.

Fighting along the thousands of kilometres of Syrian front-lines was sporadic. For weeks on end little would happen in much of the country. When shelling or sniping occurred, there was inevitably a desire to fire back out of revenge with any weapon to hand – rifles, machine guns, rocket launchers or artillery - often with little apparent purpose.

As a result of the patchwork of control, Syria's war had become a "war of sieges" by 2015. Communities surrounded by opponents had to fend for themselves, growing food and husbanding water resources. The other way to survive was to trade with the enemy.

By the summer of 2015 many Syrian cities – Aleppo, Homs, Hama, Idlib, Dier Ez Zor and many suburbs of Damascus – had been fought over for nearly four years and whole districts were in ruins. Much of the country's transport infrastructure was shattered or blocked by front-lines. The most modern parts of Syria's infrastructure were its mobile phone and internet networks, thanks to the widespread addiction to social-media across much of the country. The need to keep smartphones charged in a country with erratic power supplies resulted in Syria having one of highest take up rates for solar panels – the sun, too, was neutral.

Chapter 3
Intervention, Putin Style

At the height of the Russian operation to seize Crimea in February and March 2014 a torrent of video clips and photographs started appearing on-line. Across southern Russian and in Ukraine everyone with a smartphones started uploading images of military activity. Some of it was completely innocuous but a lot of it showed history unfolding as Russian troops and their local supporters took control of the Crimea. As I reviewed this footage on a daily basis one clip jumped out as very telling. A Russian motorist had filmed a convoy of military vehicles heading to Kerch port to be loaded on a ferry to be transported across the waterway to Crimea. There were scores of BTR wheeled armoured troop carriers, BM-21 rocket launchers, artillery pieces and supply trucks in a huge convoy. This was a complete Russian motor rifle regiment on the move. The vehicles looked well maintained, equipment was stowed neatly on top of the troop carriers and the soldiers in the turrets were waving at the passing civilian cars, whose drivers were blowing their horns to cheer the convoy along. At the front of the convoy, the regiment's colonel could be seen standing in the turret of this command vehicle and behind him his unit's battle standard had been unfurled. It looked like a Napoleonic-era battle flag complete with a huge Russian eagle.

This was an army that was proud of its history, that seemed to have confidence in its mission and appeared to have support ordinary Russians. A few weeks later the Ukrainian garrison on Crimea had either surrendered or defected to the Russians. It was a bloodless victory. By the summer, Russian troops and locally recruited militia fighters were locked in intense combat with Ukrainian troops across the Donbass region.

In July 2014 Russian troops conducted a rocket attack on a Ukrainian battalion moving close to the Russian border at a village called Zelenopillya that dramatically demonstrated that Moscow's military could also do serious combat operations, as well dramatic *coup de main* against unprepared opponents. Russian unmanned aerial vehicles, or drones, had spotted the Ukrainian column leave their base and in a matter of minutes a salvo of more than 40 rockets fired from a battery of BM-21 rocket launchers based across the border in Russia proper, had found their mark. These are the 21st Century successors to the World War Two "Stalin's Organs". The rockets, fitted with armour penetrating sub-munitions, detonated over the column. Several hundred sub-munitions rained down, destroying or severely damaging every vehicle. Casualties were heavy, with between 19 and 30 dead and more than 90 soldiers badly wounded. Dozens were killed or wounded in the back of open-top trucks at the end of the column. This was a deadly attack, carried out with ruthless efficiency - but it also showed in dramatic fashion that the Russian military had mastered the combining drone surveillance technology with long-range rocket systems. In western armies the attack sent a shiver down the spines of senior officers, who began to fear what would happen to their own troops if they had to go up against Russian forces. Whole battalions could be annihilated, with no way to defend themselves.

The 2014 Crimea and Donbass crisis demonstrated to the West that Russia's armed forces had regained the self-confidence and competence they had lost in the 1990s during the chaotic rule of Russian President Boris Yeltsin. The brutal and shambolic performance of the Russian military during the wars in Chechnya tarnished both its international and domestic reputation. Soviet-era generals, tactics and equipment had all failed dramatically in fast-moving battles with Chechen insurgents, resulting in thousands of Russian conscripts dying in horrific circumstances. It was worse than Afghanistan. Attempts to avoid military service among young Russian men reached unprecedented levels and the Kremlin began to look to professionalise its armed forces. The brief 2008 war against Georgia had shown that Russia's army was trying to turn itself around but it rapidly needed an injection of 21st Century technology to really transform itself.

Fortunately for Russia's armed forces, the country's president for much of the 21st Century, Vladimir Putin, was a keen supporter of military reform. Although he had never served in the Soviet Army, Putin had long associated military power with national and political power. After becoming president for the first time in 2000 he backed increased military budgets, military reform and improved professionalism. For the first time since the Second World War, Putin approved the purchase of new hardware from overseas, including amphibious landing ships from France, surveillance drones from Israel and armoured troop carriers from Italy. He took every opportunity to be photographed with soldiers and military hardware, including famously taking the controls of a Tupolev Tu-160 strategic bomber and sporting naval uniforms when visiting warships, as part of his macho image.

Moscow's top brass, while welcoming Putin's interest in promoting military modernisation, came to fear their new president. Failures that embarrassed Putin were dealt with ruthlessly and a dozen senior naval officers linked to the sinking of the submarine Kursk in 2000 were removed from their posts. In a sign that 21st Century Russia was not Stalin's Soviet Union, the disgraced officers were not shot or shipped to the Arctic Gulag on prison trains but were allowed to shuffle off to become bureaucratic functionaries in local government far away from Moscow. The Crimea crisis was a major turning point for Russian foreign policy under Putin. His nostalgia for the Soviet Union's great-power status was well known, but events in Ukraine in February 2014 were a major challenge to the Russian president. His ambitions to regain Russia's international position as a major power were a key part of his internal agenda, which portrayed him as the leader who had returned stability to the country and made the world respect Russia again. For Putin, the previous 20 years had been dominated by a litany of attempts by the West, led by the United States, to topple and overthrow Russia's traditional allies. The 2011 intervention against Libya had been the last straw for Putin, as he believed the US and its allies had overstepped their authority from the United Nations Security Council to protect civilians. Instead, the West had overthrown the Libyan strongman Muammar Gaddafi, a long-time Soviet and Russian ally.

Fast forward to February 2014 and the street protests that were swirling around Kiev and ultimately led to Putin's ally, Viktor Yanukovych, fleeing to Russia. Attempts by the European Union to entice Ukraine to take up associated membership were seen by Putin as another Western plot to undermine Russia's strategic influence in an important neighbouring country. This could not be allowed to stand, said Putin. Within a matter of days, he had ordered the operation to seize Crimea. This, in-effect, became a new "Putin doctrine". Russia's friends and allies around the world could, in future, rely on Moscow's protection.

The Crimea operation proved popular at home, despite the impact of western economic sanctions. The Crimea peninsula had a large ethnic Russian population and was home to the headquarters of the Russian Black Sea Fleet, so its return to "mother Russia" was a major coup for Putin. The war that broke out in the Donbass soon afterwards was less popular but it was nevertheless portrayed as a drive to protect Russians from foreign oppression. The lessons of Chechnya weighed heavily on Putin and the involvement of Russian soldiers was cloaked in secrecy. Only professional or contract soldiers were deployed into the Donbass region to avoid the ire of the parents of conscripts. The relatives of combat casualties were told they had been killed in training accidents.

In this context, it was not a surprise when, in the late spring and summer of 2015 that Putin reacted the way he did when reports of battlefield reverses for President Bashar al-Assad's forces started to reach Moscow. Putin had already intervened diplomatically once before to help Assad in 2013, when he brokered a deal with the Americans to disarm Syria of its chemical weapons to head off US airstrikes after a poison gas attack in a Damascus suburb.

This time the situation appeared even more dangerous. Assad's troops looked beleaguered on several fronts. An alliance of Jihadi and "moderate" rebels backed by the US, Turkey and the Arab Gulf states had advanced and captured Idlib. They were pushing towards Latakia and Hama in a bid to cut the capital, Damascus, off from the Mediterranean coast. All of eastern Syria, except for small enclaves in Dier Ez Zor and the north-eastern Kurdish regions, were controlled by the Islamic State. The ancient ruins of Palmyra in the centre of the country had been seized by Islamic State forces and they were continuing to push westward to take control of all of Syria's oil and gas fields. Damascus was ringed by several rebel enclaves and the city centre was regularly being shelled, mortared and rocketed.

Another alliance of rebels, backed by the US and Gulf Arab states was pushing north across the Jordanian border. In the north west, government troops in Syria's second city, Aleppo, were only supplied by a precarious desert road that was regularly cut by rebel and Islamic State raids. Morale in Syria's army was at rock bottom after a string of defeats. It only seemed a matter of time before the Syrian military suffered an unrecoverable battlefield reverse.

Putin's decision-making in the run-up to the Russian intervention is shrouded in secrecy. This is the Russian leader's modus operandi and few people outside his inner circle know exactly what he is going to do next. As per the new "Putin doctrine", the Russian leader was not prepared to allow the Assad government to fall, permitting the West and its allies in Turkey and the Arabian Gulf to "claim his scalp". Russia was going to come to his help.

From the timeline of when Russian ships and aircraft began deploying to Syria it is clear that the major strategic decisions and planning took place in late June or July. The first ships carrying the equipment, materiel and personnel began to sail from Black Sea ports in early August and were spotted by observers in Turkish capital Istanbul as they passed through the Bosphorus.

Some of the most detailed insights into Putin's decision-making come from Iranian and Israeli sources. Surprisingly they both identify Major General Qassem Soleimani, the commander of the Iranian Revolutionary Guards Corps Quds Force, as the driving forces behind persuading the Russian leader to intervene in Syria in the way he did. As commander of the Quds Force, Soleimani knew Syria and Lebanon well from his role in working with the Lebanese Shia military force, Hizbullah. The Iranians had come to similar conclusions that the war in Syria was approaching a tipping point. The Tehran government was particularly worried about Islamic State, which had pushed into Iraq from its bases in eastern Syria and was threatening to overthrow the pro-Iranian government in Baghdad. Syria was seen by Tehran as a vital bridge to Hizbullah in Lebanon that must not be allowed to fall.

Across the Middle East, Soleimani, is a legendary or infamous figure, depending on which side of the region's political, sectarian and religious divides you sit. For Iranians, the charismatic 60-year-old is the country's best battlefield commander who rose to command a combat division in the Iran-Iraq war while still in his 20s. He then commanded the Quds Force, which ran clandestine missions across the Middle East, helping Hizbullah to fight and blunt Israel's 2006 invasion of Lebanon and then controlling Shia militia forces in Iraq during the American occupation between 2003 and 2009. As a result of these activities, and his role advising Assad during the early years of the Syrian civil war he was put on United Nations, US and European Union sanctions lists, accused of human-rights abuses and links to terrorism.

Despite his international notoriety, Soleimani is closely linked to the highest levels in the Iranian government and religious authorities, so he routinely undertakes very sensitive military, political and military missions on behalf of Tehran. Although the US State Department has him on one of their terrorism watch-lists, the US military and Central Intelligence Agency, certainly respect his expertise and realise he has been an important ally in the war against the Sunni Jihadis of Islamic State. When the Iraqi government was on the verge of collapse in the summer of 2014 as Islamic State fighters rampaged into Mosul, Tikrit and Fallujah, it was Soleimani who rallied the Iraqi military and Shia militia fighters to hold the line outside Baghdad.

Soleimani reportedly made a number of trips to Moscow in early summer of 2015 to meet Russian military chiefs, including defence minister Sergey Shoygu, to pitch his plans to help prop up the Syrian army. Russian officials also visited Tehran to meet their Iranian counter parts. The plans proposed by Soleimani envisaged Russian air power, arms supplies and advisors bolstering the Syrian military. While Iranian-led, trained and equipped groups of Shia militia forces to fight on the ground alongside Assad's troops.

The first phase of the intervention would to be establish firm blocking positions to stop further rebel advances and restore the morale of the Syrian military. Once the situation was stabilised, offensive operations could be launched to retake key land, cities and towns. Changing the psychological dynamic of the war appeared to be central to Soleimani's plans, which was why Russia's intervention had to be public, dramatic and big enough to make it clear to everyone – inside and outside Syria – that Russia was throwing its full military, political and diplomatic weight behind the Assad regime. This was not to be a limited intervention but a decisive stroke to change the course of the war - and everyone needed to know this. It would have a decisive impact inside Syria, hopefully breaking the morale and will to fight of the main rebel groups. When the Iranian general's plans made their way to Putin, he apparently was enthusiastic. It would stop the fall of a key Russian ally to Western-backed rebels by keeping Syria's government structure intact, give Moscow a top seat at any peace talks to end the Syrian conflict, and so re-establish Russia as a Middle East power. An important by-product of this would be gaining access for Russian companies to Syrian oil and gas resources, as well as re-opening Syria as a market for Moscow's defence companies. By limiting Russia's involvement to predominately air power and professional soldiers on the ground, Putin would not risk another bloody Afghan or Chechen quagmire that would costs the lives of conscript soldiers and generate a "coffin factor" back home.

Soleimani's plans would also have appealed to Putin's reputed interest in covert operations, as well as his sense of political theatre. Just as in Crimea, Russia's intervention would wrong foot the Americans and show Putin as a decisive leader. If Putin ever had any doubts about intervening in Syria, he has not shown it. He publicly announced the intervention at the United Nations in September 2015, hosted Assad in Moscow and Sochi, and welcomed home Russian veterans from Syria at lavish medal ceremonies in Kremlin.

Chapter 4
The Execution

On a rainy morning in October 2015 the huge silhouette of a 4,000-ton Russian Navy tank-landing ship could just be seen in the gloom of the Bosphorous Straits. A Turkish Navy cutter guided the Russian vessel - loaded with arms and supplies destined for Syria - through the ferries and merchant ships which criss-cross the busy waterway that divides Asia and Europe.

The Aleksander Otrakovskiy was one of six Russian ships to head south to Syria over the previous week, putting flesh on President Vladimir Putin's rhetoric of support for Bashar al Assad in the Kremlin only days before. The relentless shuttle of supply ships prompted the Turks to nickname the armada the "Syria Express".

At the heart of Putin's decision to intervene in Syria was a major logistic operation to set up and sustain the Russian military contingent in the country, as well as provide the Syrian military with new arms and equipment. This complex logistic operation was one of the most visible aspects of the Russian mission to Syria thanks to a mix of open-source monitoring tools, such as live air-traffic control websites. Photographs, apparently posted by Russian military personnel in Syria, have added further details of the logistic build-up that had been underway around Latakia in Syria.

The build-up of Russian forces in Syria was also recorded in detail by Turkish amateur ship-spotters, who begun posting photographs and videos of Moscow's ships online. In July 2015 only two supply ships headed south but in August one of the ship photographers, Yörük Işık, started to post pictures showing trucks, cargo containers and other military kit hidden under camouflage nets on the decks of seven Russian ships. Işık described the ships as "packed to the gunnels with military equipment". In September, the number of ships heading south reached 12 and during October it surged to 17 ships, rising to 74 in total by the end of the year. "The pace of this traffic has revved up our hobby — we almost can't keep up with all the ships," said Işık.

Although Turkey has vigorously denounced Putin's intervention in the Syrian war and incursions in its airspace by Russian jets, it was powerless to stop the "Syria Express" because of international treaties guaranteeing free navigation through the Bosphorous Straits.

The Russians made little effort to hide their power play, with sailors and soldiers on the decks of the ships in the Bosphorous using selfie sticks to take pictures with Istanbul's historic landmarks as the background. Moscow's soldiers also uploaded pictures online from Syria's Tartus port, showing hundreds of troops, scores of vehicles and tons of hardware being off-loaded.

British military sources said the "Syria Express" quickly had an impact, with deliveries of munitions and spare parts for the Syrian air force allowing the regime to increase its rate of air strikes by 40% during October 2015.

With the war in Syria escalating as the Russian-backed offensive against rebel fighters gained momentum, the demand for arms grew so much that the Russian Navy began to hire civilian cargo ships to bolster the "Syria Express". It had bought up two ex-Turkish freighters, the Alican Deval and Dadali - soon renamed respectively, Dvinista 50 and Vologda 50 – and they were soon flying the flag used by Russian Navy auxiliaries. Shipping industry sources said the purchase of these ships was needed because much Russian ammunition and artillery propellant charges was so unstable that they would fail international health and safety rules and could not be carried on chartered vessels without invalidating their insurance cover.

While Russian supply ships had begun moving during the summer months of 2015, the major airlift operations involving Russian, Syrian and Iranian aircraft only got high gear in mid-September.

The Russian Aerospace Force launched an "airbridge" to sustain its military contingent in Syria with 39 flights by a variety of transport aircraft in September and some 44 flights the following month. These flights passed through controlled civil airspace in Iran, Iraq and Syria and so were visible on live air traffic control monitoring websites, which used open-source ADS-B transponder-based tracking data.

There were almost daily flights by cargo-carrying Antonov An-124 Ruslan and Ilyushin Il-76 transport aircraft into Lakatia and every three or four days a passenger-carrying Tupolev Tu-154 made the hop to the main hub for Russian combat aircraft in Syria. A number of Tu-154s also staged via airports in Tehran, suggesting they were moving Iranian personnel into Syria.

This huge logistic operation was aimed at delivering the Russian Aerospace Force's air group of strike jets to Bassel al-Assad International Airport in Latakia province, which as well as being the regional civilian airport for Syria's coast region was also home to the helicopter squadron of the Syrian Navy.

During late August and early September satellite imagery showed the Russians were installing hundreds of prefabricated buildings, new air traffic control facilities, aircraft fuel stores, maintenance hangers and ammunition bunkers. Imagery from inside the Russian airbase, posted on social media in September and October, showed the widespread use of prefabricated building to accommodate Russian service personnel. A ring of earthwork defence was also thrown up around the base. Fuel trucks and other vehicles needed to support the aircraft were unloaded at the Russian-controlled section of the port at Tartus, just down the coast. More than a dozen T-90 tanks and more than 30 BTR-82 troop carrying vehicles soon arrived to protect the base, along with hundreds of Russian marines from the 810th Naval Infantry Brigade of the Black Sea Fleet. These were the very soldiers who had spearheaded the seizure of Crimea from the Ukrainians the year before and became famous as Putin's "little green men".

On 18th September the first Russian combat aircraft began arriving at what had now been re-named Hmeinyan airbase. This was now almost exclusively a Russian base – the Syrian Navy had to move their helicopters to a newly constructed heliport a few miles away and civilian flights were temporarily halted to free up landing slots for Russian military aircraft.

The Russian jets arrived in three waves. First were four Sukhoi Su-30 fighters on 18th September which took off from an airbase in southern Russian, flew over Iranian and Iraqi airspace, and were refuelled in flight from an Ilyushin Il-78 Midas tanker to allow them to reach Latakia. These were Russia's most powerful fighters and they immediately changed the balance of air power over Syria and the Eastern Mediterranean. The next day, a squadron of a dozen Sukhoi Su-25 ground attack jets, known as Rooks by the Russian aviators, flew into after a refuelling stop at an airbase in Iran. A Russian Ilyushin Il-76 transport "shepherded" each cell of four Su-25s on their ferry flight to Syria. This was the first time foreign aircraft had operated from an Iranian airfield since the 1979 Islamic Revolution and it demonstrated in graphic form that Moscow and Tehran were united in their endeavour to support Damascus. On 20th September, the next contingent of Russian jets, some 12 Sukhoi Su-24Ms made the journey to Hmeinyan airbase, again with the aid of air-to-refuelling from Il-78s.

The Russian strike force was completed on 26th September when four Sukhoi Su-34s arrived at Hmeinyan airbase. These jets are capable of dropping western-style smart munitions and they gave the Russian Air Group in Syria a precision strike capability. While each squadron of aircraft came from a specific airbase, the pilots were drawn from the across the Russian Aerospace Force to ensure the most experienced personnel were involved in the most high-profile operation ever undertaken by the service. When President Putin hosted a glitzy Kremlin ceremony in March 2017 to decorate veterans of the Syrian campaign it became clear that many of the pilots of the first squadrons deployed to Hmeinyan airbase were instructors and test pilots. A strong contingent of technical experts from the Sukhoi enterprise and other Russian aerospace companies also went to Syria to make sure there were no technical glitches. A number of the ferry flights of the Russian jets to Hmeinyan airbase were filmed by rebel activists in north-west Syria as they flew overhead in formation with the Il-76s and Il-78s. This footage was quickly posted on-line. The transport and tanker aircraft "shepherding" the jets also showed up on the Flightfinder Radar 24 website as they moved across Iranian, Iraqi and Syrian air space. Within days, satellite images had appeared on major media outlets around the world showing rows of Russian fighter jets at Hmeinyan airbase.

This was a very public display of Moscow's air power and it appeared to have been deliberately done to demonstrate to the United States and its allies across the Middle East that Russia was a player again in the region. That fact that Iraq, nominally a major US ally in the Middle East, had granted the Russians overflight rights, probably at the behest of Tehran, was a very public slap in the face to Washington. Only days before, the US State Department had requested US allies in Europe and the Middle East not allow Russian aircraft overflight rights.

As the Russian fighter jets were making their way to Syria and generating huge headlines, giant Antonov An-124s delivered more than a dozen Mil Mi-24P attack helicopters to Hmeinyan, along with five Mil Mi-8AMTSh transport helicopters. The Mi-24Ps had been the mainstay of the Russian attack helicopter force since the 1970s and had achieved fame in the Afghan campaign in the 1980s. Known as the "Crocodile" or the "flying tank" to its crews, the Mi-24 is heavily armoured and can fire unguided rockets and guided anti-tank missiles. It has a 30mm cannon fitted under in a turret under its nose.

The final elements of the Russian Group of Forces in Syria began arriving between mid September and early October, with an artillery and rocket contingent from the Russian Ground Forces unloading its equipment at Tartus. Built around the 120th Artillery Brigade, but with sub-units from a number of other artillery brigades, this force boasted an array of powerful weapons, including a battery of around eight 2A65 MSTA-B 152mm towed howitzers, a battery of half a dozen BM-21 multiple-launch rocket launchers and a battery of a dozen D-30 122mm towed howitzers. The brigade also had several TOS-1A rocket launchers that were fitted with thermobaric warhead-tip rockets and a handful of BM-30 Smerch long range rocket launchers. While the D-30 guns would be positioned to defend Hmeinyan airbase, the remainder of the brigade's weapons, as well as several teams of artillery spotters and a number of command post vehicles, started to move away from Tartus in early October and began moving towards front-line positions in Latakia and Hama provinces to support the Syrian army.

Across Syria in September, small teams of Russian officers started to spread out to Syrian army headquarters to set up liaison teams. They worked to establish a "ground truth" of the battlefield and pass on requests for air support. Small detachments of Russian Special Forces, or Spetsnaz, and Russian Airborne Forces were also sent out to act as advisors and trainers to Syrian army units in key sections of the front-line.

They were accompanied by forward air controllers to direct air strikes onto their targets.

Photographs of these Russians and their GAZ Tigr utility vehicles because increasingly common on social media sites linked to the Syrian military at this time. The Russian soldiers all appeared to have very new uniforms, helmets and body armour.

In Damascus, the commander of the Russian Group of Forces in Syria, Colonel General Alexander Dvornikov, set up his headquarters in the Ministry of Defence building in the centre of the city to work with his Syrian and Iranian counter parts. Dvornikov had been personally selected by Putin over an air force officer, despite the mission being heavily dependent on air power. Apparently the general first met the Russian president in Berlin in the final days of the Soviet presence in East Germany and had gained his trust. He had also served with some distinction in the North Caucasus operations between 2000 and 2003.

To help make their coalition with the Iranians and Iraqis work smoothly, military liaison teams headed by senior generals were also sent to Tehran and Baghdad to work in the Russian embassies there and establish contact with the Iraqi and Iranian governments and military. Securing and co-ordinating overflight rights was vital to the Russian operation and these teams also included intelligence operatives to pick up information on Syrian rebels and Islamic State. The Baghdad liaison team would also have the job of telling the Americans when the first Russian air strikes were to begin, although the timing of this was a closely guarded secret.

By the end of September the Russians probably had around 5,000 military personnel in Syria. All of them were professional, known to Russians as contract soldiers. Many of the officers were veterans of the conflicts in the Caucasus in the 1990s and early 2000s but few had any experience of the type of operation they were about to participate in. During the 1970s the Soviets launched intervention missions in Ethiopia, Angola and Afghanistan with mixed results but few of the veterans of these operations were left in uniform. The Russians had participated in UN and NATO peacekeeping missions in the Balkans and had closely studied US-led interventions in Iraq and Afghanistan. Russian military literature was full of articles analysing the lessons of these missions. The Russian operation in Syria seemed to copy many aspects of western intervention forces, such as prefabricated accommodation and mess halls, media briefings and a focus on humanitarian aid to the civil population. But the Russians also applied a big lesson from recent western interventions and their own failed Afghan campaign. They did not put a big force of conventional troops on the ground in Syria.

Just as the Russians were building up their forces, the Iranians also began a smaller-scale airlift to move their own military personnel and hundreds of Shia militia fighters to Syria.

Open-source flight tracking also revealed many details of a surge in flights from Tehran to Syrian airports. Several large transport aircraft were identified in September and December 2015 flying back and forth across Iraqi airspace to both the Syrian capital Damascus and Latakia airport, in north-west Syria, which had become the hub of Russian military air operations in the country.

In the period from 17th September, two flight to Damascus by the Islamic Republic of Iran Air Force (IRIAF) Boeing 747 Jumbo jets were recorded by ADS-B flight tracking systems and posted on open-source websites. The second flight was identified taking off from Damascus on 14th October and then headed east but its transponder was switched off as it approached Iraqi air space.

The IRIAF's four Boeing 747-200s and five Boeing 747-100s have a passenger capacity of between 450 and 550, which made them the likely means of moving significant numbers of Iranian troops to Syria. Depending on the configuration employed, the Iranian 747 could also carry large volumes of cargo - between 5,700 and 300 cubic feet - allowing them to carry significant amounts of military supplies.

Two flights by Mahan Air BAe Avro RJ-85s, which can carry up to 112 passengers, were also identified flying into Latakia airport from Tehran during the third week of October. According to local media reports, the airport had been closed to civilian air traffic since early October due to Russian military presence so the flights by the Mahan Air jets suggested a military purpose. The airline had been accused by the US Treasury of providing logistic support to the Iranian Revolutionary Guards Quds Force, adding to the evidence of a military nature of the flights.

Moscow's involvement in the Syria-Iran "air-bridge" emerged when two Russian Air Force Tupolev Tu-154s, with a capacity of up to 180 passengers, were tracked flying from Tehran to Damascus and Latakia.

The Syrian Arab Air Force was also involved in the operation, dispatching one of its four Ilyushin Il-74M/T airlifters to Tehran on at least four occasions during September. These jet transports can carry up to 120 passengers, depending on the configuration.

All the flights between Syria and Iran involved the aircraft routing over Iraqi airspace, suggesting the open co-operation of Iraqi authorities and subsequently the acquiesce of the US-led coalition air forces which operated combat aircraft in Iraqi and Syrian airspace.

The ADS-B tracking data is openly available on several websites but is not considered a complete record of all aircraft in the Middle East because it does not include older aircraft not fitted with the devices and operators can turn the devices off if they wish their aircraft to "disappear". Although it is possible to identify aircraft movements from ADS-B transponder data it is not possible to gain any insight of their cargoes. If all the identified aircraft were carrying passengers, then in the region of 1,600 Iranian and Shia militia personnel could have been carried to Syria during a four-week period in September and October 2015. This would confirm media reports that "high hundreds" of Iranian military and Shia militia personnel had been moved to Syria, rather than the "thousands" as some reports suggested.

As well as stepping up its air bridge to Syria, the Iranians also dispatched two Lockheed C-130 Hercules aircraft to Damascus International Airport to begin airdropping supplies to predominately Shia besieged enclaves in north-west Syria. The Zahraa-Nubul, Foua and Kefraya enclaves had be left surrounded by rebel offensives in Idlib and Aleppo provinces, leaving several thousand people cut off. The Iranian government was very concerned about the fate of these enclaves. The opening of land corridors to them was a top priority for the Iranian-backed Shia militia forces in Syria and this featured heavily in recruiting material for militia fighters in Iran, Iraq and Afghanistan. By sending its C-130s to Damascus, the Iranians were deploying their air force outside their home territory for the first time since the 1979 revolution. Interestingly, the Iranians did not send any combat aircraft to Syria to support the Russian air group: perhaps they calculated that the Israelis would consider this a provocation and strike at them.

Although most US and European airlines had steered clear of Syrian airspace since 2011, the beleaguered Middle East country's government had made great efforts to keep open civil aircraft routes into Damascus, so flight tracking data was still made available. This revealed that the Syrian air force's fleet of four Ilyushin Il-76s, which operate under the flag of the country's state-owned airline, were making up to three daily flights from Damascus to airbases in front-line areas near Hama and Homs, close to combat zones with rebel forces. A Syria Air Airbus A320-232 was identified making night-time flights to al Qamishli airport in an enclave in the north-east of the country, held by regime troops and allied Kurdish forces of the YPG. Land routes to this enclave had been cut by Islamic State fighters for more than 18 months. Syrian Il-76s were also identified making night-time flights to al Qamishli. Syrian air-transport operations also showed the importance of control of the air to the ability of the Assad regime to sustain its beleaguered outposts and forces in isolated enclaves.

The reaction of the US and its allies to this ramping-up of air and naval movements, as well as the surge in construction activity in Syria was very low-key. Western intelligence and surveillance assets easily picked up the Russian and Iranian activity but it seems there was considerable confusion about Moscow and Tehran's intentions. The Israelis had also been watching the Russian and Iranian build-up with some concern, including sending up special missions by the Gulfstream G550 AWACS radar surveillance planes to monitor the arrival of the Russian air group. Soon, plane and ship spotters across Europe and Turkey were tracking what the Russians were doing. In the first week of September several media reports appeared describing the first phases of the Russian deployment. US diplomatic and military sources criticised the Russian moves but they did not offer any firm conclusions about Moscow's intentions. The build up at Hmeinyan airbase could just be a move to facilitate the delivery of more arms to the Syrian military or to set up a base for 1,000 Russian military trainers and advisors, said senior US sources in response to journalists' questions. The possibility of a major Russian intervention was given little prominence. US intelligence also picked up the visit of Major General Qassem Soleimani to Moscow in July, but this was also not linked to any Russian-Iranian military planning for intervention in Syria. In comments to the New York Times, Soleimani visit was attributed by US government sources to dealing with fallout from the international agreement to limit Iran's nuclear sector.

The US Secretary of State John Kerry, met his Russian counterpart Sergey Lavrov twice in early September 2015 and efforts to kick-start peace talks to end the Syrian conflict was top of the agenda. If the US was concerned about the possibility of Russian intervention, Kerry did not use the press conferences after his meetings with Lavrov to issue any sort of public *demarche* or warning. US allies were asked in early September to deny Russian aircraft heading to Syria overflight rights but this was a routine reiteration of established US policy rather than as part of a co-ordinated new effort to thwart Moscow's build up.

It has been suggested to me by senior western intelligence sources that US and British intelligence agencies could not agree on what the Russians were up to, so Kerry had conflicting advice. America's top diplomat apparently did not feel confident enough to issue any warning to the Russians on the basis of uncertain intelligence assessments.

The US National Security Agency and British GCHQ eavesdropping agencies have a major facility on the island of Cyprus, some 200 kilometres from Syria, and, according to documents released by the whistle blower Edward Snowden, they had considerable success in cracking the communications of the Syrian and Iranian militaries, including breaking into the video transmission links of Iranian unmanned aerial vehicles to enable the British and Americans to watch what the drones were filming. This generated over-confidence in London and Washington about the ability of their intelligence agencies to monitor events in Syria, and possibility led to a misunderstanding of the situation. Putin and other Russian leaders are – with some justification – notoriously paranoid about eavesdropping by western intelligence agencies so conduct much of their business in face-to-face meetings, and only issue orders for sensitive missions to senior military commanders in person. This makes it very difficult to monitor what they are doing by using technical means, such as listening into cell phones or tapping email or video conferencing links.

This appears to have been what happened with the high-level planning of the Russian deployment to Syrian, making it difficult for western intelligence to realise what was Moscow's strategic intent. The Russian commander in Syria in late 2015 and early 2016, General Dvornikov, boasted that the deployment of the Russian air group was a "bolt from the blue" that took the West by surprise. Russian commanders and units had regularly practiced no-notice deployments in a series of exercises in 2014 and 2015, so the air force was ready to dispatch aircraft to Syria at a few days' notice, said the general, in one of his few media interviews. On top of this, senior Russian leaders, including Putin and Lavrov, made a series of public comments in early and mid-September, suggesting that the early signs of the Russian deployment were little more than a continuation of the long-established policy of supplying arms and technical advisors to the Syrian military.

So, when the first flights of Russian fighter aircraft were picked up on the radar of a US Air Force Boeing E-3 Sentry AWACS aircraft monitoring Iranian, Iraqi and Syrian airspace, it was news to coalition military commanders and western leaders. The Russian move into Syria had kept everyone guessing until the very last minute. More surprises were in store.

Chapter 5
The Holding Action in Hama and Homs

From a distance the flickering red lights looked like a firework display - but this was the front-line in Syria's Hama province in October 2015. An area covering hundreds of metres looked like it was on fire. Hundreds of detonations were rippling across the impact area for more than a minute. Fireballs and smoke plumes could be seen consuming a stretch of land that included several buildings.

This was the first combat use in Syria of a Russian TOS-1A multiple-launch rocket system. Unlike the BM-21 multiple-launch rocket systems which had been in widespread use with the Syrian army since the 1980s and fired high-explosive warheads, the TOS-1A fires rockets fitted with thermobaric warheads that use a highly combustible fuel to generate a power shock wave that crushes anyone or anything caught in the blast area. Russian soldiers nicknamed it the Solntsepyok or Sun-heat. It is officially termed a flame-thrower by the Russian army and the weapons are issued to chemical and nuclear protection units because of the toxic nature of the fuel used in the warheads.

The TOS-1A strike was filmed by rebel fighters in northern Hama and the fear and shock in their voices could be clearly heard as the rockets impacted. They had obviously never experienced anything like this before. Only three days later, this section of front-line would be the scene of the first Syria offensive after the arrival of the Russian military contingent in the country.

As the first Russian cargo ships and transport aircraft started to arrive in Syria in increasing numbers during late August and into September, the first detachment of military advisors and senior officers began to fan out across the country to try to establish some sort of "ground truth" of what was actually happening. Colonel General Alexander Dvornikov, the overall Russian commander of the mission, was already in Damascus to get up to speed with the senior Syrian military leadership and to oil the wheels to allow the smooth entry of the bulk of the Russian forces into Latakia province. Dvornikov had only a limited number of advisors and staff officers at this point and they were concentrated on a few front-line zones. According to images posted on social-media, the bulk of them went to Hama and Latakia provinces, some more went to Aleppo to work with the Iranians who were preparing their own offensive in this region, and others went to Homs where Islamic State fighters were threatening the main north-south road from Damascus.

Russian soldiers are prodigious users of social media and many of the servicemen being sent to Syria started to post pictures and other information about their time in the country. In September the first of these posts showed Russian soldiers driving in convoys of vehicles out of the cities of Latakia and Tartus into the interior of Syria. The main destination of these soldiers appeared to be the central province of Hama where Syrian troops had set up a defensive line to hold the provincial capital from the rebel alliance driving south out of Idlib province. A contingent of reconnaissance troops and officers of the 74th Motor Rifle Brigade set up a base in a village to the west of Hama city, just as the Syrian army units in the region were preparing for an offensive. Photographs of Russian 2A65 MSTA-B 152mm howitzers also appeared from this region, indicating that a Russian artillery unit, identified from social media posts by Russian soldiers as the 291st Artillery Brigade, had moved out to support the offensive.

Earlier in September, a video clip appeared online showing a BTR-82A armoured troop carrier crewed by Russian-speaking soldiers in a fire-fight with rebels in a mountainous area of Lakatia province. This incident occurred on a ridge line that overlooked the Shal al Ghab valley, which was on the western edge of the rebel advance position along the Idlib-Hama provincial boundary. The Russian soldiers appeared to be carrying out a reconnaissance mission to get the lie of the land on this key terrain in the run-up to the offensive.

As these preparatory moves were under way on the ground, President Vladimir Putin was heading to New York to address the United Nations General Assembly on 28th September. The Russian president told the assembled world leaders and diplomats that the world should come together to fight Islamic State in the same way as it joined forces to fight Hitler in the Second World War. He insisted that defeat of Islamic State and other "terrorists" could only be achieved by support of the "legitimate government" of Syria. Putin said President Bashar al-Assad's regime was "fighting valiantly against terror face-to-face in Syria". Up to then Syrian forces had been struggling almost alone, said Putin.

This state of affairs was about to end. Two days later, the Russian State Duma (parliament) approved Putin's request to allow him to order Russian forces in to action in Syria. This was an act of pure theatre as there was little chance that a parliament dominated by Putin allies would vote down the president's proposal. Later that day, Russian jets took off from Hmeinyan airbase to strike at targets across Syria. For the next six days the Russian aircraft hit a wide range of targets but the raids did not seem to be concentrated in any specific part of the country. Russian intelligence on the rebel forces and their bases appeared limited. From video clips released by the Russian Ministry of Defence of the strikes, several targets appeared to be buildings far behind the front lines rather than deployed troops. Accusations started to be made that the Russian strikes were causing widespread civilian casualties.

These raids were only preparatory strikes ahead of the main Syrian ground operation - to attack north from Hama province, in the Shal al

Ghab valley, and against the rebel-held Rastan pocket north of Homs - that was to start on the morning of 7th October. This was the first serious operation to be carried out by the Syrian with direct Russian assistance. The Russian navy was now brought in to play in a move that was clearly designed to emphasise that Moscow was bringing all its military power to bear in Syria. Four corvettes of the Caspian Sea Flotilla launched a salvo of 26 Kalibr cruise missiles at targets across northern Syria. They flew across Iran and Iraq to hit their targets. In a move of grand political theatre, the Russian Ministry of Defence later that day released a series of video clips showing the missiles being launched. The Kremlin was trying to show Russia was a super power on a par with the United States – the only other country that had so far fired long-range cruise missiles from warships in time of war. The missile attacked created a media frenzy across the world as, up to then, few mainstream media commentators realised that the Russian navy had such weapons. Within Syria, the strike was aimed at boosting the morale of government troops by showing that they were now backed by a superpower. It was also sending a message to rebel fighters, whose foreign backers in Washington, Paris, London, Ankara and the Gulf were not willing to directly intervene on their side. A new war for the hearts and minds of Syria's population had begun in earnest.

In the countryside of Hama, the war would be fought with more basic weapons. Columns of Syrian tanks and armoured vehicles, backed by multiple-launch rocket launchers, artillery batteries and Russian air power, were pitted against assorted rebel groups dug in around village strong points, employing improvised gun-armed trucks, recoilless rifles, towed indirect rocket launchers, mortars and Raytheon BGM-71 TOW wired guided anti-tank missiles.

Video imagery - taken from multiple sources and vantage points - of these battles, which began in earnest on 7th October, paints a picture of rebel fighters deploying to fire positions in the countryside to try to establish "gun lines" with the assorted types of improvised heavy weapons and TOW missiles to blunt Syrian armoured columns. The TOWs scored several hits on Syrian tanks advancing from around the town of Morek. Rebel fighters received the missiles from a US-run depot in Turkey and only got replacement missiles if they were able to provide the Central Intelligence Agency operatives running this covert arms supply operation with video evidence they had fired the weapons in anger. So over the next week a slew of video clips started to appear online showing Syrian tanks and armoured vehicles being hit by TOW missiles. One particularly graphic set shows a Syrian tank column coming under fire and the crews jumping out of the turrets of burning tanks. The hapless crewmen can then be seen diving into ditches to take cover as their tanks explode.

The Syrian advance seemed to stall but the intervention of low-flying Russian aircraft and helicopters appeared to force the rebel missile and mortar teams to seek cover. Dramatic video footage shot around Morek and on the Shal al Ghab plain showed Russian Mi-24s flying at under 100 feet to launch rocket attacks on rebel positions and then the helicopters circling to stalk rebels in agricultural fields and village streets. Su-25s were also filmed in action at low level over the battlefield. Russian artillery and the handful of TOS-1A rocket systems in Hama province joined the battle as it unfolded.

The intervention of the Russian helicopters, based at Hmeinyan airbase, appears to have been decisive in the first days of this battle, with the presence overhead of flights of up to four Mi-24s at a time allowing the Syrian troops to make advances across these battle zones, capturing several villages. Under this air cover, Syrian infantry columns operating side by side with T-55 and T-72 tanks moved in to mop up and secure the first line of villages in a series of slow-moving battles.

High on the wooded ridge line overlooking the Shal al Ghab plain more Syrian troops were poised to attack, and they snaked down through the woods to strike at villages on the flank of the rebel front-lines. Artillery, BM-21 rocket launchers and tanks up on the ridge line supported the attack over the next 10 days. Each day Mi-24s from Hmeinyan airbase made the short journey over the Latakia mountains to support the Syrian advance. Russian Aerospace Force ground personnel had set up arming and refuelling points next to the runway at the main Russian so the helicopters could be turned around quickly between missions.

Although the Syrian troops from the 47th and 87th Tank Brigades seemed to make some progress during the first week or so of the offensive, however, the fighting soon bogged down after an initial line of villages had been captured, with the front-line only moving a couple of kilometres.

The Syrian attacks took back several villages along the front-line and some of these devastated and abandoned settlements were soon visited by a news team from the Russian state-owned network, Russia Today, or RT. Its English-speaking correspondent, Murad Gazdiev, filmed and interviewed seemingly happy villagers returning to the homes thanks to the Syrian soldiers standing nearby. This was a new phenomenon. The Kremlin had invested heavily in building up RT to challenge pre-eminent position of Western and Middle Eastern rolling news networks - BBC News 24, CNN, Fox and Al Jazeera - in the global media hierarchy. These networks were unwilling or unable to report from the Syrian government side of the conflict so Gazdiev's reports, as well as those of his colleagues who replaced him later in the year, brought a very different perspective on the Syrian conflict. Moscow was waging a war on multiple fronts.

The Russian advisors learnt some important lessons about the nature of the war in Syria and the capabilities of their new allies. Despite having an impressive pre-war strength and huge equipment inventories, the Syrian Arab Army (SAA) of 2015 was a shadow of the pre-civil war force. More than three quarters of its conscript soldiers had deserted in 2012-13. By 2015 the number of effective combat brigades had dropped from more than 40 to just under 20. These "brigades" were also very different from their pre-war counterparts. The two army brigades that attacked in north Hama in October 2015 were less than 1,000 men strong and only around 400 of these were combat infantrymen. Supporting them were tank companies with between 10 and 20 tanks, as well as a similar number of BMP tracked armoured troop carriers, an artillery group with a dozen or so guns and BM-21s rocket launchers. Direct firepower for infantry assaults was provided by ZSU-23-4 tracked anti-aircraft guns or twin 23mm cannons mounted on the back of SUV pick-ups, known as "technicals". These new-look Syrian brigades could launch very effective attacks to seize ground but there were limits to the amount of terrain they could hold, making them vulnerable to counter-attacks.

The officers of these brigades were old SAA professional officers but the soldiers were conscripts who had been drafted before the civil war started and not allowed to return home after their initial two years of military service. This meant they had a high degree of technical competence at driving their tanks and putting down artillery fire support, but there was little appetite to conduct risky operations that would result in significant casualties. So it was rare for Syrian army units to actually get involved in close-quarter fighting. When determined dug-in enemy were encountered, Syrian soldiers usually pulled back and tried to kill any defenders with tank, artillery, rocket, cannon or guided-missile fire. Often a combination of all these heavy weapons were used in spectacular bombardments. This usually meant Syrian offensives were never fast-moving affairs but slow and deliberate exercises.

Syrian soldiers also needed to be rested after periods of intense combat so a programme of rotations was put in place to give them time away from the front. A month was a very long period of front-line duty for Syrian regular soldiers, which meant combat brigades had to be carefully husbanded and nurtured for specific operations.

This left the burden of holding ground and manning a series of checkpoints to the locally recruited National Defence Force (NDF) militia. These were the men and women who, day-in and day-out, manned a series of checkpoints and strong points around government-held towns and villages. The Russian military had a very negative view of these NDF militia units, with several Russian officers making comments to the Moscow media and military pundits about their poor morale, leadership and fighting qualities. The Syrian army would not be in shape to launch a major nation-wide counter-offensive for some time.

Some 80 kilometres to the south of Hama a very different type of war was being fought by the Syrian army against the fighters of the Islamic State, who had surged across the central desert region in the later summer, capturing the iconic ancient ruins of Palmyra and then pushing down the Homs-Damascus road towards the giant airbase at T-4, or Tiyas. Several gas fields to the north of the Palmyra-Homs road had fallen to a roving group of Islamic State troops operating in fast-moving columns mounted in heavily armed SUVs. To the south, another group of Islamic State fighters had pushed westwards, first capturing the key cross roads town of Qaryatayn and moving north west to threaten the ancient Christian town of Mahin, which in turn threatened Homs and the nearby Shayrat airbase. These groups of Islamic State fighters were probably not very big, probably not having more than a couple of hundred fighters each. They were highly mobile, with many fighters travelling is heavily armed "Jihadi cars," or SUVs, and were backed up by very accurate artillery and rocket batteries. Many of these columns were led by determined commanders who loved to launch surprise attacks to keep their opponents off balance.

The morale of the Syrian troops in the desert was lamentable. Dozens of Syrian troops had been captured during the fall of Palmyra in May 2015 and been executed in a grim ceremony in the city's ancient Roman amphitheatre. The survivors of the units that fled Palmyra were terrified of their enemies.

This desperate situation turned into a crisis at the end of October when an Islamic State column staged a surprise raid across the desert and stormed Mahin. Syrian NDF militia men fled rather than standing and fighting. A Jihadi column then pushed towards the predominately Christian town of Sadad, some 10km from the Damascus-Homs highway. If they could cut this key north-south route they would have cut off the north of the country from the capital.

An improvised defence line was set up outside Sadad and occasional Syrian and Russian air strikes were called down to try to blunt the Islamic State advance. Soldiers were desperately needed to man the front-line. The Syrians turned to the Russians to help bring in reinforcements. A pair of Ilyushin Il-76s were kept at Hmeinyan airbase to fly supplies around the country and one of them was ordered to make a night flight up to the far north east of Syria. The town of Qamishli was home to Syria's Christian Assyrian community and they had offered to provide militia fighters to defend the Christian villages around Mahin and help recapture the town.

A pro-Assyria social media page published a photograph on 2nd November showing Assyrian fighters of Gozarto Protection Forces in front of a Russian Il-76 on a darkened Qamishli airfield. They were en route to Shayrat airbase to the east of Homs city. The commitment of Russia's air force to intra-theatre airlift missions was also confirmed on flight-tracking websites, which picked up another Russian Il-76 taking off from Shayrat on 5th November.

To neutralise this growing threat and bolster the morale of the Syrian soldiers, towards the end of October the Russians began moving the bulk of their artillery, grouped under the command of the 120th Artillery Brigade, to fire positions to the south-east of Shayrat airbase. The airbase itself was soon a forward operating base for four Russian Mi-24P attack helicopters and a team of Russian advisors joined the headquarters of the Syrian 18th Tank Division, which controlled the central desert front, to plan a wide-ranging operation to take back Mahin, Qaryatayn and, ultimately, Palmyra.

The arrival of the Russian Mi-24s was a big boost to morale of the Syrian troops holding a string of desert outposts around the giant T-4 and Shayrat airbases. In the final week of October 2015, a Russian landing ship docked at Tartus with a cargo of T-72B tanks fitted with explosive reactive armour to give them protection from TOW missiles and several BMP-2 armoured troop carriers. These vehicles were soon moved on low-loaders out to T-4 airbase to re-equip the elite 555th Brigade of the Syrian 4th Mechanised Division and make it ready for offensive operations.

The first counter-move got underway on 4th November when Syrian troops started advancing towards Palmyra and its ancient ruins. Pairs of Mi-24s were filmed making low level rocket attacks in a desert region, hitting Islamic State positions on the hilltops and ridge lines that dominated the approach to Palmyra. Russian Sukhoi Su-24Ms bombed Islamic State armoured vehicles and troop positions in Palmyra on 5th and 6th November. The valley to the west of Palmyra was a dead flat desert region that provided little cover from air surveillance or attack. The only place to hide was in a series of ravines that rose up the sides of the hills and ridges to the north and south of Palmyra.

The Syrians pushed a small armoured force from the 67th Tank Brigade and 555th Brigade along the main road into Palmyra from the west, while troops of the elite Tiger Forces moved through the desert to attack the city from the north-west. Militia fighters from the Homs National Defence Force also participated in the offensive.

While the first advances made some progress, the Syrians just did not have enough soldiers to clear the hills that dominate the approaches to Palmyra, and by the end of November a stalemate had taken hold of the desert front.

The Syrian offensive against Palmyra coincided with another operation to drive back an Islamic State fighters from Mahin and then push on to take their base at Qaryatayn. The 5th Battery of the 120th Artillery Brigade was positioned south of Shayrat airbase to fire half a dozen 2A65 MSTA-B 152mm howitzers in support of the advancing Syrian troops. Television crews from Damascus filmed the battery in action but the identity of the crews was not mentioned in their reports. The presence of the Russian soldiers was revealed in a media briefing in the Moscow Ministry of Defence when a map of the battlefield situation was posted on a huge plasma screen on the wall behind the phalanx of generals giving the briefing. Amid the map markings showing the position of air raids and troops concentrations was a caption showing the presence of the Russian artillery unit and the Mi-24s at Shayrat.

Mahin was a small, dust-encrusted desert town. All its population had long fled to safety in Homs. There were only a few hundred Islamic State fighters in the town and they were soon out-flanked by Syrian columns which seized high ground around it. On 23rd November the Jihadis pulled out of the town when it looked like the Syrians would close the last escape route. They were pursued towards Qaryatayn but there Islamic State put up a determined resistance. Just two weeks later, the Jihadis had regained their strength and made a new foray across the desert that caught the small Syrian garrison in Mahin by surprise, and they fled. The Syrians re-organised themselves and launched another drive to re-capture Mahin. After almost a repeat of the last offensive, the Syrians drove into Mahin again on 29th December.

In December a new drive was launched against Palmyra and this time the Syrians were more successful, thanks to an increase in Russian air support. By Christmas, the Syrians could see the distinctive outline of Palmyra's 13th Century castle across the desert.

Russian attack helicopters had proved decisive in these desert battles, flying at low level to deliver barrages of rockets or cannon fire. The open desert terrain outside Palmyra was an ideal place for the Mi-24s to prowl, looking for exposed targets. When combined with the accurate and sustained artillery fire of the MSTA-B battery, the Russian helicopters provided a decisive edge against Islamic State. However, they could not overcome the shortcomings of the weakened and poorly equipped Syrian army.

Chapter 6
Red Air

When the first Sukhoi Su-30SMs fighters began their final approach to Hmeinyan airbase in Syria's Latakia province they were making history in more ways than one. The Russian intervention in Syria would soon change the course of the Middle East country's civil war, but the way Moscow choose to intervene in the war was also very unusual.

Russia - and before it the Soviet Union – has traditionally been a land power and its army has borne the burden of its foreign wars. Never before had a major Russian military campaign been so dependent for its success or failure on the country's air force.

President Putin was turning over a new leaf in Russian military history when he put his trust in the Russian Aerospace Force (RuAF), as it is now titled, backed up by cruise-missile-firing warships and submarines to win the war in Syria. In a further military first, the Russian Navy's only aircraft carrier would launch bombers off its deck on combat missions for the first time in Russian military history.

Soon after the Su-30s arrived in Syria, more waves of jets touched down at Russia's newest airbase. Russian and international news crews were soon invited to the base to see the aircraft and crews preparing for action. It was a great show, with jets roaring down the runway and Mil Mi-24 attack helicopters circling overhead to add to the impression of military might. Some western observers noted that the bulk of the Russian aircraft seemed to date from the 1970s or 1980s and few boasted the precision guided "smart" bombs that adorned western jets. The red stars on the jets tails suggested this was just "another failed Soviet intervention", or so said the critics. The presence of the Mi-24s, nicknamed "Crocodiles" by the Russian aircrews, just added to the impression that this was going to be a re-run of Afghanistan in the 1980s.

The "Russian Air Group in Syria", as the contingent at Hmeinyan airbase was formally titled, eventually boasted more than 30 fast jets and was supported by over 4,000 support and security personnel. This was the largest air force contingent dispatched overseas by Moscow since Soviet times and it was meant to showcase the Russian armed forces at their best. The ground technicians and repair crews all had new uniforms. They lived in brand new prefabricated house units and ate in purpose-built mess halls. Bomb dumps, maintenance hangers, fuel dumps and air-traffic control radars had all been installed at the base ahead of the arrival of the jets themselves.

The composition of the air group showed that Russian air commanders wanted to have a balanced force, with fighters, strike bombers and ground attack jets to cover multiple tasks. This was a force designed to be able to look after itself.

As with other branches of the Russian military, the air force in 2015 was a mix of old and new. The vast bulk of Moscow's air force flew jets built in the 1980s but there were new aircraft around that had comparable capabilities to advanced western combat aircraft. The best jet on the ramp at Hmeinyan airbase was the Sukhoi Su-34. Its crew sat side-by-side in the jet's cockpit and were able to monitor computer screens displaying radar returns and video images from heat-detecting thermal cameras. The crew could then dial the co-ordinates of targets into their precision-guided bombs and missiles. The Su-34 was one of the most recent aircraft to enter Russian service so only eight could be mustered to head to Syria; and the Sukhoi company sent a contingent of engineers and technicians to ensure nothing went wrong during the combat debut of the jets. According to biographic data on the Su-34 pilots sent to Syria collected by the Ukrainian internet monitoring group InformNaphalm, the majority were senior majors, lieutenant colonel and full colonels with several decades of cockpit experience. The 47th Separate Mixed Aviation Regiment, which operated the jets, was clearly considered an elite unit and it was expected to play a key role in the coming operation. To make sure the American, Turkish or Israeli air forces did not interfere with the Russian operation a contingent of top line fighters was sent to Syria. First to arrive were Sukhoi Su-30SMs and then a quartet of Su-35Ss. These are Russia's classic "super fighters," known as Flankers by NATO, which boast a fearsome reputation for close-range dogfighting, as well as supersonic performance and beyond-visual-range missiles to engage targets from dozens of miles away. Although not in the same class as US Lockheed F-22 Raptor stealth fighters that were already flying over Syria, the Russian jets were more than a match for anything else flying around the Middle East. As with the Su-34 regiment sent to Syria, the Su-30 and Su-35s were piloted by veterans with plenty of fight experience.

The real burden of the looming bombing campaign would fall on the crews of the RuAF Sukhoi Su-24 strike jets and the Su-25 ground attack jets. Both jets were originally designed in the 1960s and the airframes in Syria were probably built in the mid- to late-1980s. A dozen or so of each type of jet was sent to Syria. The Su-24 is broadly equivalent to the early models of the European Tornado jet, featuring swing wings and pylons to carry bombs on its wings or underneath its fuselage. The Su-24 regiment sent to Syria came from the 6980th Airbase at Shogol and it was equipped with the SM variant of the jet, which allowed it to drop a limited number of smart munitions. The jets also benefited from an avionics upgrade that included the incorporation of a new navigation computer, as well as having handheld GPS navigation devices mounted on their cockpit's dashboards. This all meant that the "dumb" or "iron" bombing accuracy of the aircraft had been dramatically improved, with some reports suggesting the new variant could put bombs within 25 metres of the aim point compared to 200 metres with the old system. The US-made Paveway laser guided bomb, by comparison is accurate up one metre. While the Russian jets were obviously not as precise as their western counterparts, their accuracy was good enough to hit a street of houses or an artillery battery position.

The Su-24 regiment in Syria had a far wider age and experience spread than other units, with a mix of veteran majors and colonels as well as young captains and lieutenants. The two-seat Su-24 allows for less-experienced crew to be paired with seasoned veterans.

The Su-25, which is known as the Rook by the Russians, is of a similar vintage to the Su-24 but is meant for a very different job. In World War Two the Red Air Force's most famous aircraft was the Sturmovik, which was built to find and kill German tanks. The Su-25 was meant to the be the successor to the Sturmovik and the Cold War equivalent of the American A-10A Warthog tank buster jet and it had an armoured cockpit, reinforced fuselage and a canopy with a bigger field of view so the pilot could look for enemy tanks to attack. As with the Su-24, the Rook's cockpit had been upgraded and the latest variant could hit targets with far greater accuracy than older models. The Rook's most devastating weapons were its 23mm and 30mm nose-mounted cannons and under-wing unguided rocket pods. If an Su-25 could line up a target and then dive at it, a salvo of rockets and a ripple of cannon fire would inflict heavy losses on enemy tank columns, artillery positions or infantry trench lines.

The Rook pilots of the Russian air force were an elite group. The 960th Attack Aviation Regiment that provided the Su-25 detachment in Syria contained many combat veterans. Several of its pilots had served in the Caucasus conflicts in the 1990s and in Georgia in 2008 but the Syria operation was a new endeavour for them.

While the Moscow government's propaganda machine went into overdrive to show off the air group in Syria to the Russian and international media, other parts of Russia's armed forces were also being readied to support the war in Syria. A major objective of the intervention in Syria was to project Russia as a global superpower with armed forces and weapon systems that could rival those of the United States and its close allies, Britain and France. This would also have the secondary benefit of boosting sales of Russian military hardware in export markets around the world. Wars are good for business.

The high commands of both the Russian Aerospace Force and Navy had studied recent intervention operations by the US military in Kosovo, Afghanistan, Iraq and Libya and were keen to show they had similar power-projection capabilities.

Russian Long Range Aviation was put on stand-by to strike at Syria with its manned Tupolev Tu-22M3, Tu-95 and Tu-160 heavy bombers. These bombers were classic Soviet-era nuclear war machines which had been re-roled for conventional warfare. The Tu-95 was perhaps the most famous of the bombers and was known in the West as the Bear. Its four counter-rotating engines and swept-back wings gave it a distinctive silhouette. A Tu-95 famously dropped the most powerful ever thermo-nuclear bomb, the Tsar Bomba, in 1961. In the later years of the Cold War the Tu-95s were re-equipped with long-range cruise missiles to fire at targets from outside NATO air defences. By 2015, the Tu-95 force was re-equipped with conventionally armed variants of the Kh-55 cruise missile. Although the Bears had regularly been intercepted by NATO fighters over the North Atlantic during the Cold War, the Tu-95 had never been used in action before the Syria conflict. Just over 50 were in use with the Russian air force in 2015.

The Tu-95's big brother was the Tu-160, or as it was code-named by NATO, the Blackjack. This was a supersonic bomber, known to the Russians as the White Swan, that was designed to penetrate NATO air defences at low level. It first entered Soviet service in 1987 but only just over two dozen were actually built before the Berlin Wall collapsed and production ground to a halt. By 2015 some 16 remained airworthy and were the pride and joy of Russian Long Range Aviation. President Putin famously once took the controls of Tu-160 during a training mission and he liked the experience so much he approved plans to re-start production of an upgraded version.

The most numerous Russian heavy bomber in 2015 was the Tu-22M3 which was famously code-named the Backfire by NATO. It was originally designed to make low-level raids into NATO airspace to launch cruise missiles at land targets or ships. They had been used to drop bombs on Afghanistan in the 1980s, Chechnya in the 1990s and South Georgia in 2008. Between 50 and 70 were in service in 2015.

In the decade up to 2015, the Long Range Aviation force had undergone renewed investment with more money being spent on spares, maintenance and training for strategic strike operations with conventional-weapons. The Tu-95s and Tu-160s concentrated on strike operations with long range, air-launched cruise missiles, while the Tu-22M3s would focus on carrying out "carpet bombing" strikes with "iron bombs" against area targets. This recreated the "Arc Light" strikes of the Vietnam war by the US Air Force B-52 bombers. The commanders of Long Range Aviation had been progressively stepping up the operational readiness of their bomber squadrons by holding a series of short notice or snap scrambles or by sending aircraft on long-range patrols in the North Atlantic, Arctic or Pacific regions.

After the start of the Russian mission in Syria, the Tu-95s and Tu-160s were held at their home bases in central Russia or in the Arctic near

Murmansk. But the shorter-range Tu-22M3s needed a base closer to Syria so Mozdok airbase in the Caucasus was prepared to host a detachment of the bombers.

Russia's Navy was also keen to enhance its conventional strike capabilities and since 2012 had been progressively equipping its surface fleets and submarines with the 3M14 Kalibr cruise missile. It reportedly had a range of up to 2,500 kilometres and Moscow touted it as a rival to the US Tomahawk Land Attack Missile. One version could be launched from a Kilo-class submarine's torpedo tube and another from the vertical-launch tubes of a frigate or corvette. For Putin, the Kalibr was the ultimate military machismo symbol, with only the US and Britain ever using such weapons in combat before.

As part of the build-up to the Syria operation, a number of warships and submarines of the Black Sea Fleet and Caspian Sea Flotilla equipped to fire the Kalibr were put on alert.

Co-ordinating bringing together aircraft, missiles and warships across several times zones and arranging diplomatic clearances for aircraft and missiles to overfly a number of neighbouring countries, as well as international sea and air routes, was a complex task that fell to members of the Russian General Staff's new National Defence Command Centre in Moscow. This was opened in December 2014 as the nerve centre of Russia's armed forces and it boasted a network of computer links to airbases, naval vessels and army bases across Russia and outside the country. During the Syria crisis, the command post would become famous as the venue of media briefings by top Russian generals. Photographs from inside the command centre showed scores of Russian staff officers at work behind ranks of computer screens. It also had wall-sized computer screens able to display maps and drone imagery, as well as allowing video conferencing with commanders at remote locations to take place. Once the Syrian campaign got underway, Russian generals began to appear at almost daily media briefings in the Moscow Ministry of Defence. Behind them would be slick Microsoft Powerpoint presentations of maps, photos and video clips of the Russian air force's "greatest bombing hits". Some of the video show also appeared to have been recorded by the Sukhoi Su-34's thermal-imaging cameras. This was the main Russian jet in Syria that could delivery western style "smart bombs", so it was used for raids that needed pin point accuracy, such as strikes on suspected rebel commanders.

Russian air operations in Syria during the final three months of 2015 underwent rapid evolution through a number of very distinct phases. The identities of senior Russian air commanders in Syria remain a closely guarded secret and none of these officers have been named in the Moscow media. Nor have senior Russian air force officers discussed the evolution of their air campaign in an open forum. To build up an accurate picture of events it is necessary to piece together accounts of Russian pilots and forward air controllers, conduct analysis of video of Russian air operations, and look at open-source tracking of Russian and Syrian aircraft.

The first six weeks of the air campaign were characterised by tightly controlled air strikes, with the majority of targets being pre-selected by the Russian headquarters in Syria for attack. According to multiple accounts by pilots, they were briefed at Hmeinyan airbase before their missions and then would take off to head out to attack their targets.

These strikes would generally be carried out from medium altitudes of around 10-15,000 feet using their aircraft's bombing computers to calculate bomb release points. Except for the Su-34s, which used a number of precision guided or "smart" weapons, all the other strikes were carried out with unguided "dumb" or "iron" bombs. All the strikes were carried out under tight direction from a ground control centre at Hmeinyan airbase. There appear to have been occasions when Russian jets were directed to attack targets of opportunity but all these involved hitting co-ordinates passed to the pilots from the ground control centre. Russian strike-jet pilots did not have much freedom of action to find and engage targets.

Different arrangements appear to have been in place for attack helicopter pilots who operated at low level over battlefields and were given permission to engage targets that popped up or were located by forward air controllers on the ground.

One Russian pilot based in Syria described his regiment's tactics in a media interview, saying; "In the Western press, there are sometimes reports that, they say, Russian pilots somewhere hit a peaceful object. All this is a lie. We use weapons only on the co-ordinates that come from the higher headquarters, and, therefore, have already been clarified, reconciled. Therefore, if I strike, I am convinced: this is a blow to terrorists."

An account of the Su-25 regiments' operations in Syria in late 2015 and early 2016 appeared in the Russian media in 2017. It said the "main method of conducting combat operations by the Su-25SM crews in Syria was the successive infliction of air strikes against predetermined land at a fixed time in the navigational bombing mode."

It revealed that surveillance aircraft first scouted out the targets and then groups of between two and six aircraft would be sent to attack one or two minutes after the targets were detected. The attack wave would circle over their targets at between 3,500 and 4,000 feet for up to 40 minutes at a time to keep the enemy's heads down, said the report. During this time, each Su-25 would take turns to drop bombs.

"The hits were made point-by-point - for each air bomb had its own purpose," said the report. "The principle of one bomb - one goal was for the modernized Su-25SM like a law. [The Su-25SM] ensured the accuracy of target destruction of several tens of metres."

Interestingly, the report confirmed that for targeting large groups of enemy soldiers the Su-25 crews would drop weapons fitted with sub-munitions.

The next major escalation of the Russian air campaign in Syria unfolded after the loss of a Metrojet Airbus A321 airliner over Sinai on 31st October 2015, just after it had taken off from the Sharm al Sheikh holiday resort. The deaths of 219 Russian, four Ukrainian and one Belarus tourists and aircrew caused outrage in Moscow. Two weeks later the Russian government accused Islamic State terrorists of planting a bomb on the aircraft. President Putin ordered a military response. This unfolded on the morning of 17th November.

A dozen Tu-22M3 bombers took off from Mozdok airbase in South Ossetia and headed to eastern Syria to unload their cargo of dumb bombs on targets near Raqqa and Dier Ez Zor between 5am and 5.30am. Some four hours later, a second wave of Tu-95 and Tu-160 bombers took off from Engles-2 airbase, the home of the 6950th Aviation Base unit, in central Russia and headed south towards Iran, before turning west and into Syrian air space. They launched 34 air-based Kh-55 and Kh-101 cruise missiles at targets around Aleppo and Idlib.

The first public indication of the strike came early on the morning of 17th November when still and video imagery appeared on social media showing what appeared to be a Russian cruise missile overflying northern Syria. Images of debris from other large missiles, possibly Kh-55s, also appeared online.

Later that day President Putin strode into the National Command Centre in Moscow to hold a remarkable event. Putin took a seat on the stage and started to issue orders to his military commanders for a series of further strikes in full view of the cameras, live on Russian television. He also ordered the Russian navy cruiser Moskova to co-operate with the French aircraft carrier, Charles de Gaulle, which was to sail for the Eastern Mediterranean on 18th November in the wake of a major Islamic State terrorist attack on Paris that left 130 dead and 368 people injured.

Over four days, the Russian bombers repeatedly returned to targets over Syria, with the Tu-22M3s continuing their carpet bombing and the bigger Tu-95s and Tu-160s firing volleys of cruise missiles. Smaller strike jets based in Syria also surged their efforts.

The finale of the bombing campaign was an audacious raid by two Tupolev Tu-160 bombers on 20th November. They were launched from an airbase in Russia's Arctic north and made a 13,000 km flight around the west coast of Ireland and through the Straits of Gibraltar to fire cruise missiles at Syria from the eastern Mediterranean, before proceeding via Iraq and Iran to land back in Russia. The strike caught Britain and other NATO allies by surprise and it took them several hours to work out actually what the Russian bombers had done. A rather bemused RAF press spokesmen in Ministry of Defence in London initially laughed at the idea when they were asked questions by reporters about the raid. He had to make apologetic phone calls back to the journalists several hours later to confirm the raids.

After the conclusion of the Long Range Aviation campaign on 20 November, the Russian Ministry of Defence issued statistics for the bombing effort. It said 101 cruise missiles had been fired, including 18 from naval vessels. When added to dumb bombs dropped by the Tu-22M3s the total of ordnance dropped ran to 1,400 tons. This was the largest operation by the Long-Range Aviation branch of the Russian air force since the Second World War.

Senior Russian government leaders and military commanders claimed success for their strikes, but independent bomb damage assessment was unavailable. Imagery that appeared on social media showed at least one Russian cruise missile apparently detonating prematurely in mid-air over Aleppo province and another, apparently a Kh-55, crashed in Iran.

Nevertheless, the four days of activity suggested that efforts by its commander Lieutenant General Anatoly Zhikharev, to rejuvenate the Long Range Aviation Command had made progress. Equally important had been the ability of the Russians to marry its operations with an information operation to not only project firepower onto targets in Syria, but to reap political and diplomatic benefits from the bombing campaign both at home and abroad.

The four days of intensified bombing demonstrated Russia's long-range strike capability. It also allowed Russia to target Islamic State without distracting its air group in Syria from its core task of supporting the on-going Syrian ground offensive. In that way, Russia could be seen to be indirectly retaliating for the airliner bombing and demonstrating solidarity with France in the wake of the 13th November Paris attacks, thereby presenting itself as a credible partner in the fight against Islamic State.

There remains considerable controversy over the effectiveness of the Russian air campaign during its first six weeks. The effectiveness of Russian air strikes was only as good as the intelligence they were based on. At this stage in the campaign, the Russian appeared to have not built up detailed understanding of the Syrian battlefield.

Interestingly, there were accusations at this time that the Russian air force targeting officers were harvesting intelligence from online posts by a Russian blogger called Ivan Sidorenko, who trawled through Jihadi posts on Twitter and Facebook and identified military bases and other locations of significance. Several of these locations were subsequently bombed by Russian and Syrian aircraft. This use of what is known as "open-source" intelligence is widespread in western air forces but it was a new development for the Russian air force and showed they were on a steep learning curve. Breaches in operational security, or OPSEC, by rebel groups through their online postings would continue to be exploited by the Russian military as the campaign unfolded.

At the regular media briefings in Moscow, senior Russian generals routinely boasted of the effectiveness of their air strikes. But still and video imagery posted on social media on both the rebel and government sides, as well as in bomb damage video released by Moscow, suggested that the impact of Russian air strikes was less than optimal in this period of the campaign. The bulk of targets for Russian jets appeared to be fixed – buildings, bridges and fortified positions – not moving targets. Repeatedly the Russians described these positions as rebel command posts, ammunition factories or troop concentrations. The imagery of strikes suggested that many of the targets were empty buildings, or otherwise, not what Moscow said they were. On one occasion, the Russian military released imagery of what was described as an Islamic State oil refinery, whereas independent analysts suggested it was a water-treatment plant. There were repeated accusations from rebel sources and western governments that the Russian air attacks were causing widespread civilian casualties.

The imagery released in Russian media briefings appeared to have been either satellite imagery or cockpit video from the Su-34 jets. There was no live drone video footage, suggesting that the Russians did not have the ability to monitor targets in real time over extended periods. Repeatedly, pictures emerged during this period of crashed Russian Orlan-10 drones in rebel areas - but these were small hand-launched drones that could not transmit their pictures back to the Russian air headquarters at Hmeinyan airbase. These drones helped front line commanders but could not be used to plan and conduct what the western military termed "time-sensitive targeting", i.e to strike at moving targets. Russian commanders clearly realised this was a major shortcoming and they moved to try to redress this capability gap, to establish a working "kill chain".

The best evidence that the Russians had brought a time-sensitive targeting capability online in Syria emerged in early January 2016, when commercial satellite imagery of Hmeinyan airbase started to show large Forpost surveillance drones and their distinctive hangar. During December 2015, Forpost video imagery started to appear in Moscow Ministry of Defence briefings, to illustrate claims of attacks on rebel supply convoys and targeted strikes on senior rebel commanders.

The Forpost drone came to be central to Russian air operations in Syria, in effect becoming Moscow's "ace in the hole". Time after time, Forpost imagery was used in press briefings about Russian heavy bomber and cruise-missile strikes, fighter jet attacks and ground operations. These showed before-and-after imagery, revealing that the Russians regularly had Forposts up to find targets for air strikes and then to film their progress, all live while senior commanders watched the imagery back at Hmeinyan. Subsequently, further imagery showed that the Russians had found ways to distribute the imagery, so commanders away from Hmeinyan could view it in real time. This was a major advance for the Russians, which gave them an advantage in many battles during the remainder of the campaign.

The fact that the Russian military were dependent on an Israeli-supplied drone was not something either Moscow or Tel Aviv wanted to talk up at this point in the campaign. After the poor performance of Russian air strikes against Georgia in the brief 2008 war, Putin had brokered a deal with the Israeli Prime Minister Bibi Netanyahu to buy a batch of Searcher 2 drones from the Israel Aircraft Industry (IAI) company and then to set up a factory in Russia to assemble them. The Israelis had pioneered the use of drones in combat, ironically against the Syrians in the 1982 Lebanon war, and they were the only "western" country that was willing to share drone technology with Russia. It would have taken Russian scientists several years to catch up with their western rivals without the help of the Israelis.

The Russian OPK Oboronprom company and IAI subsequently established a UAV partnership which led to the Joint Stock Company Ural Works of Civil Aviation in Ekaterinburg setting up an assembly line to put together the drones from kits supplied by Israel. The drones were renamed the Fortress by the Russians, which translated into English as Forpost.

Moscow has not released much information about its UAV units but it is believed that, as per Russian military doctrine, the Forposts are operated by the Russian General Staff's Main Intelligence Directorate, or GRU, rather than the Russian Aerospace Force. At least one Forpost has been lost in operations over the Pro-Russian separatist enclave in eastern Ukraine since 2014 and another was lost over Syria in January 2018.

The Forpost could beam live video picture back to the Russian air operations centre from hundreds of miles away, which revolutionised how the Russian air force did business. The new drones and the video imagery they recorded also transformed how the Russian military and the Kremlin carried out information operations - or as it is better known - propaganda.

In June 2017, the Russians finally unveiled the Forpost to Moscow media. The Russian Ministry of Defence's Star television network sent a team of its finest presenters to Hmeinyan to talk up the role of the Forpost. For the first time, it showed the inside of a Forpost ground control cabin at Hmeinyan airbase. This revealed that the cabin was a standard Israel Aircraft Industries MALAT Division Advanced Ground Control

Station product, which was likely to have been delivered as part of the original sales contract. An IAI MALAT Division logo can be seen on one of the work stations. The logos of the US computer company APC can be seen on what appears to be server rack, and one of the computer displays has the logo of the Japanese company NEC. Flight and sensor controls had English-language markings on them, further indicating they had been supplied by IAI as part of the original Forpost/Searcher contract. A Russian military telephone handset appears to be the only non-Israeli supplied piece of hardware in the ground station.

Russia's air offensive got off to a slow start but by the end of 2015 Moscow's airmen began to get into their stride. During the first months of 2016, Russian air power would start to swing the balance across several battlefields in favour of forces loyal to the Damascus government.

Chapter 7
Iran's War

Amid the early morning fog and gloom the Syrian Jihadi fighters were picking over the remains of a series of bunkers and trenches a few miles south-west of Aleppo. The debris of war was everywhere – abandoned AK-47 rifles, ammunition boxes, chairs, mattresses and lifeless bodies. Only a few hours earlier this had been a front-line position of an Iraqi Shia militia unit. In the fog, the Jihadis had been able to approach the position, drop grenades in the bunkers and kill all the surprised occupants.

From the dead fighters' passports, it was possible to conclude they came from the Shia heartland in central Iraq. It is not clear what happened to dead fighters. There was a strong likelihood that they were just left where they had fallen, for the elements and stray dogs to sort out. The Jihadis did not stay around to admire their victory. If the fog lifted, Syrian artillery fire would soon start falling on the newly captured position. This was not the place for the Jihadi fighters to hang around and celebrate their very small victory.

The fate of these unfortunate Shia fighters was not uncommon on the battlefields south-west of Aleppo. For several months in late 2015 and into 2016, the rolling farm land to the south-west of Aleppo city was the scene of duels between the religious zealots of the Syrian Jihadi rebels and a group of Shia militias organised and funded by the Iranian Revolutionary Guard Corps. Fighting flowed back and forth before both sides stepped back and looked at alternative means of victory.

Iran is a long-standing backer of Syria's President Bashar al Assad and, in alliance with Lebanon's Hizbullah movement, had dispatched arms, advisors and fighters to help the Damascus regime in the early days of the civil war in 2011. As well as seeing Syria as a key gateway to Lebanon to keep up a supply route to Hizbullah, Tehran was also keen to defend several Shia communities and holy shrines in Syria which were under threat from the predominately Sunni rebels and Islamic State. When Major General Qassem Soleimani went to Moscow in the summer of 2015 to plan the Russian-Iranian campaign to prop up the Damascus government, he offered to organise more Shia militia groups to help mount an offensive to the south of Aleppo. This would aim to cut the Idlib-Aleppo motorway and isolate the rebel enclave in eastern Aleppo city, as well as breaking the sieges of four predominately Shia enclaves in western Aleppo province and northern Idlib province.

Iran's contribution would involve them mobilising thousands of Shia militia fighters from across the Middle East, deploying armed drones and Lockheed C-130 Hercules transport aircraft to air-drop supplies to the Shia enclaves. Hizbullah pledged to dispatch some of its best fighters to Aleppo to spearhead the new offensive, in co-operation with the Syrian Army's 4th Mechanised Division. Soleimani promised to organise and lead the offensive.

During September 2015, Russian, Syrian and Iranian aircraft began shuttling between Tehran, Baghdad and Hmeinyan airbase, moving hundreds of Shia fighters. Images appeared on social-networking sites of bewildered Shia fighters sitting on the floors of giant Il-76 transport aircraft as they prepared for their flights to Syria.

Once at the new Russian airbase in Syria, coaches took the Shia fighters to a helicopter landing site a few kilometres down the road towards Latakia. Syrian and Russian Mi-8 transport helicopters then shuttled them northwards to the Al Safirah garrison, south east of Aleppo city. This huge, sprawling military base was once home to Syria's secret ballistic-missile programmes but it was now a huge garrison for Syrian, Hizbullah and Shia forces. General Soleimani had set up his headquarters in the grounds and other buildings had been turned into training halls for the Shia fighters as they started to arrive. Revolutionary Guards instructors began teaching the Shia volunteers how to fire AK-47s, march and put on their new camouflage combat uniforms. The recruits began posting scores of images of their training on social-media sites to show the folks back home in Iraq, Iran and Afghanistan that they soon would be ready to take the fight to the enemy. Some of the fighters looked as if they had some experience of Iraq's long civil war but most of them looked like callow youths who had no idea what they were getting themselves into.

Nearby to the Al Shafirah complex some rather more experienced soldiers were preparing for battle. Several hundred professional Hizbullah special forces soldiers had been attached to a brigade of the Syrian 4th Mechanised Division. These were the best soldiers in the ranks of the Lebanese groups, who had years of experience fighting the Israelis. They were equipped with night-vision goggles and encoded radios and so were easy to spot on video footage posted on social-media, by their distinctive desert camouflage uniforms and US-made M16 rifles.

The Syrian soldiers were to provide armour and firepower support for the Hizbullah offensive, setting up an artillery fire base in the countryside just outside Al Safirah with a several BM-21 rocket launchers and 2S1 122mm self-propelled guns. Trucks brought up hundreds of rockets and shells which were piled next to the launchers and guns.

In this sector, the Syrian Tiger Force was also gathering to strike eastwards in an attempt to lift the siege of Kweires airbase to the east of Aleppo city and north of Safirah. Some 300 Syrian air force personnel were trapped behind Islamic State lines and it would be a major boost for the Damascus government if they could be freed. Between 500 and 1,000 Tiger Force soldiers, led by their infamous commander, Colonel

Suheil al-Hassan, would take part in this phase of the battle. The Tiger Force set up a fire base with artillery and rocket launchers to support the coming battle, but the Colonel was a very aggressive commander. So he brought his artillery pieces and ZSU-23-4 anti-aircraft guns right up to the front-line to fire directly at the Islamic State trench lines. The Tiger Force commander revelled in his ruthless image and reputedly would tune his walkie-talkie radio into the frequency used by the enemy commander on the other side of the front-line. He would then inform his opponent that he and all his men were about to die unless they fled. The close proximity of all these forces meant that a joint Syrian-Russian-Iranian headquarters had to be set up inside the Al Shafirah base. This became known as the Central Command, or "Centcom", of the Aleppo front and was needed to co-ordinate all the fighter jets, attack helicopters, rockets and artillery of three armies and two air forces that would soon be flying around over the congested battlefield.

Pictures of Soleimani working in the headquarters appeared repeatedly during this time, and Russian soldiers also posted details of their presence at the base on social-media sites. As well as having radio communications links, images of the headquarters suggested that Soleimani and other senior officers had electronic downlinks to watch video imagery from drones and view satellite imagery of the battlefield. It is not clear if this satellite imagery was supplied by Russians or was just downloaded from the Google Earth website. Either way, it showed a degree of sophistication that surprised many western observers.

The offensive south-west of Aleppo started on 16th October, a week or so after the Syrian attack in northern Hama and Latakia provinces. This meant the bulk of Russian and Syrian air support was switched northwards, after the Syrians had achieved their initial objectives to the south. BM-21 rocket and 122mm artillery barrages from the 4th Division's artillery group opened the offensive, hitting a series of rebel positions in a string of villages that lay parallel to the only road in government hands which ran south from Aleppo to Al Safirah and then to Hama, via Khrassaner and Ithriya. This road ran down a narrow corridor that was less than five kilometres wide at some points, and it needed to be widened to protect the only supply road into Aleppo. The 4th Division's T-72 tanks and Hizbullah special forces met little resistance from the rebel defenders. Video imagery shows the Syrian-Hizbullah columns advancing south on 19th October through the village of Kadar, heading towards Ithriya, in Homs province. Columns of T-72s, with lines of infantry alongside them, moved through a string of villages meeting minimal resistance. This force advanced more than 20 kilometres south of Aleppo in four days. This was the easy bit.

The attack force then swung around by 90 degrees and prepared to attack due west towards the M5 highway linking Idlib with Aleppo. Again the Hizbullah special forces, backed by the 4th Division's artillery, led the way, making the initial attacks on the string of villages that dominated the Qinnasrin Plain to the south west of Aleppo. In a series of brutal attacks, the Hizbullah special forces stormed rebel trench lines to capture important hill tops. Dramatic video imagery showed the Hizbullah soldiers dropping hand grenades into trenches and then "fire and manoeuvring" across open ground to storm the next rebel positions. Only highly skilled and motivated troops would even attempt this type of attack in the face of resistance.

The ambitious nature of the offensive now meant that the Shia militia forces gathering at Al Safirah had to be committed to hold the ground captured by the first wave of Hizbullah assault troops and then begin to take over the advance themselves. The three best Shia militia units – the Harakat Al-Nujaba, the Iraqi Kataeb Hezbollah militia and the Afghan Shia Firqa Fatayyemoun militia – were now thrown into the battle, with their Iranian commanders and advisors to the fore. From images of these militia groups preparing to attack and receiving "motivational talks" from their commanders, each of these groups probably only mustered between 300 and 400 fighters, backed by a handful of tanks and rocket launchers.

The villages and towns above the Qinnasrin Plain had been fortified and reinforced by heavily armed and experienced rebel fighters. Shia militia assault troops started to be hit by rocket and artillery barrages as they advanced. Rebels put up small drones to monitor the Shia fighters' movement and the rebels repeatedly launched surprise counter attacks that left the attackers running for their lives. The rebel propaganda film crews produced dramatic video reports filmed from drones showing a couple of their tanks storming into a Shia militia-held village and the shell-shocked defenders running out of the other end of the village.

Even when the Shia fighters managed to hold firm, they began taking heavy losses from rebel artillery and rocket fire. The rebels also began posting a string of video clips showing them picking off Shia militia positions, tanks and other vehicles with US-supplied TOW missiles. To help generate the proof needed to get replacement missiles from the CIA, the rebels filmed every missile launch and posted clips of them on the internet. Analysis of these clips showed that, during the last week of October 2015, on average more than a dozen TOW missiles were being fired daily, this dropped to between four and eight daily in the first half of November. More than half of these were in south west Aleppo where the open and rolling terrain was ideally suited to the US-made wire-guided anti-tank missile.

The TOW "greatest hits" videos became a staple of rebel internet propaganda campaigns, but they illustrated some interesting shortcomings of the Shia militia fighters operating in southern Aleppo province. The videos invariably show that Shia fighters had no idea they were being targeted until the missiles hit, with fighters being filmed walking around in the open next to tanks, vehicles or field guns. Shia fighters also seemed to have little idea how to position their tanks and heavy equipment so they were out of view of rebel missile teams. Overall, the Shia militias seemed ill-prepared and unready to fight enemies equipped with modern weapons or surveillance systems. It was telling that the Syrian 4th Division avoided putting its troops in front-line positions, where they would suffer daily attrition from TOW missiles and other rebel heavy weapons. The Shia militias appeared to be expendable cannon fodder.

The Iranian media also began to report a steady stream of casualties among the country's military personnel in Syria as the fighting south of Aleppo intensified. Between September and December 2015, it named 14 military officers as being killed in Syria, along with one senior Hizbullah commander.

All along the Qinnasrin Plain fighting see-sawed back and forth with villages changing hands on a daily basis. The Iranians brought up more Shia militia fighters to help swing the balance but the rebels threw in their own reinforcements. To try to give them an advantage, for the first time the Iranians used their missile-armed Shahed-129 drone, and video imagery was posted online showing missiles being fired from them at rebels in villages to the south-west of Aleppo. Even with this air support, the rebel defences were proving a tough nut to crack, and, although by late November the Shia forces got within sight of the M5 highway it would prove impossible to cut it.

The vulnerability of Syrian tanks to TOW missiles had already been proven during the fighting in Hama in October, and the Russian military had set in train the delivery of a batch of T-90 main battle tanks to Syria in a bid to neutralise the missile threat.

The T-90 is one of the first tanks ever to be fitted with a missile-defence system to neutralise and spoof inbound guided missiles such as the TOW, known as the Shtora-1. This system incorporates laser detectors around the tank's turret to automatically alert it to being marked by the laser guidance system of some versions of the TOW. If a threat is detected, the turret can be automatically slewed in the relevant direction so that smoke grenades can be launched to produce a screen that blocks the designator, giving the tank time to move to a new position.

The Shtora-1 is also designed to defeat missiles, which use an infrared (IR) beacon to track and guide them to their target. These include the version of the TOW system that was in widespread service with Syrian rebels. When the infra-red detectors alert the tank to an inbound missile, the Shorta-1 automatically slews the turret in the direction of the threat. Then two large heat sources, or emitters, on the turret are powered up and used to confuse the missile launcher's tracking and guidance system. In addition to these active defences, the T-90 is fitted with a layer of Kontakt-5 explosive-reactive armour blocks which prematurely detonate the warheads of in-bound TOW missiles before they can penetrate the tank's main armour.

Photographs of the new tanks first began appearing on social media on 23rd November, and six days later the Iranian State-owned news agency FARS began reporting that the tanks had been delivered to the Syrian 4th Division, based south of Aleppo. Images of a T-90 tank appeared at what seemed to be media facility at a Syrian army base on 28th November, with Syrian soldiers preparing the tanks for battle.

From the social-media images from this period, six tanks with factory fresh paint schemes can be identified being moved on a convoy of tank transporters on a country road in a region that bore similarities to the Khrassaner–Ithriya logistic road.

Although only a handful of tanks appear to have been involved, their delivery showed the importance the Russians placed on countering the rebel TOW threat. Not only were the missiles inhibiting the important advance south of Aleppo but they seemed to be undermining the morale of Syrian tank crews. They needed to be convinced that they would not be sitting ducks in "death-trap" tanks. The publicity given to the delivery of the new tanks and their defensive systems showed that a propaganda battle was underway to demonstrate that Russian tank technology was better than American missile technology.

To the east of Aleppo, a very different type of battle was underway. Colonel Hassan's Tiger Force was given the mission of punching a 20-kilometre corridor through Islamic State lines to Kweires airbase. The Jihadi fighters had fortified a string of villages, fields and farm complexes around the airbase.

The Tiger Force was one of the most experienced Syrian combat units and was invariably called upon to carry out full-front assaults. There was no finesse about Colonel Hassan's tactics. He also delighted in inviting Syrian television crews to film his victories. The advance on Kweires airbase was a text-book Tiger Force operation. Each village on the route to the airbase was subject to a withering barrage of air strikes, rockets, artillery and tanks firing directly at Islamic State positions. Only when the enemy positions had been flattened would Colonel Hassan send in his infantry or intrusion groups to capture the ground. They would advance under covering fire from ZSU-23-4 quad anti-aircraft guns, which sprayed out a rain of tracer shells. The Colonel was repeatedly filmed standing on top of a trench or a tank, personally directing attacks via multiple hand held radios. He would then take Syrian news crews to tour the site of his victories to show off the bodies of dead Islamic State fighters. There was nothing subtle about this and the Colonel appeared to delight in demonstrating to both friends and foes that his troops would kill every enemy fighter they met on the battlefield. It was psychological warfare of a very brutal sort.

Colonel Hassan's performances were pure bravado but often in the propaganda clips of Tiger Force battles it was possible to see his professional staff officers co-ordinating the complex fire-support missions that made its attacks possible. Many of officers could be seen using tablet computers to look at satellite imagery or using maps with target positions and code names of targets marked on them.

This ritual was repeated on a daily basis for nearly three weeks until a corridor of devastation had opened a route to the 300 Syrian airmen trapped inside the base. They had been besieged since 2013 and their relief was a major boost to the Damascus government. Syrian state television conducted a live outside broadcast from Kweires airbase on 11th December to demonstrate to the population that the tide of war had turned in its favour.

Chapter 8
Russia's War with Turkey

In some of the most dramatic images to emerge from the Syrian conflict, the Russian Sukhoi Su-24 strike jet could be seen being engulfed in a fireball over northern Syria on 24th November 2015. As the aircraft dropped to earth, two parachutes were seen as the crew made their escape.

The crew floated to earth and rebel fighters broke from cover to start shooting at the Russian airmen with rifles and machine guns. One of the Russians was hit by the fire but the other airman was able to land safely in the wooded hills of northern Latakia, only a few miles from the border with Turkey.

To the south at Hmeinyan airbase, officers in the Russian air group command post soon began to monitor radio signals from the emergency beacon of the Su-24's navigator, Captain Konstantin Murakhtin. A pair of Mil Mi-8 transport helicopters and two Mil Mi-24 attack helicopters were scrambled from the base, with a contingent of marines from the 810th Naval Infantry Brigade on board to rescue the downed airman.

Video footage shot by rebel fighters during the battle showed the Russian helicopters flying low over the forested hills in a bid to find their downed comrade. The rebels opened fire on the helicopters and one of the Mi-8s had to make an emergency landing. Mortar shells started to drop around the grounded helicopter, forcing the crew and its marines to take cover nearby. One of the marines was killed by this fire but his comrades managed to raise the other Mi-8 on the radio and it returned to lift them to safety.

A rebel TOW missile team had now climbed up to the top of a ridge line over-looking the grounded helicopter and they were filmed calmly setting up their launcher. Then they launched a missile at the helicopter, turning it into a huge fireball.

Fortunately for Captain Murakhtin, a group of Syrian soldiers had also been watching the action and saw where he came to earth. These were local men who knew the lie of the land in the heavily wooded region. The Syrian officers told their senior commanders that they thought they could get to the pilot and bring him out to safety. Russian air commanders agreed to launch a series of air strikes along the Turkish border to distract the rebels, as a team of Syrian and Hizbullah commandos infiltrated through the woods in a bid to find the downed airman. The soldiers then shepherded the pilot to safety and within hours he was back at Hmeinyan airbase, telling Russian journalists how he wanted to return to duty to avenge his dead comrade.

The whole incident was over in a matter of hours but it had a profound influence on the course of the Syrian conflict. Ever since the Russian air force began operating over Syria at the end of September 2015, there had been repeated accusations from Ankara that Russian aircraft were regularly infringing Turkish air space. The Turkish air force was put on alert and warning were issued that any aircraft entering Turkish air space would be shot down. This was a hair trigger.

The border between Turkey and Syria's Latakia province is winding and not obvious from the air. Syrian and rebel soldiers were locked in heavy fighting close to the border. The rebel fighters were heavily dependent on a series of roads and border crossing points that weaved over the mountain ridges the border followed. The presence of Turkish combat air patrols in this sensitive border region also served the purpose of deterring Russian and Syrian air attacks on the rebel supply lines, close to the border. Pairs of Turkish Lockheed Martin F-16 Fighting Falcons circled continuously at strategic points, monitoring Russian and Syrian air operations a few miles to the south and east.

The Russians were not going to be put off by the Turkish air presence. They repeatedly flew bombing missions against rebel targets close to the border and dared the Turks to do their worst. This all came to a head on the morning of 24th November when a Su-24 was launched on an air patrol over northern Syria. In this tense situation, the Russian jet was ordered by flight controllers to bomb a rebel target in northern Latakia. After successfully carrying out this strike, the Sukhoi was ordered to turn around and carry out another strike in the same area. As it came around and headed westwards on its second bombing run, a Turkish F-16 was ordered to head south to intercept to the Russian jet that appeared to heading directly towards Turkish airspace. The accounts from Ankara and Moscow on what happened next still conflict on whether the Russian aircraft actually crossed into Turkish airspace. With reaction times measured in seconds, the Turkish pilot was ordered to shoot down the Sukhoi. He launched an AIM-9X Sidewinder heat-seeking missile at the Su-24 and seconds later it exploded in a fireball.

The aftermath to the incident was even more incendiary than the attack itself. President Putin was outraged. He ordered economic sanctions worth billions of dollars against Turkey's holiday and other industries. To prevent any more incidents, the Russian president ordered a battery of S-400 strategic surface-to-air-missiles to Hmeinyan airbase in Syria. These were the most powerful missiles in the Russian air defence arsenal and could potentially shoot down Turkish aircraft as they took off from airfields hundreds of miles inside their country. A Russian Navy flotilla, led by the air-defence missile cruiser, the Moskova, was also ordered to patrol the Syrian coastline to add to the air defence "umbrella". Putin stepped back from a direct military confrontation with the Turkish armed forces but he ordered a major stepping-up of attacks on the rebels backed by Ankara in Idlib and Aleppo provinces. At the same time a propaganda campaign was launched accusing the Turks of assisting the Islamic State through the buying of oil from the Jihadi group. In a series of blistering Moscow press conferences, Russian generals showed video imagery shot by Forpost drones of convoys of trucks and oil tankers crossing into Syria and heading for Islamic State territory.

Russian jets were then ordered to bomb these crossing points and truck convoys. Across north-western Aleppo province, social-media footage began appearing showing burning trucks and oil tankers. Moscow accused these vehicles of being rebel supply convoys but they all appeared to be civilian vehicles. It was not possible to determine their cargoes but they all seemed to burn furiously. Any trucks moving along the main roads in Aleppo and Idlib provinces were fair game for the Russian strike jets. In a significant change in tactics, the Russian pilots were given permission to attack targets at will in several "kill boxes" along the Turkish border zone.

A Russian report of the Su-25 regiment's operations in Syria during this period included an account of these interdiction strikes. "Since November 2015 Su-25s have begun to fly reconnaissance and strike operations - the so-called "free hunt"," it said. "Take-offs were carried out singly or in pairs (after which each aircraft departed along its own route) and then they carried out independent search to [find] and destroy mobile targets. [The Su-25s] hunted for columns as well as for single military vehicles (trucks, wagons, gasoline tankers), thereby suppressing the supply of weapons, ammunition, fuel, food, medicines and other logistics to bandit [rebel] formations. Sometimes four PTB-800 [drop tanks] and two NAR B-8 [rocket pods] were hung on planes, and then they were [on patrol] in the [mission zones] for two hours.

These were classic air interdiction tactics, as practiced by allied air forces in World War Two, the Vietnam and 1991 Iraq wars. However, western air forces were no longer happy with these tactics, viewing them as indiscriminate and far too likely to cause civilian casualties.

In some of the video clips, the Russians claimed they were bombing large Islamic State truck parks in Raqqa and Dier Ez Zor provinces that contained hundreds of vehicles. Only a few weeks before, a British journalist from the Sunday Times had flown on a Royal Air Force Sentinel R1 radar surveillance aircraft over eastern Syria and the aircraft's crew had detected the truck parks but coalition commanders decided not to attack the vehicles. It seems that because they thought the truck drivers might not have been Islamic State fighters but press-ganged civilians they had been spared from attack. When Russian drone surveillance spotted the truck parks, they showed no such scruples and a series of air strikes were ordered to hit the vehicles; video imagery of the truck parks exploding in huge fireballs was subsequently show at a Moscow Ministry of Defence media briefing.

On the ground, the Russian, Syrian and Iranian military commands in northern Syria were busy working out how to put real pressure on the rebel forces in north-western Aleppo province. The Shia militia had made some advances to the south-west of Aleppo city but the strong rebel defences had proved impossible to break. The Syrians had also made advances on northern Latakia, but this was also proving too tough. Planners and intelligence officers at the "Centcom" headquarters at Al Safirah had to look at a new sector where they could strike.

They turned their attention to the north of Aleppo city, which was less than 10 kilometres from the pro-government Zahraa-Nubul enclave. It in turn was attached to the large Afrin enclave, which was controlled Kurdish YPG, or People's Defence Units, militia group. Although officially not allied to the Damascus regime and nominally an active part of the US-led anti-Islamic State coalition, the YPG was a sworn enemy of the Turkish government. Ankara viewed the YPG as an adjunct of the Kurdish Workers Party, or PKK, and described both the YPG and PKK as terrorists. The Turkish army regularly shelled Afrin and clashed with YPG fighters over the border. Some 300,000 people lived in the Kurdish enclave and some 20,000 in the Zahraa-Nubul enclave.

In this environment, the Kurds in Afrin were open to offers to co-operate against Turkey. A series of night-time helicopter flights took senior Syrian army officers into Afrin during January 2016 to co-ordinate the coming offensive. The YPG commanders were attracted to the idea of the Syrians opening a land corridor from Aleppo, which would mean they were no longer dependent on the Turks and their Jihadi rebel allies for supplies. As a sign of good faith, Russian Ilyushin Il-76 and Iranian Lockheed C-130 Hercules transport aircraft flew several missions to parachute supplies to the enclave. Soon the deal was done and the Syrian operation was set to start at the end of January.

The aim of the attack would be to punch a corridor through to Zahraa-Nubul but this in turn would cut in half the rebel alliance known as the Army of Conquest, which was the predominant rebel group in the region from the Turkish border down to Idlib. The advance would cut the sole metalled road that ran south from the Kilis border crossing to Aleppo and then Idlib. This would in turn force the rump of the Army of Conquest to re-orient its supply line via roads and tracks into Turkey over high mountains to the west of Idlib. The Kurds would in turn then be able to try to link with other YPG units around Kobani, to the east. The unification of Kurdish enclaves along the Turkish border was Ankara's worst nightmare. So not surprisingly, the Russians and Syrians were set to stir the pot with their new offensive.

With the Kurdish YPG and Syrian National Defence Force (NDF) militia in Zahraa-Nubul region squared away, the build-up of forces began in earnest in January in the north west of Aleppo city. The 4th Mechanised Division was given overall command of the operation and it deployed two of its own brigades, along with the Hizbullah special forces again. For the second time a major Syrian offensive would be led by a detachment of T-90 tanks. Other tanks and armoured vehicles of the 4th Division were fitted with Syrian-made missile jammers, called Sarab-1 or Mirage-1 in English, to blind the guidance systems of the rebel TOW missiles. All told, some 2,000 troops were massed for the operation.

Other units of the 4th Division were sent to the south-west of Aleppo to confuse the rebels and keep them guessing as to where the main offensive would fall and when.

Russian aircraft, Syrian rockets and artillery started to bombard the villages along the line of advance on 1st February. Over the next three days some 280 air strikes hit rebel trench lines, mortar positions and dug-in tanks on a very narrow front. The intensity of the bombardment had not been seen before in the Syrian war. Other Russian and Syrian aircraft bombed the approach routes to the battle zone to try to stop any reinforcements being dispatched from both Idlib to the south and Azaz to the north. At least five SS-21 Tochka ballistic missiles were fired by the Syrians at key road junctions and border crossings just behind the battle zone.

Hizbullah special-forces infantry, accompanied by 4th Division T-90s, led the ground assault, which first secured the village of Rityan. From video imagery of the battles, the defenders did not appear to put up much resistance. The assault troops linked up with the NDF pushing eastward from Zahraa between the small villages of Meyer and Mu'arrast al Khan on 3rd February, cutting the northern routes out of Aleppo to Turkey.

Army of Conquest fighters tried to stage repeated counter-attacks to hold back the Syrian advance. The intensity of the fighting was indicated by reports from Syrian and Iranian media sources that one Syrian army brigadier general and an Iranian Revolutionary Guards Corps brigadier general, as well as 11 Iranian "military advisors", had been killed in fighting around Aleppo on 2nd and 3rd February.

YPG fighters in Afrin took advantage of the chaos in the Army of Conquest ranks to stage their own offensive, eastwards out of their enclave and rapidly seized several towns and villages, as well as Menagh . Some 70,000 refugees headed into Azaz and then towards, the Turkish border. This prompted Ankara to respond and Turkish artillery began shelling the YPG fighters on Menagh .

At the same time as this, the Syrian army had advanced to the north-west of Aleppo, units of its Tiger Force moving to complete the encirclement of several hundred Islamic State fighters dug in between the eastern edge of Aleppo city and Kweires . These fighters staged a night time retreat rather than fight to the death.

The offensive north of Aleppo was by far the most ambitious and complex operation mounted by the Russian-led coalition in Syria since Moscow began its intervention in the Middle East in September 2015. As an exercise in hurting Turkey and its militia allies in Syria, the north Aleppo offensive certainly fitted the bill.

Chapter 9
The Battle of Palmyra, March 2016

Gruesome execution videos have become the trade mark of the Islamic State's publicity machine. So when it posted a film on line of its fighters displaying the body of a dead Russian soldier in desert outside Palmyra on 17th March, no-one was really surprised.

The unfortunate soldier had suffered multiple injuries and his uniform was soaked in blood – much of which had not yet dried. These were not pictures for the faint hearted. His weapons and equipment were displayed around the body, suggesting this was no ordinary Russian soldier but part of the elite special forces unit known as Spetsnaz. The soldier's affiliation appeared to be confirmed by other photographs posted at the same time, which were taken inside a Russian barracks showing his comrades displaying the distinctive flag with the "bat" insignia of the General Staff Intelligence directorate, or GRU, Spetsnaz. For several days after the pictures appeared online there was silence from the Kremlin, prompting wild speculation about their authenticity. It would be a full week before the Russian military confirmed that one of its men had been killed in action in the Syrian desert.

Yet only days before, Russian President Vladimir Putin had taken the world by surprise when he announced that Russia's combat operations in Syria were over and that the main part of his military contingent would soon be returning to their home bases.

Russian media reports said the Kremlin was now focused on the UN-sponsored Geneva peace process. Moscow's diplomats were ordered to redouble their efforts bring the Syrian government to the negotiating table and to help set up a nationwide cessation-of-hostilities agreement. This was the time for Moscow to try to seize diplomatic and political advantages from the first six months of the Russian military intervention in Syria. The military campaign in Syria would be downplayed by Putin to allow him to leverage concessions out of the US and its allies. The public narrative of Russian intervention was dramatically re-jigged to suit the new circumstances.

Within days of Putin's withdrawal announcement on 14th March, a series of parades were being held by the runway at Hmeinyan airbase to say farewell to contingents of Russian aircraft. Bands played, flags waved and the jets disappeared into the skies, heading home to Mother Russia. At airbases across Russia, the aircraft arrived to a great fanfare. The impression was that it was "mission accomplished", although Putin did not repeat the famous catch phrase of US President George W Bush from 2003.

On 17th March during a glitzy ceremony in the Kremlin's Hall of the Order of St. George, Putin fuelled the feel-good factor by presenting medals to Russian military personnel who served in the operation in Syria. He revealed that Russia's six-month long military intervention cost 66 billion roubles ($464 million US) and also paid tribute to the army's heroes who had died in Syria. He confirmed that five Russian servicemen had died in Syria, including a GRU Spetsnaz special forces operator, whose death had previously not been revealed and was mentioned at the start of this chapter.

In the ceremony, Putin presented medals and decorations to 17 service personnel, including making four Heroes of the Russian Federation, the country's highest honour. Awards were made to a "missile artillery" commander from the 810th Naval Infantry Brigade and an officer of the 120th Artillery Brigade. A Russian army drone operator was also honoured, as well as a female engineering officer from an air-defence unit. The senior ground forces officer who oversaw the Russian intervention, Colonel General Alexander Dvornikov, was named in public by the Kremlin for the first time.

Putin lavished praise on the pilots and commanders of the Russian Aerospace Force (RuAF) and several were honoured, including a number of senior test pilots. The role of the Russian aerospace industry in sustaining the operation of deployed combat aircraft was highlighted by Putin, with Sergei Smirnov, deputy director-general of Sukhoi's Novosibirsk Aircraft Works, being honoured with a medal.

Putin confirmed during his speech that Russian forces would continue to support the Syrian military as they sustained operations against what he termed "terrorist" groups and to protect Syrian sovereignty from outside interference. He declared that Russian air power could return to Syria rapidly if the current cessation of hostilities broke down. "If necessary, Russia is capable of building up its forces just in a few hours to a scale that is appropriate for the developing situation, and using the whole arsenal of available capabilities," Putin said.

The Russian president did not go into many details about the residual force that would remain in Syria, beyond mentioning that it would be "well-protected on the ground, on the sea and in the air." He specifically said that Tartus port and Hmeinyan airbase would be protected by Russian Pantsir and S-400 air defence systems. The Russian Conciliation Centre at Hmeinyan airbase, which had been set up to monitor the cessation of hostilities agreement, was also to remain in Syria, along with the officers who deconflict airspace with the US-led coalition.

Amid this massive exercise in news management, Moscow's real intentions were cleverly concealed. The veil, however, began to slip once analysts started to pore through the video footage from the withdrawal ceremonies Hmeinyan airbase. Far from withdrawing the bulk of its air power, the Russian air force in fact had only in fact pulled back home its squadron of Sukhoi Su-25 ground-attack jets, along with four of the eight Sukhoi Su-34 strike-aircraft and a couple of Sukhoi Su-24 bombers. This in effect reduced the fixed-wing strike force in Syria by a third. While some of the older Russian fixed-wing aircraft were being withdrawn, a number of the country's newest attack helicopters were being sent to Syria.

In the background of some of this video footage, the distinctive shape of one of Russia's newest attack helicopters, the Kamov Ka-52 Alligator, could be seen partly assembled outside a hangar on the edge of Hmeinyan airbase on 16th March. Later that day more footage was broadcast by the Russian media that showed another advanced attack helicopter, a Mil Mi-28, flying around the base in what appeared to be a flight test. The Russian Ministry of Defence's own Star television network played its part in revealing the changing nature of the Russian deployment 10 days later when filming a giant Antonov An-124 lifting off from the Syrian with a cargo of three Mi-24 and 35s being flown back to their home base as part of the "withdrawal". On the far side of the runway the distinctive launcher vehicle of a Iskander M tactical ballistic missile could be seen. Its 400 kilometre-plus range meant it could hit targets in central Syria without even leaving the Russian base on the Mediterranean coast. Far from withdrawing from battle, the Russian force in Syria was clearly being reconfigured for a new phase of the war. *

The focus of the Russian air power would now be the desert region of central and eastern Syria where fighters of the Islamic State held sway. This fitted the new Russian political and diplomatic narrative, that Moscow could say it was the West's partner in the fight against the radical Jihadi group and be a full player in the international diplomatic efforts to end the Syrian civil war.

Syria's central desert region was overrun by Islamic State fighters in May 2015, culminating in the capture of the ancient city of Palmyra. During its lightning advance the Jihadi group also overran several of Syria's biggest oil and gas fields, as well as cutting off the only supply route to the city of Dier Ez Zor, leaving its 5,000-strong Syrian army garrison and 100,000 civilian population cut off.

Islamic State columns rampaged across the region for several months and as late as October 2015, were still threatening the eastern edge of the Syrian capital, Damascus, and the city of Homs. In November 2015, the Syrian high command and its Russian allies decided to strike back on this front and turn around the Islamic State advance.

A remote desert airbase at Shayrat in the central Homs region of Syria soon became the home for a contingent of Mi-24P gunships which flew down from Hmeinyan to set up a forward-operating site. The first target for the Syrian counter-attack was the town of Qaryatayn, just to the south of Palmyra. Pairs of Mi-24Ps made daily sweeps across the desert, firing barrages of free-flight rockets at Islamic State positions on mountain tops dominating desert valleys. For almost three months, these battles swung back and forth as Islamic State columns staged counter-attacks on Syrian army units advancing along roads.

A detachment of four Mi-24Ps and a single Mi-8AMShT was kept at the base throughout December 2015 and into January 2016, according to commercial satellite imagery. Video imagery released by pro-Syrian army bloggers showed the details of Russian helicopters operating at Shayrat airbase, where they flew from a flight line next to Syrian Arab Air Force (SyAAF) hardened aircraft shelters. When they launched for missions, the Mi-8s would take off and follow behind the gunships, apparently to provide immediate recovery if any of the helicopters should go down in the remote desert region.

The Islamic State siege of Dier Ez Zor was tightened in January 2016 with a large-scale offensive that overran an important part of the Syrian defence lines. In response, some 18 heavy bomber sorties were flown against the Islamic State positions around the city by eight Russian Long Range Aviation Tupolev Tu-22M3 bombers between 22nd and 24th January. The 2,000-kilometre-long missions were launched from the RuAF base at Mozdok airbase, in Ossetia, where the RuAF's Reinforced Air Wing had been set up to support Moscow's operation in Syria. In Russian Ministry of Defence video of one of the Dier Ez Zor missions, two Tu-22M3s were shown each dropping sticks of around a dozen FAB-250-270 266kg unguided bombs in an attempt to "carpet bomb" Islamic State fighters pressing the city's defence lines.

For more than a year, Dier Ez Zor's garrison and population had relied on SyAAF Mi-8 helicopters as their only lifeline. In a bid to increase the supplies reaching the city, the RuAF began flying air-drop missions to the city. At first the Russians tried to portray the air drops as "Syrian" by painting a Syrian flag on the tail of its Ilyushin Il-76 based at Hmeinyan airbase. The aircraft retained its Russian military serial and the crew which appeared in videos of the airdrops, were all wearing Russian flight suits and behaved like Russian military pilots. Later in January 2016, video also appeared showing a Lockheed C-130 Hercules making another air drop over Dier Ez Zor, suggesting that the Islamic Republic of Iran Air Force (IRIAF) had joined the effort to support the city. As the only operator of C-130s allied to the Syrian government, the Iranians seemed the prime suspects, although Tehran did not formally acknowledge the missions.

The United Nations World Food Programme attempted its own air drops to Dier Ez Zor on 24th February, using a chartered Il-76 flying from Amman in Jordan but high winds and technical difficulties hampered the air drop to the city. Four pallets were damaged because their parachutes failed to open properly, seven landed in no man's land and 10 drifted away and remained unaccounted for, according to a WFP announcement. Russian Su-30 fighters escorted the UN aircraft on the mission. The Russian pilots filmed the mission from the cockpits of their jets and their foray into the skies of eastern Syria during broad daylight was a graphic demonstration of RuAF air power in a region normally dominated by US and British combat aircraft striking at Islamic State held oil fields around Dier Ez Zor.

The support for the Dier Ez Zor garrison was only the first phase of a major Russian operation against Islamic State in the central Syrian desert. Even before the official announcement of the Russian "withdrawal" from Syria, General Dvornikov had put in place the necessary planning and deployments to enable the Syrian army, backed by a sizeable contingent of Russian advisors and supporting artillery, to attack and seize the city of Palmyra and its ancient ruins – a UNESCO World Heritage site. The public relations impact of Syrian and Russian troops liberating Palmyra would be immense.

The preparations for the attack got under way in February 2016, when the Syrian high command began massing thousands of extra troops in the desert ready for the operation against Palmyra. The RuAF helicopter detachment at Shayrat was also doubled in strength in time for the offensive, with eight Mi-24 or new Mi-35s and one Mi-8 routinely on the flight line at the base.

The attack force concentrated for the attack around the Syrian airbase at T-4 and was soon joined by a Russian artillery detachment equipped with some of the most modern weapons in Moscow's arsenal. The Russia 24 television network broadcast a report from the Palmyra region on 13th March showing two BM-30 Smerch and a TOS-1A multiple rocket system in action. During this period a Russian soldier from the 120th Artillery Brigade uploaded pictures onto his social media account from a patch of desert just to the west of Palmyra, confirming the presence of Moscow's men in the battle. Neither BM-30 or TOS-1A had been noted before in the Palmyra region, previously being heavily committed to action in the north of Lakatia province. The Smerch rocket had a range of 80 kilometres and the TOS-1A fired a barrage of thermobaric or fuel air explosive-tipped rockets, which first sprayed a film of kerosene over a target and then detonated it to create a devastating explosion.

During February and into March 2016, Syrian media had been reporting a steady stream of reinforcements being dispatched to boost the advance on Palmyra. These included the elite Tiger Force under the command of Colonel Suheil al-Hassan, the Liwa Suqour Al-Sahra, or Desert Hawks, Brigade of Colonel Muhammed Jaber, the Quneitra and Golan regiments of the National Defence Force militia, and the Syrian Marine battalion. Units from the Lebanese Hizbullah, the Afghan Shia Liwa Al-Fatemiyoun militia and a small detachment of Iranian Republican Guard special forces were also identified as arriving in the Palmyra region. The al

Masdar News Agency reported that by 23rd March, over 6,000 Syrian and allied troops were participating in the new offensive.

Despite the reports of thousands of Syrian troops massing in the desert to attack Palmyra, the war on this remote and brutal front was far from glamorous. Syria troops and their Islamic State opponents lived in makeshift bunkers, trenches and checkpoints spread out across the desert. Video imagery posted online from this time showed many of these positions, which were often no more than a couple of sandbags arrayed around trenches. Sometimes the occupants - often less than a dozen soldiers - had built sleeping quarters out of old crates or planks of wood and tried to make them more comfortable with looted furniture. Supplies were meagre, often no more than several plastic water bottles and pitta-bread sandwiches. The soldiers were completely dependent on supplies dropped off by their comrades. There was no point in trying to flee – all around was nothing but empty desert with no food or water to be had. The risk of being picked up by enemy patrols was too great. For the Syrians, the prospect of being captured by Islamic State fighters was too grim to contemplate.

Death did not usually could come not from attack by enemy infantry but by guided anti-tank missiles, tank fire or artillery strikes. Time and again on this desert front, the rival armies would take potshots at each other with long-range weapons. The aftermath of these attacks was usually a shattered bunker or trench with bits of bodies left scattered around them. From this period, video clips filmed by victorious soldiers inspecting captured trenches showed that, often, there was no-one left to bury the dead or treat the wounded. The losers in these desert battles faced lonely and lingering deaths.

February and March saw the Russian helicopter crews striking targets closer and closer to the gates of Palmyra. An opposition blogger in the town posted an online video in late February showing an Mi-24 strike against a hill a few hundred yards from Palmyra's historic medieval castle.

The battle turned on the control of several ridge lines around Palmyra and to increase the accuracy of the RuAF helicopter and fixed wing strikes on Islamic State positions, the GRU dispatched several teams of special forces to act as forward air controllers with Syrian spearhead units. These teams increased the effectiveness of RuAF air strikes dramatically, but the Islamic State defenders still had plenty of fight left in them. They located one of the Spetsnaz forward air controllers on 17th March on a remote hill top and moved to overrun his position. According, details subsequently revealed by the Kremlin, the Spetsnaz officer called down an air strike on his position just as the Islamic State fighters were closing in rather than risk capture. The Russian GRU operative was killed and Islamic State later displayed his body and equipment in an online video.

The battle for Palmyra reached a climax in the last week of March, with Mi-24 and newly arrived Mi-28s mounting hourly strikes in and around the ancient city. Video footage from the battlefield showed both types of Russian helicopters making low-level strikes with rockets and guided anti-tank missiles. Russian helicopters were flying between 20 and 25 strike missions a day against Islamic State targets in and around city Islamic State fighters held a last line ridges to the west, south and north of Palmyra until the Russian TOS-1A rocket launcher was move forward to position within range of a key road junction, known as the Palmyra Triangle, to bring down its devastating firepower. A mine-clearing line charge (MCLC) system was filmed by the Russian Life News network being used outside Palmyra to blast a route through Islamic State minefields. The system appeared to be fired from an Ural truck and then detonated several hundred metres away.

On top of the ridge lines, Islamic State anti-tank missile teams tried to put up resistance and pick off Syrian tanks moving across the desert plain. A suicide bomber in a pick-up truck was sent to attack a group of newly arrived Syrian Marines in a village as they prepared to move into the front on 21st March, killing several of them.

The decisive breakthrough was made on the Hayyan ridge line to the south west of Palmyra from 18th March by the Tiger Force troops who staged a series of running battles with stay-behind teams of Islamic State fighters dug in to rocky outcrops. It was not a surprise that the Tiger Force, as the most battle-hardened and professional Syrian unit, were given this key mission. They had to work closely with Russian forward air controllers during the battle. Once it was over several pictures emerged of the Russian Spetsnaz operatives and their Syrian allies relaxing on the ridge's crest. This further cemented the links between the Tiger Force and the Russian military that would be repeated in subsequent battles later in the year.

By 23rd March, the Tiger Force had pushed along the Hayyan ridge and was overlooking the Palmyra Triangle road junction. This allowed the Desert Hawk Brigade riding in their "Mad Max" armoured pick-up trucks and gun wagons to drive up to the hill directly over looking Palmyra's ancient ruins. At the same time, on the northern axis the Syrian Marines pushed forward with strong support from Russian Mi-28 gunships and Syrian Gazelle helicopters firing anti-tank missiles. Palmyra's medieval castle was captured on 26th March and it was only a matter of time before the city below fell. This was the key day of the battle - the Russian Ministry of Defence said its aircraft flew 40 sorties and engaged 158 targets, resulting in 100 Jihadi fighters being killed, as well as four tanks, three artillery pieces, four ammunition dumps and five other vehicles being destroyed. With Syrian troops controlling the commanding heights around Palmyra, the Islamic State fighters in the city now staged a tactical retreat, mounting up in a column of pick-up trucks and heading east along the road towards Dier Ez Zor, leaving a small rear guard at the Palmyra grain silo position to hold up any pursuit. The Islamic State left improvised road side-bombs and mines around the city but the advancing Syrian troops on 27th March found few dead bodies of their enemies. Immediately behind the assault troops were a strong contingent of Russian and Syrian journalists who were rapidly broadcasting images of the liberated ancient ruins of Palmyra to the world. It was a public relations triumph for the Kremlin. The first major city to be liberated from Islamic State had been freed by Syrian troops, backed by Russian air power. The US and its allies could no longer claim that Russia was not fighting Islamic State.

The British-based Syrian Observatory for Human Rights reported on 27th March that an estimated 400 Islamic State fighters and around 180 government troops had been killed in the fighting for Palmyra. Photographs released by Getty Images suggested one of these fatalities was a Syrian colonel, killed by Islamic State mortar fire on Palmyra Castle just after it had been captured. However, once the Syrian and Russian media entered Palmyra, their reports and imagery did not suggest that heavy fighting had taken place in the city's streets. If hundreds of Jihadis and Syrian soldiers had been killed then they must have fallen in the battles that took place in the desert and mountain ranges in the weeks immediately before the final dénouement. Not for the first time, a Syrian battle been hyped up by media reports into a massive engagement but had in fact ended in a whimper as one side fled the battlefield rather than suffering heavy losses. The Islamic State forces retreat from Palmyra went against the popular narrative that they preferred death or martyrdom to defeat. The defenders of Palmyra certainly wanted to live to fight another day.

With Palmyra and its ancient ruins secure, the Russians and Syrians set about building a security cordon around the city to allow them to milk the victory for maximum political and diplomatic advantage. There were few people in the city that needed any sort of humanitarian aid – the vast majority had fled Islamic State's barbaric rule months before. A Russian army de-mining team was flown to Syria and then moved to Palmyra to start clearing the city's ancient ruins of improvised explosive devices, mines and unexploded ordnance.

Russian troops then began setting up a forward operating base in the city and installed an air-defence system to protect the strategic site. Video imagery broadcast by the AFP news agency showed the Russian base had been built within a few hundred metres of the iconic Palmyra Castle, on the city's western fringe. The base was secured by a high chain-link fence topped with razor wire, and included prefabricated container buildings, large tents for equipment maintenance and a field kitchen, as well as satellite communications dishes. A Russian flag could be seen flying in the compound. One Pantsir-S1 72V6-E4 point-defence anti-aircraft system was seen on the video clip, as well as several BTR-82A armoured personnel carriers. The number of BTR-82As filmed suggests nearly 100 Russian combat troops were stationed at the base, probably to provide close protection of mine-clearing troops operating in Palmyra and for high level-Russian visitors to the city. Logistic supply and recovery vehicles were also visible in the footage.

Work on the base probably began in April after the Russians deployed a mine -clearing unit too Palmyra to help Syrian troops clear unexploded ordnance and improvised explosive devices left behind by retreating Islamic State fighters.

Russia continued to maintain a strong military presence in the central desert region at Shayrat and T-4 airbases.

The RuAF helicopter detachment at Shayrat had been joined by four Kamov Ka-52 attack helicopters in time for the final assault on nearby town of Qaryatayn in early April. Satellite imagery of Shayrat airbase and the nearby T-4 airbase taken on 31st March showed a combined Russian helicopter force of four Ka-52s, three Mi-28s, seven Mi-24s and two Mi-8s in place.

The attack on Qaryatayn tidied up the front to the south of Palmyra and helped hinder Islamic State fighters re-organise their defences. The new Ka-52s and Mi-28s had night-attack systems that allowed them to patrol along roads and tracks in darkness to strike at Islamic State vehicles moving troops into new defensive positions. Video of a night-time missile engagement released by the Russian military showed that the helicopter's targets had no idea they were under attack when the missiles hit them. Night-time operations are not risk-free and on 12th April an Mi-28 crashed near Homs city, with the loss of its two crew. The TASS news agency later reported that an investigation attributed the crash to the crew losing orientation in the featureless desert, causing them to fly into the ground, which seemed plausible.

Moscow's helicopters were seen escorting a large convoy of dignitaries and journalists to Palmyra on 6th May to attend an orchestral concert in Palmyra's ancient theatre. This event was major success for the Kremlin and was broadcast live around the world, including on western news channels, such as the BBC and CNN. The operation to move several coach loads of more than 100 international journalists was a major logistic exercise for the Russian military, who not only provided an air escort but laid on several dozen armoured vehicles containing hundreds of troops to accompany the convoy. Thousands of Syrian troops secured the outer cordon around Palmyra as the concert by Russia's Mariinskiy Theatre Orchestra was underway. President Putin appeared on video link from Moscow to congratulate everyone for a job well done. The continued Russian presence in the Palmyra region was also linked to the continuing Syrian operations against Islamic State, which was holding a series of oil and gas wells to the north and east of Palmyra. At the start of May 2016 local media reported that Syrian Tiger Force units began advancing eastward into the Arak gas field which is 20 kilometres west of Al-Sukhnah on the Palmyra-Deir Ez Zor Highway. Video footage showed formations of between three and seven Russian attack helicopters launching strikes along this road in a bid to break the siege of Dier Ez Zor.

Despite their defeat in Palmyra at the end of March, Islamic State forces in the region staged several major counter-attacks during April and early May, including a large operation that seized a large section of the Shaer and al-Mahr gas fields 40 kilometres to the north-west of Palmyra. Imagery posted online by the Jihadi group appeared to show a large amount of ammunition seized from the Syrian military in the gas fields. The Damascus-based al Masdar News Agency reported that Tiger Force units had to be re-deployed from the drive on Dier Ez Zor in a bid to counter this Islamic State advance along the mountain range that dominates the supply route between Palmyra and Homs city.

The Syrian and Russian advance on Palmyra in March was not the only operation launched in the central desert region during this period. A Syrian army column had began advancing on the Islamic State capital of Raqqa in an unexpected move during February. News of the operation first emerged in the second week of February after Syrian soldiers began posting images of deployments along the border of Hama and Raqqa provinces on social media sites. Damascus-based news media and the Syrian Observatory for Human Rights also reported on the advance by regular Syrian Arab Army troops and National Defence Force militia units.

The Syrian force gathered at the desert garrison town of Ithriya in the east of Hama province in early February before beginning to advance eastward along the main road to Raqqa. A series of skirmishes with Islamic State fighters was then reported and by 14th February there were reports of fighting across the provincial boundary. This is the first time Syrian troops had been present in Raqqa province since August 2014 when Tabqa airbase, to the south of Raqqa city, was seized by Islamic State. Some 200 captured Syrian soldiers were subsequently filmed being beheaded and shot in one of the Jihadi group's most infamous atrocity videos.

Social-media posts and local news reports suggested the Syrian force involved several units, including the 555th Brigade of the 4th Mechanised Division, which had been operating in the Ithriya region since December. Brigades of the elite 4th Division usually boasted around

1,000 troops, equipped with T-72 tanks and other armoured vehicles. Reinforcing units included the Golan Regiment of the National Defence Force militia, which was filmed driving through Damascus in a convoy on 31st January from its base in Quneitra. The convoy included three T-55 tanks, a BMP-1 infantry fighting vehicle and one 2S1 122mm self-propelled gun on low loaders, as well as four towed artillery pieces, a BM-21 multiple launch rocket system, three towed MLRS and more than fourteen "technical" gun-equipped pick-up trucks. The Desert Hawks Brigade, the "Liwa Al-Quds" Palestinian militia and Brigade Group 134 of the Ba'ath Party militia were also identified as being part of the Syrian force. Media reports suggested that the reinforcing units totalled some 800 troops.

The Syrian government took the US news network CNN up to Ithriya to watch this operation against Islamic State, to add to the public-relations narrative devised by their Russian allies. They filmed an artillery battery on the edge of the town firing at Jihadi forces out in the desert. Closer examination of the video footage revealed the 2A65 MSTA-B 152mm guns and their tow trucks to be from the Russian 120th Artillery Brigade. There was even a contingent of Russian T-90 tanks and BTR troop carriers providing protection for the artillery battery.

Despite the media coverage of the build-up around Ithriya, the attack never made much progress. It seemed that it was a feint designed to confuse the Islamic State military commanders and cause them to divert forces from the looming battle around Palmyra. If this was the case, it was a successful move.

The Ithriya front remained largely inactive as fighting escalated around Palmyra - some 100 kilometres to the south - in March, April and into May. As Islamic State began to strike back around Palmyra the Syrian High Command decided to re-activate its offensive against Raqqa. The 555th Brigade, backed by the Desert Hawk Brigade and an assortment of other units, pushed across the Hama-Raqqa provincial boundary in the first days of June.

They made good progress for over two weeks, easily advancing to the key crossroads south of the Sfarieyh oil field and then turning north along the road to Tabqa airbase. This success proved illusory. Islamic State commanders were just waiting for the best time to strike. They sent up unmanned aerial vehicles (UAVs), or drones, during these battles to try to find the Syrian spearheads in the desert. Locating Syrian columns in the barren desert region was a major challenge.

One Islamic State drone was shot down by a Syrian Arab Army anti-aircraft gun, manned by the 555th Brigade during fighting around the Sfarieyh oil field on 11th June. Video imagery broadcast by the Abkhazian Network News Agency (ANNA), showed a piston-engine-powered drone crashing into the desert outside Sfarieyh after being engaged by

Syrian air-defence gunners. The identity of the drone was not clear but markings on the wreckage of its engine appeared to be written in English, suggesting this was an imported "hobby" product.

The intelligence gathered by the drones was soon put to good use and the Syrian advance guard at the Sfarieyh oil field was attacked from multiple fronts by Islamic State columns, backed by heavy artillery support. Fearing they would be cut off in the desert, the Syrian force was ordered to withdraw and by 22nd June it was back at Ithriya.

At the same time further south, Islamic State fighters had pursued the Syrians back towards the eastern outskirts of Palmyra. There just were not enough Syrian troops to hold all the territory they had captured to the east of Palmyra a few weeks earlier. The Russian helicopter group continued to fly daily missions to limit the ability of the Islamic State to concentrate their forces to strike at Syrian outposts. On 8th July, they shot down an Mi-35 attack helicopter in the region, with the loss of two Russian aircrew.

In a bid to try to turn back this threat, the Russians now ramped up their air support and re-activated the Long Range Aviation detachment at Mozdok airbase, in Ossetia. Six Tu-22M3 heavy bombers made their first strike against targets in central Syria on 12th July. Video footage released by the Russian Ministry of Defence showed formations of six Tu-22M3s simultaneously releasing sticks of unguided iron bombs in a bid to saturate targets with high explosive.

Two days later, six more Tu-22M3s were dispatched to attack central Syria, striking a command centre, a field training camp and two oil re-fuelling facilities at T-3 airport, according to the Russian Ministry of Defence. Russian heavy bombers staged their third wave of air strikes on 21st July to hit Islamic State facilities east of Palmyra, as well as in the areas of the cities Sukhnah, Arak and Et-Teibe in the Homs province. The seriousness of the situation in central and eastern Syria, meant that more Tu-22M3 raids had to be flown during August. Strikes were flown from Mozdok on 7th and 11th August against east Palmyra and Raqqa provinces respectively, but the need to extend construction work on a second runway at Mozdok airbase meant that other bases were used to the launch further raids.

A Tu-22M3 strike was flown from Engels in central Russia on 14th August. The Russian air command wanted a base closer to their bomber's targets so Iran was approached to make Hamadan airbase in the west of the country available. On 15th August four Tu-22M3s and four Sukhoi Su-34s, as well as Il-76s carrying support equipment, arrived at the desert airbase for a rapid refuel, before taking off to hit targets across Syria. Two days later the Su-34s hit Syria again from Hamadan.

When the details of the deployment were leaked by the Russian Ministry of Defence there was considerable disquiet in the Iranian parliament about foreign forces being based in their country. As a result, the deployment was curtailed after the Tu-22M3s flew their last mission on 18th August. Four days later the last Russian aircraft returned home.

The Syrian and Russian campaign in the central desert region against Islamic State had provided initial gains but the Jihadi group proved more resilient and stronger than many had expected. The terrain worked to their advantage and the Syrian army just did not have enough troops or logistic support to defend their limited gains. Russian air power – attack helicopters and heavy bombers – was committed in strength to help the Syrians but this did not in the end prove decisive.

For the Kremlin and the Russian military command in Syria, the fight for Palmyra and the central desert region provided good headlines but it was not central to their strategy in the first half of 2016. Securing a successful outcome from the UN-sponsored Geneva peace talks and the cessation-of-hostilities agreement between the Damascus government and the moderate rebel groups were the top priorities for Moscow. This would boost President Putin's international prestige, perhaps open the way for the US and EU to drop or modify the economic sanctions imposed after the 2014 Russian occupation of Crimea, and lead to the US and its allies recognising the Russian and Syrian governments as allies in the war against Islamic State.

As a result, Russian air support for Syrian operations against rebel forces across the country was scaled back in a bid to show that Moscow was abiding by the ceasefire, although the Russians and Syrians reserved the right to hit so-called terrorist groups, such as the Al Qaeda-affiliated Nusra Front and Islamic State. This gave them plenty of wriggle room to use airpower when they wanted.

While the Russian Foreign Minister Sergey Lavrov grandstanded at the Geneva talks with US Secretary of State John Kerry, it soon emerged that the Russian military had its own agenda for moulding the shape of Syria's future.

During his first months in Damascus, the Russian commander in Syria, General Dvornikov had found that the Syrian government had set up a ministry of reconciliation to try to peel away support from rebel groups. This ministry, headed by Ali Haider of the Syrian Social Nationalist Party (SSNP), had been in the forefront of negotiating the end of several sieges in major Syrian towns. These agreements resulted in rebel fighters and their families being evacuated from besieged enclaves to the major rebel stronghold in Idlib province. People and fighters who choose to stay behind received amnesties from the Damascus government, were re-connected to electricity and other utilities, and were given aid to begin repairing war damage.

Haider and his ministry's negotiators first brokered local ceasefires, then established contacts to allow public utilities that crossed front-lines to be got working again, before moving to pitch relocation deals. The Russian intervention and the failure of the US and its allies to intervene militarily on the side of the rebels fundamentally changed the political dynamic within besieged communities across Syria. The rebel forces were clearly not going to sweep away the Damascus government so, to besieged rebel groups, the opportunity to get safe passage to Idlib had a strong attraction, as the only way escape certain death at the hands of Russian bombing or Syrian army attack. For the besieged communities, the evacuation deals offered a way to put an end to the fighting as quickly as possible.

According to a senior official of the SSNP interviewed by the author, Haider and Dvornikov wanted to talk about how the Russians could get involved in what became known as the "reconciliation" strategy. The official described the Russian general as "the Big Man", who obviously had the ear of Putin.

"They had a dialogue about the Russians becoming engaged in reconciliation at a local level while everyone waited for a national solution to the crisis," said the SSNP official. "When they first arrived in Syria in September 2015 they carried out an assessment on which areas were occupied by the opposition and which supported the government. We worked very closely with the Russians from their reconciliation centres and they in turn worked closely with the representatives of our military in every area where they operated. The opposition liked working with the Russians – often more than working with us. So we said OK, if it works."

Dvornikov and his officers saw this as the model for winning over communities that had "soft" or "shallow" support for rebel fighters to the cause of the Damascus government. This was a classic counter-insurgency strategy to win the "hearts and minds" of the bulk of the population and isolate them from rebel fighters. This was aimed at capitalising on the war weariness of Syrian communities, who were fed up with the fighting and the privations caused by sieges. With many of the most hard-line rebel fighters being outsiders from the communities in which they were fighting, this divide and rule tactic clearly had some potential. Not everyone in the Syrian government, security apparatus and military was happy with the reconciliation strategy, although some hard-liners wanted to fight to the death and kill all the rebels and their supporters. These arguments swirled around in Damascus in late 2015 but it seems Russian support for the reconciliation strategy was instrumental in convincing Assad to give it greater prominence. Russian support also meant that the Syrian military threw its weight behind the strategy. It was noticeable that, during these evacuation operations, Syria troops and police behaved with discipline, treating evacuees with respect to ensure the process went to plan.

To capitalise on the work of the Syrian reconciliation ministry, Dvornikov set up the Russian Centre for Reconciliation of Opposing Sides in the Syrian Arab Republic in February 2016 at Hmeinyan airbase. He drafted some 60 staff officers to run the centre and Lieutenant General Sergei Kuralenko was moved from Baghdad, where he was leading the intelligence sharing centre with the Iraqi and Iranian governments, to head it up.

The reconciliation centre sent small negotiating teams to join their Syrian counterparts across the country during 2016. They were often assisted by other Russian troops who delivered humanitarian aid or set up field hospitals to help build trust and relationships with Syrian communities. Across Syria, the pace of these evacuation deals gained momentum during 2016 with some nine agreements being reached between the Syrians, Russians, local communities and rebel fighters by the end of the year. As well as these high-profile deals involving urban enclaves, the Russian reconciliation centre was involved in scores of ceasefire deals where rural villages switched sides to support the government in return for security guarantees, amnesty for local fighters, the delivery of humanitarian aid and reconnection to utilities.

While opposition supporters have described the evacuation deals as a form of "ethnic cleansing" the details of the deals suggest that the majority - usually more than 80% - of the populations of besieged enclaves remained behind to live under government control.

The rolling programme of evacuation and ceasefire deals through 2016 changed the nature of the Syrian war in ways that many outside observers, who relied on opposition groups for their information, did not appreciate. Progressively, the Syrian government had been removing a string of rebel controlled enclaves that surrounded the capital, Damascus, and other major cities. The way that this had been achieved - through negotiations, the successful exchange of prisoners and movement of fighters and their families safely to Idlib – built trust and momentum, prompting more communities to join the process. This in turn added to the success of the Russian and Syrian government "hearts and minds" strategy to win over more of the population to their cause.

The reconciliation centre also proved central to Russian attempts to map the "human geography" of the Syria conflict. From accounts of Russian forward air controllers and advisors in Syria, before air strikes could be authorised the reconciliation centre was consulted to ensure that the targets were not in communities loyal to the Damascus government.

UN-sponsored Geneva peace process and the associated cessation-of-hostilities agreement ground to a halt in May and June. The peace talks had gone nowhere and fighting was raging on most front lines.

Moscow's participation in the peace process had not brought any of the benefits it had expected. In late June, the Russian, Syrian and Iranian governments decided to accelerate the twin track strategy of brokering evacuation deals and at the same time launching a major military operation to capture the rebel held enclave in eastern Aleppo. Moscow was moving to change the facts on the ground in Syria.

Chapter 10
Little Moscow – The Russians in Syria

Contingents of soldiers, airmen, sailors and medics stood to attention on a hot May morning as the two reviewing officers standing in the back of UAZ jeeps passed along the formation.

The military band struck up patriotic tunes, leading off the march-past. First came the formations of the units assigned to the airbase – the airmen, air-defence troops, army artillery, naval infantry. Field guns fired in salute and then a column of armoured vehicles, missile launchers and towed guns passed by. A pair of Mil Mi-24 gunships passed over the parade line and then two Su-34s made a low pass.

The format of Victory Day parades at Russian military bases and cities has not changed much since 1945 when the defeat of Nazi Germany in the Great Patriotic War - World War Two - was first celebrated. This parade, however, was different. It was taking place on the aircraft taxi-way at Hmeinyan airbase in Syria's Latakia province. A giant Il-76 transport aircraft landed half way though the parade, adding to the feel that this was an operational airbase in a war zone. A formation of young Syrian soldiers in ill-fitting uniforms were arrayed on the side the parade, providing an interesting contrast to the well-equipped and perfectly turned-out Russian servicemen.

Although the Kremlin has never formally published the number of its troops in Syria, the best estimate is the turn-out figures from the September 2016 Russian Duma, or parliamentary, elections. The Central Electoral Commission recorded 4,571 Russians voting in Syria, including 193 at the Russian embassy in Damascus. As it is unlikely these were expatriate Russians, there were most probably all of Moscow's soldiers. According the commission's data, around 63% of voters in Syria cast their ballots for Putin's United Russia party, which was nearly 10% more than the percentage the president's party won back at home.

By May 2016, Russian troops were well established at a string of bases across Syria, ranging from the sprawling Hmeinyan airbase and the large naval and logistics base in Tartus port, through to small detachments of advisors working inside Syrian army outposts in the central desert. Cargo ships and transport planes arrived and departed on an almost daily basis delivering supplies and bringing in fresh contingents of troops. Moscow-based media organisations regularly reported from Russian bases, which appeared to be well supplied and looked like they were well built. Russia's Group of Forces in Syria appeared to be in the Middle Eastern country for the long haul. The Russian operation in Syria had turned into Moscow's most ambitious overseas combat mission since the Soviet intervention in Afghanistan in the 1980s.

Eight months on from the start of Moscow's intervention, the Russian military in Syria had settled in to a routine, of sorts. From Russian media reports, social-media posts by Russian servicemen, obituaries of dead soldiers and analysis of satellite imagery of Russian bases it was possible to build up a detailed picture of how Moscow's men and women lived and fought in Syria.

The Russian mission in Syria was very different from the Soviet intervention in Afghanistan. The biggest difference was that Moscow only sent professional soldiers or "contract" soldiers to Syria. Since, Afghanistan and then the collapse of the Soviet Union in the early 1990s, the Russian military had undergone a transformation. In the Soviet Union, conscript soldiers had been the bedrock of the Red Army. For millions of Soviet men, the two-year period of national service was a rite of passage. Conscript Red Army soldiers, non-commissioned officers and junior officers spent two years training to be ready for combat and then returned to civilian life after their service ended. The Red Army was in perpetual state of turmoil as hundreds of thousands of conscripts arrived and then left two years later. In the navy and air force, conscripts were used for menial or non-technical jobs, such as guarding airbases, working in kitchens or driving trucks.

A core of professional officers and technicians kept the Soviet military going. These men flew Soviet air force's aircraft, manned its missile batteries, commanded warships and provided the officers for army regiments and divisions. These career officers were often the sons of military men. For professional officers, service in the military was a "cradle-to-grave" experience. Officers generally served their whole careers in the same army regiment, airbase or ship, lived in military housing with their families, sent their children to military schools and then spent their retirement in military facilities.

Even after the demise of the Soviet Union, the conscript system staggered on until the Chechen wars, which began in 1994, led to it being discredited. The deaths of several thousand conscripts and the failure of the Russian army to rapidly defeat Chechen insurgents led to calls for the professionalisation of Moscow's military. This pressure gained further momentum after Vladimir Putin became president in 2000.

The former Soviet professional officer class remained the bedrock of the Russian armed forces - but with whole units now fully manned by contract soldiers the character of the Russian military changed dramatically. Many of the contract soldiers were also the sons of professional officers who would sign up as a means to prove themselves before applying for places in prestigious officer- training academies. Young men from remote regions outside the main cities also saw military service as a way to get a well relatively well-paid job and the chance of a career. There is a strong and prevalent macho culture in Russia, which generates a steady stream of young men wanting to try out to join elite airborne,

Spetsnaz or naval infantry units.

Russia has moved on dramatically from Soviet times, with the growth of a prosperous middle class in the major cities and a widespread addiction to social media among all sections of Russian society. The salaries of military officers has been left behind by the civilian economy, but service in military is still seen as a relatively secure career, retaining a certain degree of social prestige and many of the fringe benefits for officers remained. Military service continued to attract the sons of military families in significant numbers.

Almost every Russian officer above the rank of colonel had served in the Soviet army and then seen their armed forces sink into a rapid decline during the 1990s. Defence budgets collapsed, morale of conscripts went in to freefall after the Chechen wars, NATO swallowed up the states of the old Warsaw Pact and the former Soviet republics in the Baltics. Not surprisingly, many were natural supporters of Putin and his agenda to restore Russia's national pride and its military strength. So, for many senior Russian officers, the Syria mission was a chance to restore their county's position in the world.

In their interviews with both the Russian and international media, senior Russian officers in Syria appeared highly motivated and determined to ensure the success of their mission. Syrian army officers and government officials also noted that their new allies were not the overbearing and rigid Soviet officers they knew from the Cold-War period. Senior Russian officers in Syria seemed keen to learn from mistakes, had an understanding of local culture, and repeatedly put together complex but effective plans.

British journalist Vanessa Beeley met Russian soldiers and officers during the siege of Aleppo and recalled they had been extensively briefed and trained to build strong good relations with Syrian military and civilian population.

"They were ordered to connect with the people, to behave in a non-threatening way and be kind to them", she said. "This very much came from above. They came to Syria with Arabic speakers, and many of the Russian soldiers were Muslims who understood Middle-Eastern culture. The Russians clearly made an effort to connect with the Syrian people at a cultural, linguistic and social level."

The rank and file of the Russian contingent in Syria were all professional or contract soldiers but they came from a different generation to the colonels and generals. According to their media interviews and social media posts, they were motivated by a desire for promotion and money, and a sense of adventure. This generation of Russians were completely addicted to social-media and many could not resist posting pictures and video of their exotic trip to the Middle East. They were seen attending musical concerts, living in Syrian army camps, and shopping in local bazaars.

Many of the units that got sent to Syria – airborne forces, naval infantry, Spetsnaz and rocket artillery – were treated as elite units, containing the fittest and most motivated soldiers and officers in the Russian military. So the soldiers in Syria appeared to have good morale and went about their business in a professional manner. There does not seem to have been any significant morale problems within the Russian contingent in Syria.

The Russian military put considerable efforts into maintaining that morale. Soldiers only spent six months on duty in Syria before they would rotate back home. Prefabricated barracks, mess halls, field kitchens and medical facilities were all flown or shipped to Syria so soldiers would live in conditions that would have made Afghan war veterans deeply envious.

The Kremlin decided from the outset of the Syria intervention that this was going to be a "good war". It openly acknowledged the presence of Russian troops in Syria, allowed the Moscow media to follow the progress of its forces, publicly dished out gallantry medals to brave soldiers, and dead servicemen were returned home to full military funerals. President Putin even greeted the widows of dead soldiers in the Kremlin. This contrasted with the "secret" war in East Ukraine, where Russian participation was publicly disowned and dead servicemen were spirited home for secret funerals. The Kremlin, however, was less keen to publicise the role of the employees of Russian private military contractors or mercenaries who were hired to beef up the training mission to the Syrian army.

The Russian military operation in Syria required a number of innovations that were not immediately apparent. A unique command-and-control network had to be set up to co-ordinate the air, land and sea operation in Syria. Moscow only provided occasional "snap shots" of its command structure in Syria but it is possible to piece together information from public media briefings, open-source analysis of news and social media imagery from Syria, and analysis of the timeline of Russian military operations. These sources can be used to build up a picture of how Moscow controlled its forces in Syria. Some of these operations were highly complex, involving strategic air and naval forces operating far from Syria, indicating high-level command-and-control linkages across the Russian military.

For many months, Russia kept the name of the field commander in Syria secret and did not even acknowledge they had a deployed commander. The identities of the senior air force commanders at Hmeinyan airbase have also never been revealed, even in Russian media.

Still and video imagery from Syria, posted both on social media and available via traditional news media, along with satellite imagery of

Syrian and Russian bases, also adds much to our understanding of Russian command centres. It is possible to identify satellite-communication dishes, radio antennas, and command post vehicles and buildings. The footprint of Russian liaison vehicle and personnel deployments is illuminating. The relationship developing between senior Russians and Syrian officers can also be tracked.

From the start of its intervention, the Russian military put great effort into creating a command-and-control network that mirrored the Syrian military chain-of-command. The commander of the Russian forces, usually an officer with the rank of colonel general or lieutenant general, was based in Damascus, close to the Syrian Ministry of Defence and the military high command. Senior Russian officers of major general- and senior colonel-rank were photographed visiting Syrian army headquarters across the country, either acting as advisors on a long-term basis or on fact-finding visits.

More middle ranked officers - lieutenant colonels, and majors from the airborne and Spetsnaz - were recorded deploying in the field with Syrian army brigades and regiments as their advisors and air-support co-ordinators. Many of these advisory detachments were routinely photographed operating from light armoured vehicles, including Iveco Lynx and GAZ Tigr. They also appeared to be equipped with multiple communications devices and tablet computers to view satellite imagery and maps.

The Russians put considerable effort into the co-ordination of air operations, including setting up an air command centre at Hmeinyan airbase. Liaison teams were stationed at other Syrian airbases and air force command posts. The Syrian and Russian air defence forces appeared to have been integrated into a single organisation. Spetsnaz forward air control teams were also been seen deployed with Syrian army units to request air strikes and monitor their execution.

In addition to its co-ordination and advisory network with the Syrian military, the Russians set up another organisation, titled the Coordination Centre for Reconciliation of Opposing Sides in the Syrian Arab Republic. This organisation frequently appeared in reports from across Syria as being involved in brokering ceasefires with local communities and then securing deals for them to return to Syrian government control. As part of these deals, representatives of the reconciliation centre were often present to escort opposition fighters and their families out of enclaves and then on to other opposition-controlled territory.

Accounts from Russian forward air controllers suggest that the reconciliation centre also played an important role in intelligence-gathering and combat operations. Apparently, these forward air controllers routinely communicated with the reconciliation centre before authorising air strikes to check on the political affiliation of communities down range. This role – mapping the "human geography" of the complex and multifaceted Syrian civil war – suggests a degree of sophistication in military planning by senior Russian officers that is often not appreciated by outside observers.

The head of the centre in late 2016 was Lieutenant General Vladimir Savchenko, who replaced the first head, Lieutenant General Sergei Kuralenko. Kuralenko had previously headed the Russian-Syrian-Iraqi-Iranian intelligence sharing facility in Baghdad in 2015, which further indicated the intelligence role of the reconciliation centre.

Since 2015, the Russian military deployed a range of strategic weapons systems to Syria, including ship- and submarine-launched Kalibr cruise missiles, air-launched cruise missiles, heavy bomber strikes, land attack missiles, and carrier-launched strike aircraft. The employment of these weapon systems appeared to be co-ordinated by the Russian General Staff from the National Defence Command Centre in the heart of Moscow.

President Vladimir Putin famously ordered a major air and missile attack on Syria in November 2015 during a live media broadcast from the command centre. From imagery of the command centre, it appeared to be equipped with extensive digital communications facilities which included video-conferencing links to deployed headquarters in Syria.

As well as coming up with an innovative command network, the Russians also experimented with new weapons and equipment. Syria became a laboratory for the testing in real combat conditions of new aircraft, tanks, missiles, armoured vehicles and ships. Equipment that made its combat debut in Syrian included the Sukhoi Su-34 strike jet, the Kalibr ship and submarine cruise missile, the Kh-55 and Kh-101 air launched cruise missiles, the Tigr armoured utility vehicles, the Kamov Ka-52 and Mil Mi-28 attack helicopters, Typhoon mine- proof vehicles and the Tupolev Tu-95 and Tu-160 strategic bombers.

As well as wanting to see how these weapons performed, the Russians also saw the potential for using the war in Syria to boost the sales of hardware. In the months after the intervention multi-billion dollar orders flowed to Moscow from China, Egypt, India and Algeria.

A major area of innovation was in the Russian use of surveillance aircraft and drones. The Forpost drone's video product was a big hit with Moscow. As with their American and British counterparts at the start of the Afghanistan conflict 15 years earlier, once senior politicians and commanders had tasted the quality and quantity of the video imagery that the Forpost could generate, they wanted it more of it and they wanted it immediately.

The Forpost was soon joined in Syria by one of the handful of Tupolev Tu-214 spy planes. This was the equivalent of the US E-8 Joint-STARS or British Sentinel R.1 spy planes. The Russian jet had a radar that could track all vehicle movement across a wide area of Syria in realtime, as well as narrowing into a small area to produce three-dimensional radar pictures of tanks or other vehicles. These in effect could find tanks, trucks and field guns hidden in woods or shrouded in cloud and fog. The converted airliner also had long range thermal cameras, similar to those fitted to the Forpost. Russia's air force was not striking blind.

To enhance their air surveillance over Syria, the Russians sent their A-50 AWACS aircraft to monitor US-led coalition, Turkish and Israeli aircraft over and around Syria, as well as cruise missiles.

One of the more controversial aspects of the Russian intervention in Syria was the presence in the country of private military companies, or PMCs. These are nominally illegal within Russia but have built up large portfolios of work in foreign countries. Many of them are outgrowths of the Russian security industry, which has tens of thousands of employees who work as body guards or security personnel in shopping centres and factories. Most of them are former military personnel and their ranks include former members of the airborne forces, Spetsnaz and naval infantry.

The Russian Ministry of Defence has its own security contractors who guard barracks, dockyards, airfields and storage depots. These are understood to have moved to Syria to carry out similar work at Russian bases in the country, including guarding Moscow's embassy in downtown Damascus.

Several of these PMCs have been linked to businesses close to the Kremlin and they seem to have been awarded with contracts in Syria. The most famous of these is the PMC Wagner, and several of its senior employees have been photographed with Putin in the Kremlin. There are plenty of accusations flying around regarding PMC Wagner's activities in Syria, including that it was contracted to train and advise Syrian army units. The company has also been linked to providing security for Russian businesses working to repair and re-open oil and gas fields recently recaptured from Islamic State in central Syria. A video appeared online purportedly showing PMC Wagner staff torturing prisoners at a gas field near Palmyra in the summer of 2017. The company were also linked to several merchant ships chartered to move cargoes from Black Sea ports to Syria. Its exploits in Syria were followed closely by Ukrainian online activists who also accused the company of working with rebels in the Donbass at the behest of Moscow

Unlike regular military personnel killed in Syria the deaths of employees of PMCs received no coverage in the mainstream media in Russia. Some claims suggest more than 100 of these operatives have been killed in Syria since 2015: the names of a few dozen have been identified by independent media reports and online investigations.

By the winter of 2017 Putin's intervention in Syria remained relatively popular in Russia. The professional soldiers killed in action were returned to heroes' funerals in mother Russia so there was no repeat of the Afghan or Chechnya "coffin factor" to turn opinion against the war. Perhaps more importantly, the war appeared to be well run and was achieving its objectives.

Russian Airpower over Syria

Tupolev Tu-160s strategic bombers made several cruise missile strikes on targets in Syria, flying direct from their home base in Russia. (Russian MOD)

The Su-25 Rook was the back bone of RuAF close air support operations, flying low level strikes using unguided rockets. They operated from forward airbases in central and eastern Syria during 2017.(Star TV network)

Russian Naval Forces off Syrian Coast

The Admiral Kuznetsov aircraft carrier transited the English Channel in October 2016 en route to Syria, escorted by the Royal Navy Type 45 destroyer HMS Dragon.(UK MOD)

The Novocherkassk, a Ropucha-class landing ship, was a key player in the Syria Express, moving supplies to Tartus from Black Sea ports via the Bosphorous (@ Yörük Işık)

Syria - Russian Assessment of Military Situation September 2015

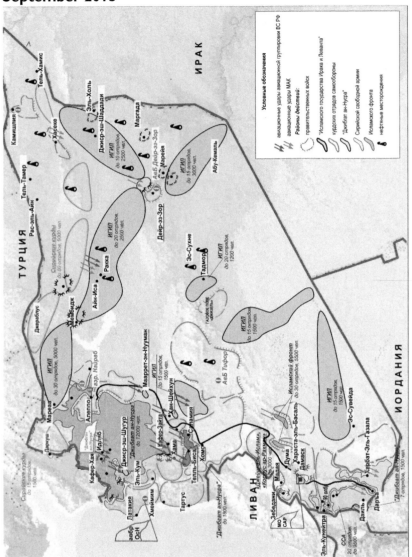

This Russian Ministry of Defence briefing map sets out the main groupings of Syrian government, rebel, Kurdish and Islamic State forces in September 2015. In the south east, centre and north east are Islamic State. The Jihadi rebel units are in the north west. The Kurdish YPG are in the north along the Turkish border and the government controlled territory is largely in the west. (Russian MOD)

Siege of Aleppo- August - December 2016

(@PetoLucem)

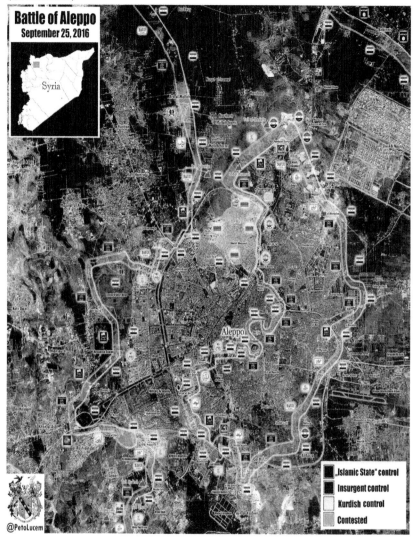

Central Syria and Dier Ez Zor - August - September 2017

(@PetoLucem)

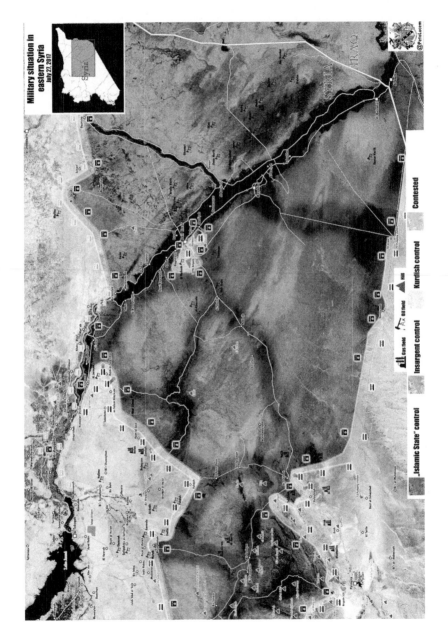

Tracking Russian Operations in Syria from Space

Russian aircraft deployments at Hmeinyan airbase in Latakia province could be tracked at regular intervals throughout the campaign by commercial satellite imagery

(Airbus/SPOT and Samir (@obretix))

Chapter 11
Aleppo Summer

The fall of the rebel enclave in the eastern half of Aleppo city in December 2016 was a major international crisis, prompting heated exchanges during United Nations Security Council sessions, intense media coverage and a scramble to provide humanitarian aid to the civilians affected by the battle.

That the Damascus government, backed by their Russian and Iranian allies, would try to achieve a major battlefield success in the latter half of 2016 was not a big surprise to close observers of the Syrian conflict. It was even more predictable that the dénouement would take place in the northern city of Aleppo.

The failure of the Geneva peace process in the late spring of 2016 made it inevitable that the Syrians would make a push to capitalise on their military success in cutting the road route from Aleppo to the Turkish border in February and then, the following month, their recapturing of Palmyra. When combined with the continued unwillingness of US President Barack Obama to intervene militarily on the side of the main rebel groups, these events created an important psychological advantage for the Damascus government. The rebels were losing ground and there was no hope of rescue by their friends in the West or the Gulf.

This was the time to try to peel the bulk of the population in rebel-controlled territory and enclaves away from the opposition cause: or so thought Damascus and their Russian military advisors. The approach of the US presidential election in the autumn of 2016 gave added impetus to achieving a decisive success before the end of the year. In the spring of 2016, Hilary Clinton seemed almost unstoppable in her bid to replace Obama. She was expressing very hawkish views about the Syrian conflict, including intervening on the side of the rebels by imposing a no fly zone and setting up "safe enclaves". To head this off, the Syrian government forces had to make dramatic progress very quickly.

With the rebel cause appearing doomed to a slow and lingering defeat, the Syrian government believed wavering communities would see the benefits of switching to the side of Damascus. Through the summer and into the autumn several besieged rebel enclaves around Damascus entered into negotiations with the Syrians and Russians before brokering agreements to allow rebel fighters and their families to be bused to the main opposition stronghold in Idlib province. This psychological "wedge" in opposition morale would be magnified dramatically if the rebel enclave in eastern Aleppo could be taken. The fall of eastern Aleppo would show that there was no hope for the rebel cause. So a major military operation was mounted to capture it and win over its population to the Damascus government.

The framing of Syrian military operations in this way is difficult for many outside observers, particularly in the West, to appreciate. A near-continuous flow of international news reports, based largely on opposition or opposition-influenced sources, portrayed the population of eastern Aleppo as universally supporting the rebel fighters who controlled the enclave. The idea that a significant chunk of the enclave's population might welcome the Syrian army as "liberators" just did not compute for many in the western media.

No definitive account has emerged from the Russian or Syrian side about the deliberations that led to the launching of the Operation Dawn of Victory, as the Aleppo campaign was code-named by Damascus. Looking back it is very clear that the operation was planned and executed over several months. It was a complex operation with many inter-connected moving parts, including the concentration of troops around the city, positioning of naval forces, the establishment of a command structure to control the assault, a build-up of supplies, the launching of psychological-warfare campaigns aimed at the enclave's civilian population, and the start of diplomatic moves to head off US and Turkish military intervention. The timelines for all these activities point to an over-arching political decision being made in late May or early June 2016 by the Damascus government and the Kremlin to begin the Aleppo operation.

This timeline places the key planners on the Russian side as the then commander of Moscow's group of forces in Syria, Colonel General Alexander Dvornikov, and his deputy, Lieutenant General Alexander Zhuravlev, who was scheduled to take over as the top Russian commander in Damascus in July 2016. Dvornikov had overseen Moscow's intervention in Syria the previous summer and was a trusted confidant of President Putin. The general was tall, well-built and charismatic and had established good relations with President Bashar al-Assad and senior Syrian military officers. He had built up a network of trusted Syrian allies and was regularly seen visiting Syrian army units to hand out Russian medals to brave or successful officers and soldiers. As many senior Syrian generals rarely left the safety of their offices in Damascus, the Syrian soldiers and officers on the front lines came to see the large Russian general as their protector.

His main success had been in crafting military operations that delivered the political results demanded by his masters in the Kremlin. Famously, when Putin held a glitzy ceremony in the Kremlin in March 2016 to award medals to servicemen who had served in Syria, Dvornikov had presented Putin with a large framed photograph of a Mil Mi-24 helicopter gunships hovering over a Syrian house near the main Russian airbase in Latakia province. On the roof of the house was a huge slogan painted in Russian, saying "Good morning, Russia. Hello. You are our friends and our brothers. Thank you". Putin loved it. The general clearly knew how to keep his boss happy.

While Dvornikov, as overall Russian commander, would have had the job of setting out the aims of the new plan for the Aleppo campaign, the detail would have been worked out by Zhuravlev and other senior staff. Zhuravlev was then made commander to execute the plan in July 2016.

The campaign plan called for eastern Aleppo first to be isolated by closing the siege lines to prevent reinforcements and supplies coming in from Idlib province. Then the aim was to separate the rebel fighters from the bulk of the population. Negotiations were to be opened with leaders in the enclave to give the population the chance to move to government controlled territory through so-called "humanitarian corridors", while rebel fighters would be offered safe passage to Idlib, as was the case in enclaves around Damascus. The need to conclude this operation before the change of US president meant ground assaults would be necessary to break into the enclave to convince rebel fighters that their position was so untenable that they should take up the offer of evacuation.

The ground force for this operation would be predominately Syrian, assisted by local Palestinian and Kurdish allied militias. Russian air power would be available, as well surveillance drones, long-range cruise missiles fired from ships, and heavy bombers. Personnel from the Russian reconciliation centre would be on hand in strength to co-ordinate any evacuation and provide humanitarian aid to the thousands of people from the enclave who it was hoped would chose to come over to the government side. In the most public sign that Moscow was preparing to bring significant additional firepower to bear in Syria, the Russian Ministry of Defence announced in July that the country's only aircraft carrier, the Admiral Kuznetsov, would sail for the eastern Mediterranean in October to "join the counter-terrorist operation in Syria". The carrier's progress towards Syria would later become central to the Aleppo operation. Cruise-missile-carrying corvettes were also dispatched to the eastern Mediterranean during the late summer of 2016.

Providing diplomatic top cover for the Syrian ground operation would fall to the Russian Foreign ministry. Since the spat with Turkey after the shooting down of the Russian jet in November 2015, the Kremlin had been working had to re-build relations with Ankara. Putin and his Turkish counterpart, Recep Tayip Erdogan, patched things up and by the summer of 2016 had come to a working arrangement over the Syria crisis. During June, the Turkish leader apologised over the downing of the Russian jet, opening the way in August for Putin and Erdogan to meet in St Petersburg. The details of their discussions were never made public but it is believed they sealed a deal under which the Syrians had a free hand against the rebels in Aleppo and, in return, the Turks would be able to launch an incursion into northern Syria to prevent a link-up of Kurdish enclaves along the length of Turkey's southern border.

As well as neutralising the possibility of Turkish intervention, Russian diplomats - led by their veteran foreign minister Sergey Lavrov and long serving UN ambassador Vitaly Churkin - engaged with the Americans to forestall US intervention. Obama had no intention of intervening militarily in the Syria crisis during the final days of his presidency, but Lavrov had the task of making sure the Americans were given no excuse to introduce new sanctions or diplomatic measures against Russia and Syria as the military operation unfolded. The US Secretary of State, John Kerry, spent most of the summer trying to negotiate a ceasefire deal in the hope that this would lead to a re-start of peace negotiations, or at least allow the delivery of humanitarian aid. He played into the Russian foreign minister's hands.

Lavrov's task was to ensure any ceasefire arrangements were couched in such a way that they did not preclude continued operations against groups defined as "terrorists" by the Russians. This labelling of different groups became central to the ceasefire negotiations, as the United Nations and western countries had designated the Islamic State, the Al Qaeda off-shoot first known as the Nusra Front and then re-named Jabhat Fateh al-Sham in July 2016, as well as a couple of other smaller armed groups in Syria, as "terrorists" as well. In the context of north-west Syria and eastern Aleppo, the Nusra Front and its allies were the main groups leading a coalition of rebel fighters that formed the core of the resistance to the Syrian military. As long as the Nusra Front was in the frame as a terrorist group, the Russians and Syrians felt they could shrug off criticism from the US of any offensive into Aleppo. Was not the US also carrying out anti-terrorist air strikes against Nusra Front leaders in Syria? Lavrov repeated this line time and time again over the summer of 2016. John Kerry would look an increasingly forlorn figure as he tried to broker ceasefire, after ceasefire knowing they were no not worth the paper they were written on because none of the warring armies around Aleppo were interested in a ceasefire.

Iranian military personnel and their Shia militia allies would not play a major direct role in the coming assault on eastern Aleppo, but they continued to hold an important section of the outer siege line along the border with Idlib province. Their task was to prevent any attempt by rebel forces to break the siege of Aleppo from the south-west.

Several of the Syrian army's best units would eventually be moved north to Aleppo to take part in the assault, and this would entail taking risks elsewhere by thinning out front lines or removing reserves from threatened sectors. By tracking these moves, it would appear that the build-up of troops around Aleppo began in late June and early July. Once these units began being committed to battle it became increasingly difficult and risky to call off the offensive.

The first major move of the campaign was the concentration of the elite

Tiger Force in northern Aleppo in mid-June. As the most battle-hardened and professional unit in the Syrian army it was no surprise that it was chosen to begin the operation to close the siege of eastern Aleppo. The Tiger Force and its infamous commander, Colonel Suheil al-Hassan, were always selected to lead important offensives or to clean up after rebel forces had broken through the lines held by less-effective regular army and militia units. It was organised into seven or eight regiments of around 500 men in each. These units were self-contained assault forces with their own mini- or hobby drones, T-72 tanks, BMP armoured troops carriers, 2S1 122mm self-propelled howitzers, BM-21 multiple rocket launchers and ZSU-23-4 anti-aircraft vehicles.

Hassan and his trusted lieutenants had become expert at co-ordinating all this firepower at small sections of the enemy's front line to literally blast holes in rebel lines. Once resistance had been neutralised, small groups of assault troops, known as intrusion units, would move forward to actually occupy objectives. Their commander was usually not far behind. Hassan's apparent coolness under fire and reckless bravery, made him highly popular with his troops. Senior Russian officers were reportedly very impressed with the professionalism of the Tiger Force and its battlefield success.

By the summer of 2016, Hassan had acquired his own Russian-made Lynx armoured utility truck which he used to tour his units. In his mobile command post, a large portrait of President Putin hung next to the one of Syria's President Assad. The Colonel had also been invited down to Hmeinyan airbase to be presented with a medal by General Dvornikov while on parade in front of a Sukhoi fighter. In an important sign of how much the Tiger Force was trusted by the Russians, it was one of the few Syrian units to have access to live video imagery from Russian surveillance drones. Hassan was also repeatedly appeared on Syrian news reports using a tablet computer to study satellite photographs of enemy positions, which most likely came from Russian surveillance satellites.

In a clear sign that the Aleppo operation was the main effort of the Syrian military by mid-June, at least seven Tiger Force regiments had been moved to the city under the direct command of their chief. No less than two brigades of the elite 4th Mechanised Division were also moved to Aleppo ahead of the offensive.

The focus of the Tiger Force operation to close the siege of eastern Aleppo was the Castello Road region, and a three- kilometre-wide corridor of rebel-held territory into the city. The whole region had been fortified over the previous four years of fighting with minefields, trench lines and barricades. Any advances had to be made over open ground or down streets that could be swept by deadly machine gun, mortar or artillery fire.

Starting on 20th June, heavy artillery and rocket barrages, backed up by air strikes pounded the rebel trenches and fortified villages that protected the shoulders of the rebel corridor into the enclave. The Tiger Force turned to its brutally effective tactics to batter through these lines. In a series of incremental attacks, Tiger Force intrusion squads moved forward taking a street or a building at a time, after their supporting artillery had latterly flattened any resistance. This was slow work but it kept Syrian casualties low, which was an important consideration for Colonel Hassan who knew his regiments would be needed later in the campaign. It took the Tiger Force just over a month to close the Castello Road corridor and advancing units of the Tiger Force joined up on 29th July closing the siege of eastern Aleppo.

This "siege" did not last for long. Rebel groups in Idlib province started to mass forces in preparation for a surprise attack to break the Syrian siege lines in south-west Aleppo. On 7th August, the Nusra Front and an alliance of rebel groups began bombarding Syrian positions around an area known as the Artillery Base and Air Force Technical College with rockets and artillery fire. This former Syrian army training base was already largely in ruins from four years of being fought over. The Syrian front was held by the 47th Regiment of the Republican Guard but it had thinned its lines out to send manpower to support the Tiger Force offensive along the Castello Road.

Rebel commanders sent up drones to spy on the Syrians as small groups of assault troops moved forward during the artillery barrage. Taken by surprise, the Syrian defenders panicked and within the space of a few hours the Artillery Base was cleared, opening a new kilometre-wide corridor into eastern Aleppo.

The rebel attack was a major disruption to the Syrian and Russian plans, showing up the weaknesses of many Syrian units, even supposedly elite Republican Guard regiments. Within hours of the rebel breakthrough, the senior Syrian commander in Aleppo, Major General Adib Mohammed, had been sacked and was replaced by the veteran Republican Guard commander, Major-General Zaid Saleh, as head of the city's security committee. From his underground command post in the Assad Military Academy complex in western Aleppo, Saleh would soon be overseeing the successful offensive to capture the rebel enclave. But first he had to deal with the crisis caused by the rebel advance which was taking place only a kilometre or so from his headquarters. This was a very serious situation and new front-lines had to be rapidly built up to prevent rebel fighters infiltrating government positions across western Aleppo. New supply lines along the recently captured Castello Road had to be opened to west Aleppo.

According to members of a delegation of British Christian clergy who met Saleh during this time, he came across as "calm" and "efficient". "We visited his office and he was very serious and business-like" recalled one of the visitors. "There were maps and plans posted all over his office walls. We were told not to photograph them. He was very clearly in charge of what was going on."

Over the days immediately after the rebel breakthrough, General Saleh began shuffling his troops around to plug the gaps in his front line. Palestinian fighters from the Liwa al Quds Militia were moved to defend the 1070 Housing Project, which was the northern shoulder of the new rebel corridor into eastern Aleppo. They were soon joined by Tiger Force officers and soldiers who were planning how to recapture the Artillery Base. Russian officers were repeatedly photographed visiting Syrian headquarters in Aleppo during this time, as planning for a counter-offensive gathered momentum.

During August, a stream of Syrian army reinforcements started to arrive from the Damascus area. A ceasefire and evacuation deal in Daraya, in southern Syria, had meant troops could be freed for the operation in Aleppo. Units identified as arriving in Aleppo at this time included elements of the 15th Special Forces Division, the Military Intelligence Shield Forces Lion's Den Battalion, and, by the end of the month the 800th Republican Guard Regiment.

In early August two Russian Navy Black Sea Fleet Buyan-M corvettes, Zeliony Dol and Serpukhov, which were both fitted to fire Kalibr cruise missiles, passed through the Bosphorous and headed for the Syrian coast. The weapons, which had an acknowledged 2,500 kilometre range, had been used three times before in the Syrian conflict. The Russian Ministry of Defence announced missile strikes by the ships on 19th August against "facilities" of the Jabhat al-Nusra group in north-west Syria. It said a command centre and a base near Dar-Taaza, as well as a mortar munition manufacturing plant in Aleppo province, were destroyed in the attacks.

For the first time, the Russian military released real-time bomb damage assessment (BDA) video of its Kalibr strikes, with appear to have been filmed by an unmanned aerial vehicle or a Sukhoi Su-34 fighter jet equipped with an advanced targeting pod. This was a new development and suggested that the Russians had been able to connect the drone surveillance operations to the targeting system of the cruise-missile-equipped warships, creating what is known in the Western military as a "kill chain".

All through August and into September, both the Government and opposition waged intense information operations to promote their rival claims during the fighting around Aleppo. From the video imagery released – by both sides – it is possible to build up a picture of the rival tactics and weaponry employed in these battles around the strategic terrain on the south-western edge of Aleppo.

One insurgent group released video footage shot from drones showing the use of artillery and rocket fire to break up and drive back a government armoured attack on the Air Force Technical College. Shells and rockets can be seen exploding around Syrian BMP armoured vehicles and T-72 tanks as they ferried assault troops up to the edge of the College. The Syrian troops then beat a hasty retreat across open ground to safety. The ferocity of the fighting can be gauged from drone imagery that shows an opposition fighter climbing on top of a Syrian T-55 armoured recover vehicle and dropping a grenade or explosive charge inside its turret hatch. Other rebel drone footage shows an opposition tank counter-attack which drives back hundreds of pro-government soldiers from a trench line in the countryside to the south of Aleppo.

Pro-government video and reports by the Abkhazi news agency, ANNA, showed Syrian troops and Palestinian fighters from the Liwa Al-Quds militia using a road protected by earth berms to cover their approach to the Technical College. Assault teams are then shown progressively clearing the buildings of the training complex and then establishing defensive positions to fend off counter-attacks. A forward logistic and casualty-clearing centre also appeared to have been set up by the Palestinian militia inside a housing complex to the north of the Technical College. One of the militia's spokesmen told the ANNA interviewer they had committed 3,000 fighters to the battles around Aleppo. A BMP vehicle with the insignia of the Syrian Republican Guard could also be seen inside the logistic base.

On 4th September, a pro-regime video was released showing the final assault on the artillery training base, including images of T-72 tanks and BMP-2 vehicles approaching the facility as air strikes, artillery and rocket fire impacted across the site. Infantry teams could also be seen moving through the walls around the base.

Video imagery appeared online on 5th September showing what appeared to be TOS-1A firing thermobaric warhead-tipped rockets at the artillery training base. The weapon had been seen in action on a number of occasions over the previous year, including in northern Latakia province in 2015 and during the battle for Palmyra in March 2016. On both occasions, these weapons appeared to be operated by Russian personnel but it was not possible to discern if Moscow's troops were involved in this action.

These operations came to a conclusion during the evening of 4th September with a ground assault, backed by air, artillery and rocket support, which penetrated into the artillery training base. The Syrian state news agency, SANA, announced that "army units, in cooperation with allied forces, carried out a special and swift military operation, that established full control over the area of the Military Academies to the [south-west] of Aleppo city and chased down the fleeing terrorists in the area".

It said Syrian troops were now "blocking all movements and supply routes of terrorist organisations from the southern countryside towards the eastern neighbourhoods [of Aleppo] and al-Ramouseh."

SANA claimed Syrian troops killed "scores" of opposition fighters and injured others but independent verification of these claims was not possible. The Reuters news agency reported Zakaria Malahifji of the Fastaqim rebel group confirming that opposition fighters had been driven from their positions and a new siege had been imposed on opposition-controlled areas inside Aleppo.

As a result of the escalating fighting around Aleppo, the US Secretary of State, John Kerry, made one more push to broker a cessation-of-hostilities (COH) agreement. After a series of meetings he claimed success and announced that the COH would come into effect on 9th September. This suited both the Syrian government and the opposition, whose forces needed resting after several weeks of intense fighting.

Moscow was enthusiastic about the deal because they claimed it opened the way for an agreement on joint US-Russian operations against "terrorist" groups in Syria. Such an interpretation would have legitimised their intervention in Syria and co-opted the US into supporting the Syrian government's war against its internal enemies, led by the Nusra Front. The US side disputed this view of the agreement and said it was just a "humanitarian" pause in the fighting to save lives. Under the COH agreement, both the US and Russian sides were to be responsible for ensuring compliance of their respective allies in Syria and monitoring of breaches of the ceasefire.

The complex and violent nature of Syria's battlefields meant both Washington and Moscow had to improvise innovative efforts to find out what was actually happening along the country's thousands of kilometres of confrontation lines. These built on procedures and organisations set up to monitor a similar ill-fated ceasefire deal in February 2016.

The Russian monitoring effort was run by their Coordination Centre for Reconciliation of Opposing Sides in the Syrian Arab Republic. Lieutenant General Vladimir Savchenko, the reconciliation centre commander, tasked his staff to monitor the latest ceasefire deal with a mix of technical and human intelligence-gathering methods. They were supported by surveillance assets of the Russian Air Group and Russian ground units in the country to help in this effort around Aleppo.

The Russian Ministry of Defence said that the cease-fire monitoring effort involved surveillance flights by unmanned aerial vehicles over Aleppo, and it started to live-stream their video on its website. Russian Naval Infantry briefly took control of checkpoints along the contested Castello Road. They were backed up by ground-based video cameras and 1L271 Aistenok mortar fire-surveillance radar. The later system was identified in a live video feed from the ground-based cameras, which the ministry also streamed on its website. Both the Naval Infantry and the

Aistenok radars were believed to have already been in the Aleppo region as part of a Russian artillery and force-protection group supporting the Syrian army. Reconciliation-centre personnel had been active in the Aleppo region for several weeks, with two of their officers among the fatalities when a Russian Mil Mi-8 helicopter was lost to the south of the city on 1st August.

For the US, monitoring ceasefire compliance was far more challenging because Washington lacked personnel on the ground near the confrontation line. The only US military forces inside Syria were operating in areas of the north-east controlled by the Kurdish YPG militia and its Syrian Democratic Forces, which were physically separated from the zones covered by the COH agreement. The US and the coalition mounted daily missions by intelligence, surveillance, target acquisition and reconnaissance (ISTAR) aircraft over Syria but they had limitations when it came to monitoring small-arms and small-calibre indirect-fire weapons over wide areas.

Much of the ceasefire-monitoring effort fell to diplomats of the US State Department, and one of its officials told the author on 16th September 2016 that it had "multiple means for tracking alleged COH violations." He said the State Department monitored a wide variety of open sources and received direct reports from the field, including civil-society, opposition groups and individuals. These reports came via the United Nations and/or directly to the US government. US diplomats also conducted "outreach to contacts in the opposition, both in Syria and in the region," the official said

"Other parts of the government also monitor the situation in Syria, but we cannot discuss those mechanisms," said a senior US government source, in an apparent reference to the covert links to opposition militia forces established by the US Central Intelligence Agency. The CIA had liaison offices in Jordan and Turkey to help funnel arms to pro-western opposition groups and these were believed to have been re-roled to use their contacts to co-ordinate cease-fire compliance.

Both Russia and the United States moved quickly to try to establish networks to monitor compliance with the 9th September COH agreement but lacked the means to put in place meaningful numbers of "eyes on the ground" to actually see what was happening along every kilometre of the front lines.

Compliance with the COH was typically patchy across Syria but events outside the eastern city of Dier Ez Zor on 17th September would lead to the agreement's dramatic collapse in very acrimonious circumstances when a group of Syrian troops holding a key hill overlooking the city were hit by 37 coalition air strikes.

Six weeks later details of the incident near were revealed during a Pentagon briefing by USAF Brigadier General Richard "Tex" Coe, who led the US Air Forces Central Command investigation team. General Coe's investigation identified a chain of events that culminated in the coalition air commanders at the Combined Air Operations Centre (CAOC) at Al Udeid airbase, Qatar, authorising 37 air strikes by US Fairchild A-10A Warthogs, Australian Boeing F/A-18 Hornets, Danish Lockheed Martin F-16 Fighting Falcons and a UK General Atomics MQ-9 Reaper on the Syrian position. Syrian government sources claimed the attacked killed 84 of its soldiers, but Coe said during the briefing on 29th November that coalition imagery analysts could only confirm 15 deaths at the location.

A redacted executive summary of General Coe's report suggests a mis-identification of tanks, other vehicles and personnel at the location of the attack two days beforehand set in train the errors that led to the incident. These errors in turn resulted in the subsequent classification of the location as being in Islamic State controlled territory and, as a result, the CAOC's Dynamic Targeting Cell (DTC) received target engagement authority (TEA) to launch an attack on 17th September. Information from intelligence analysts with a deeper understanding of the complex battle lines around the Syrian-government held enclave inside Islamic State territory at Dier Ez Zor was "not communicated" to the DTC Chief in time to prevent the attack, the redacted report said. It also emerged that CAOC staff who routinely warned Russian air commanders in Syria of intended coalition air strikes provided the Russians with the wrong position of the targets. When a Russian officer used a hotline to warn the CAOC that Syrian government troops were under coalition air attack, the US officer who was the designated point of contact was elsewhere on Al Udeid airbase and it took 27 minutes for him to return to the CAOC and establish communications with his Russian counterpart.

"Having performed a thorough review of all the facts and circumstances, as the investigating officer I found that the decision to identify the targets as [ISIL] military objectives was made in good faith, based on information reasonably available at the time to all coalition decision makers," Coe was reported as saying in a Pentagon news release. He added that the targets were struck in accordance with the law of armed conflict and applicable rules of engagement for all nations involved.

General Coe recommended a review of the CAOC's targeting process, better information-sharing to avoid "group think", a more formal lesson-learned process so CAOC personnel on short tours of duty could quickly learn from incidents, and more use of the US-Russia hotline to pass critical information. The high turnover key personnel at the CAOC was identified as an underlying cause of the 17th September incident, leading to a poor understanding of the battlespace by the DTC staff. They then did not, or were unable to, seek input from other CAOC personnel who had a greater understanding of the situation on the ground around Dier Ez Zor.

The impression created by the General Coe's report is that the US Air Force officers and their British allies running the air war against Islamic State had little understanding of the complex battlefields inside Syria and were overly fixated on killing Islamic State fighters. They had tunnel vision and could only understand the war from the perspective of the US-led coalition vs Islamic State. This would prove to be an expensive shortcoming.

Unfortunately, this chain of misfortune occurred at a critical moment in the Syrian crisis, just as the Americans and the Russians were trying to stitch together another ceasefire deal. The Syrian government accused the US of deliberately attacking its troops and decided to launch a retaliatory air strike against an aid convoy and humanitarian-aid warehouse in opposition territory near Aleppo. Russian aircraft also reportedly participated in this operation. The strike reportedly killed 12 people and destroyed 12 aid trucks.

The selection of these as targets gave an interesting insight into Russian and Syrian assessment of opposition forces around Aleppo. The warehouse was run by the famous White Helmets search-and-rescue organisation but the Syrian and Russian governments routinely accused them of being a US and UK government-funded intelligence-gathering front organisation, linked to the Nusra Front. The White Helmet base was the most vulnerable and exposed US and UK-linked target that could be hit without directly attacking western forces themselves. There was then a furious UN Security Council meeting at which the Russian, British and American Ambassadors traded accusations. Not surprisingly, the COH was now dead in the water.

Chapter 12
Aleppo: Attack and Counter-Attack

In the final week of September 2016, the Syrian and Russian offensive against the east-Aleppo enclave began in earnest. The 9th September ceasefire was left in tatters after the US-led coalition Dier Ez Zor air strike and then the retaliatory Russian-Syrian attack on the White Helmet warehouse near Aleppo.

The Syrian command around Aleppo had taken the opportunity of the ceasefire to re-shuffle its troops ready for the next attack. They had also benefited from the concentration of Russian surveillance assets over the city to monitor ceasefire compliance. At least two Russian Forpost drones had been circling over the city on a 24/7 basis since 9th September, allowing the Russians and Syrians to build up a detailed picture of rebel defensive position and the movements and habits of the civilian population in the enclave, as well as tracking a number of rebel commanders. The rebels, who had their own drones, did their best to hide their vehicles and equipment from Russian aerial surveillance. During this period one rebel group posted an online video of their armed pick-up trucks, or technicals, being prepared for action in the underground car park of an apartment building.

The Syrian and Russian battle plan was complex and sophisticated, involving ground and air forces, backed up by systematic air surveillance by Russian drones. A major part of the plan was the pre-positioning of humanitarian and medical aid for any civilians who might escape from the enclave to government controlled territory. British journalist Vanessa Beeley visited several of the Syrian and Russian-run refugee reception centres during the later stages of the siege, and described this humanitarian operation which involved the pre-positioning of field hospitals, mobile field kitchens and refugee registration facilities as "extraordinary" and "generous". "The Russians had a plan and were well organised," said Beeley.

The aim of Operation Dawn of Victory was not just to capture the territory of the rebel enclave but to win over the "hearts and minds" of its population. International aid organisations and the United Nations estimated that between 250,000 and 300,000 people were inside the enclave, including some 8,000 armed fighters. Around 1,000 of these were hard-line fighters of the Nusra Front and its Jihadi allies. The Syrians had some 10,000 troops deployed around Aleppo, although the majority of them were militia fighters of the National Defence Force who manned the siege lines around pro-government enclaves. These soldiers took turns to serve shifts at the front in between their civilian jobs in the city. The professional soldiers of the Tiger Force and several other Republican Guard units had been reinforced by some 1,200 troops in

August and additional forces were on their way to the city. In the final week of September, some 1,750 new Syrian troops arrived in Aleppo from the Damascus region, including elements 102nd and 106th Republican Guard Brigades, as well as more troops of the 4th Mechanised Division. These units were quickly moved to take up positions on the inner siege lines around the rebel enclave. Other units of Tiger Force and Desert Hawks Brigade arrived at Kweires airbase to be held in reserve.

A strong contingent of Russian advisors and surveillance experts were in the city to assist the Syrians. Every major Syrian and allied unit in the city had a team of Russian officers advising them on how to call down air strikes and to analyse video feeds from drones orbiting the city. A team of officers from the Russian reconciliation centre were also in the city to organise the delivery of humanitarian aid and medical assistance for any civilians who came out of the enclave. A Russian artillery unit, with 2A65 MSTA-B 152mm howitzers and BM-21 rocket launchers, had been filmed arriving in the Aleppo region in June and was later spotted at Kweires airbase to the east of the city in August, added to the firepower available for the offensive. A Russian jamming and signals intelligence detachment set up a base at Aleppo's civilian airport.

The commander of Russian forces in Syria, Lieutenant General Alexander Zhuravlev, was repeatedly photographed visiting Aleppo from August as he conferred with the Syrian commander in the city, Major General Zaid Saleh, and the leader of the Tiger Force, Colonel Suheil al-Hassan. The Russian General made regular appearances to decorate Syrian and Palestinian soldiers in what seemed like a concerted drive to motivate them to keep attacking.

The next phase of the Syrian battle plan involved concentrating their effort on capturing the least defended and largely uninhabited areas of northern Aleppo. This was not really surprising given the nature of the terrain in the centre of the city. Its narrow streets between high rise buildings, numerous water obstacles and elevated roads made it very difficult to employ direct-fire weapons or manoeuvre armoured vehicles. It was a moot point whether the Syrian government had the manpower to conduct a large scale and systematic house clearing operation in the centre of Aleppo. A battle that risked significant Syrian military casualties was not on the agenda.

The opening attack was led by the Palestinian Liwa al-Quds, or Jerusalem Brigade, militia, which had been recruited from refugee camps around Aleppo. Palestinian refugees were some of the most stalwart supporters of the Syrian government because it had given them shelter after the founding of Israel in 1948. The Jerusalem Brigade was one of the most highly motivated fighting forces in Aleppo and it had been hardened by four years of combat into a unit that was expert at urban warfare.

Syrian artillery and rocket launchers staged a two-day long barrage of the front lines around the abandoned Handarat Palestinian refugee camp, which was co-ordinated with several Russian air strikes. When the Jerusalem Brigade fighters began to infiltrate the camp and a neighbouring industrial zone they met hardly any resistance: just a few scattered snipers and machine gunners. The rebel defenders soon melted a way out of the camp to re-group. Photographs from inside the camp showed heavy destruction of buildings but only a handful of dead rebel fighters, appearing to confirm that the rebels had retreated from the camp. But before the Palestinian fighters had time to consolidate their positions a squad of rebel fighters counter-attacked on 25th September. Rather than suffer casualties, the Palestinians pulled back. After a couple of days re-organising, the Palestinians repeated their attack. This time, Syrian Republican Guard troops joined the assault. The camp was completely cleared of resistance by 1st October and, to make sure the rebels could not launch any counter attack, other Syrian units staged feints around the enclave to confuse defenders about what was happening.

The fighting now moved southwards into a large industrial area along the northern edge of the rebel enclave. Russian aircraft pounded a series of large abandoned factories and the ruins of a large hospital to open the way for the Palestinian militia to make steady progress over the first two weeks of October. By 16th October, the Syrian troops and Palestinian militia fighters, had pushed some four kilometres into the opposition-held enclave, across a four-kilometre- wide-front. The extent of the advance was confirmed by statements from government and opposition spokesmen, as well as analysis of news and social-media imagery showing key landmarks being occupied by government troops. Troops of the 102nd and 106th Republican Guards Brigades, supported by contingents of the Palestinian Liwa Al-Quds militia, were filmed using tanks, artillery, anti-tank guided missiles and anti-aircraft guns in the direct-fire role, backed by Russian air strikes. During their advance there appears to have been little close-quarter combat on this front. Over the five days up to 16th October, Syrian troops and their allies pushed south to a line south of the Jandoul roundabout that extended across to the Agricultural School in the Haidaiyra district.

Analysis of imagery from this period of fighting in northern Aleppo suggests that opposition fighters staged a series deliberate withdrawals in the face of the government advance. In effect they collapsed their own defences.

Syrian troops also launched a couple of other ground offensives around the fringes of the opposition's Aleppo enclave, seizing a hill on the southern edge at Sheikh Sa'eed and making a lodgement in the Bustan district in the centre of the city. But on both these fronts, the progress appears to have been measured in hundreds of metres.

This all suggested that the final phase of the Battle for Aleppo had yet to begin in earnest, with the opposition militia pulling back in a staged withdrawal from the outer fringes of the enclave into the central urban area.

It was a gruesome ritual of the Syrian war that victorious forces usually showed off the corpses of dead opponents after capturing positions - but during this fighting there was a conspicuous lack of imagery of such displays from northern Aleppo by government troops on their social-media accounts or in the official Damascus media. This suggested opposition fighters had been able to retreat in good order, carrying their dead and wounded with them. Only a handful of obituaries of government soldiers appeared in the local media, which added to the impression that few combatants from both the government or opposition side had thus far been killed in the fighting in northern Aleppo.

All through this four-week period of fighting, the international news media was dominated by reports of bombings of hospital and civilian areas in the rebel enclave. There was a daily stream of video of devastated hospitals and Skype interviews with White Helmet civil-defence workers. There were no international journalists or aid workers inside the enclave to provide any sort of objective assessment of casualties.

Compilations of reports from inside the enclave suggested a range of casualty figures. IHS Jane's Terrorism and Insurgency Centre reported on 12th October that it had recorded 362 fatalities between 19th September and 3rd October in Aleppo, of which some 51% were civilians. The United Nations Office for the Coordination of Humanitarian Affairs (OCHA) reported that 406 people had been reported killed and 1,384 wounded in eastern Aleppo from 23rd September up to 8th October. My own analysis of media reports between 22nd September and 17th October suggested some 420 were reported dead in around 170 air strikes. This averaged at six air strikes a day, causing around 17 deaths each day. In government-held western Aleppo, which was frequently targeted by rebel shelling in retaliation, 91 people including 18 children were claimed killed over a similar period by Syrian state-controlled media.

After the siege was over, on 27th February 2017, the United Nations Human Rights Council's Independent International Commission of Inquiry published a wide-ranging report into Battle of Aleppo. It was only able to confirm the deaths of 38 people in attacks on hospitals in east Aleppo and 34 civilians killed in west Aleppo by rebel fire. This suggested that both sides during the Battle of Aleppo exaggerated the number of civilian casualties for public-relations reasons in a bid to motivate their people to fight and to try to gain international sympathy.

The diplomatic and media coverage of the hospital attacks did, however, prompt the US Secretary of State, John Kerry, to make one more push for a ceasefire - but he could not broker a deal. The Russians announced a unilateral bombing pause on 18th October.

It suited both sides to go along with this proposal. The government was able to rest its assault troops and the rebels needed to rebuild their defences along the northern fringe of the enclave. So, on 20th October, the final "humanitarian ceasefire" came in to force.

Chapter 13
Aleppo Falls

Russian commanders and their Syrian allies were well prepared for the calling of the 20th October ceasefire, and by time it came into effect they had put in place an operation to activate what they dubbed "humanitarian corridors" for civilians to leave the rebel-held enclave.

Small detachments of Russian troops from the Centre for Reconciliation of Opposing Sides in the Syrian Arab Republic were positioned at eight crossing points around the rebel enclave. Helicopters dropped leaflets offering safe passage to civilians and surrendering fighters. The same messages were repeated on local television and radio stations, which could be seen and heard inside the enclave. Syrian Red Crescent aid workers and a fleet of buses from the state-owned transport company were also on hand to deal with any refugees. The green-painted buses would soon become a major feature in the Aleppo crisis. Russian Forpost drones and ground-mounted video cameras started streaming pictures of the crossing points live on the Russian Ministry of Defence website. It was not gripping viewing. Nothing happened. No civilians and only eight wounded opposition fighters took advantage of the ceasefire on 20th October to leave the besieged city, according to Moscow.

Despite the apparent lack of success, the Russian Ministry of Defence announced a 24-hour extension to the ceasefire until the evening of 21st October. Opposition groups in the city, backed by the US, UK and French governments, denounced the cease fire and opening of humanitarian corridors as a trick to try to force, first, the evacuation and then the surrender, of the city. The Syrians accused rebel fighters of threatening civilians who wanted to leave the enclave - a claim that UN human rights investigators subsequently confirmed. Throughout 20th October there were media reports of mortar and small-arms fire along the confrontation lines in the city, with the Russian military reporting three of its officers, who were manning a checkpoint on one of the humanitarian corridors, suffered "slight injuries" from opposition fire. The negative reaction of opposition groups in the city to the 20th October Russian and Syrian ceasefire suggests that at this point they had little inclination to surrender their enclave.

If offers of safe passage were the Russian "carrot" to the population of east Aleppo, at the same time Moscow unveiled its new and bigger "stick" to threaten the rebels. All through the summer the Russian media had been filled with reports of the preparations to get the country's only aircraft carrier, Admiral Kuznetsov, and a supporting naval task group ready to sail for the Mediterranean from ports around Murmansk on the Kola Peninsula in the far north of Russia. The carrier's air group of more than a dozen Sukhoi Su-33 and Mikoyan MiG-29 combat aircraft would effectively increase Russia's air power in the Syrian theatre by a third. The Russian air force could have easily deployed another dozen jet combat aircraft to Syria but Moscow had a different agenda. It wanted to deliberately ratchet up the impression that Moscow was massing overwhelming military force to back the Syrian ground assault on Aleppo. The progress of the Admiral Kuznetsov and her Northern Fleet battle group out into the Atlantic, through the North Sea and English Channel and then into the Mediterranean, would generate huge coverage in the international media. The unwillingness of the US, Britain, France and other western countries to do anything to stop the Admiral Kuznetsov would reinforce the impression that the rebels in eastern Aleppo had been abandoned to their fate by their main backers. It proved to be a master-stoke of psychological warfare.

On 15th October, Russia's state-owned news agency TASS announced that the carrier had sailed."The group consists of the aircraft-carrying heavy cruiser Admiral Kuznetsov, the Pyotr Velikiy battle cruiser, large anti-submarine ships Severomorsk and Vice-Admiral Kulakov and support vessels," said a statement from the Russian North Fleet, reported by TASS later that day.

The aim of the deployment was "to ensure naval presence in the important areas of the world ocean," said the Northern Fleet statement. "Special focus will be made on safeguarding security of maritime traffic and other types of maritime economic activity of Russia and also on responding to the new kinds of modern threats such as piracy and international terrorism."

NATO had been developing plans to monitoring the progress of Admiral Kuznetsov and her battle group as it transited through the North Atlantic and into the Mediterranean. Many of the alliance naval and air assets participating in Exercise Joint Warrior off the west coast of Scotland were drawn upon for the surveillance operation, including Canadian Air Force CP-140 Aurora and US Navy Boeing P-8A Poseidon maritime patrol aircraft temporarily deployed to RAF Lossiemouth in Scotland.

UK assets on call for the surveillance operation included a Type 23 frigate and a Type 45 destroyer to shadow the Russian ships, according to UK military sources. Royal Air Force aircraft were also being prepared for the operation. These included a Boeing RC-135 Rivet Joint electronic eavesdropping aircraft, a Lockheed C-130J Hercules transport re-roled for surface surveillance by providing the crew with additional binoculars, and Eurofighter Typhoon fighter aircraft to shadow any Sukhoi Su-33 Mikoyan MiG-29Ks fighters launched from the Admiral Kuznetsov.

Britain and NATO tried to give the impression of "business as usual", saying on 15th October, "UK and NATO assets routinely monitor warships from other nations when they enter our area of interest and this will be no different."

When the Admiral Kuznetsov passed through the English Channel on 21st October the crew taunted watching British and NATO warships by deliberately moving fighter jets and one of the Russian Navy's new Kamov Ka-52 attack helicopters up onto the carriers deck to be photographed. They were putting on a show of force and reinforcing the impression that western countries were too weak to stop the Russian Navy. The US and Britain tried to stop the Russian battle group refuelling at the Spanish enclave of Cueta on the North African coast, but Moscow had strong relations with neighbouring Algeria and the Algiers government quickly agreed to allow Russian tankers to take on fuel for the Admiral Kuznetsov. The limits of Western influence were again exposed.

Events in Aleppo now returned to centre stage. The Russian and Syrian declared ceasefire had not produced any results. Only a handful of civilians had left eastern Aleppo and rebel fighters expressed no interest in joining in with the ceasefire.

Syrian opposition fighters from several groups and units, based around Idlib, were now in the final stages of preparing a major offensive to try to break the siege of eastern Aleppo by attempting again to punch through government positions in the south-west of the city. Convoys of pick-up trucks fitted with anti-aircraft guns, artillery pieces and rocket launchers, as well as several tanks and armoured vehicles on low loaders, began to move northwards from Idlib to jumping-off points around western Aleppo. If the rebels had hoped to repeat their success in August when they surprised the government troops around Aleppo, this attempt was doomed to failure. Rebel news teams began posting videos of the massing of their troops online between 20th and 24th October. The footage showed the troop convoys moving in broad daylight along main roads. Russian and Syrian surveillance drones and other intelligence assets would have clearly spotted the convoys, even if they had not been able to find the videos of the rebel convoys on YouTube.

On 25th October a Syrian journalist photographed the army commander in Aleppo, Major General Zaid Saleh, inside his office in the city's military academy. On the wall behind the general was a large map showing the proposed attack plan for the coming Syrian offensive, but there were also arrows showing the expected attack axis of the coming rebel break-in attempt. The Russian Ministry of Defence even announced on 21st October that 1,200 rebels and 120 vehicles, including tanks, were heading towards Aleppo. It was clear this time the rebels would not have the element of surprise. Although there were some air strikes in the western Aleppo countryside as the rebel force approached the city, the suspicion remained that the Russians and Syrians let the rebel force attack so it could be devastated by their overwhelming air power, artillery and tank forces outside the western suburbs of Aleppo.

The first rebel attacks got under way in heavy rain on 28th October, which appeared to ground Syria and Russian strike aircraft and temporarily blind their air surveillance. At least three large vehicle-borne suicide bombs, including one in a modified BMP armoured vehicle, led the assault that breached government lines on the western edge of the city; then follow-up infantry, backed by tanks, exploited the confusion caused by the bombs to push into the Al Assad and Minyan suburbs. The opposition offensive was backed by rocket strikes, artillery and mortar attacks on government-held territory, including targeting Aleppo's airport.

This was the most vulnerable moment for the Syrian defenders. The devastating suicide-bomb attacks left the defenders along much of the western edge of the city stunned, leaderless and confused. Hundreds of rebel fighters were surging forward and finding no organised resistance. Just by chance, a 16-soldier-strong Russian Spetsnaz squad was based in the Assad Military Academy and rapidly moved to find out what was going on. They immediately became locked in a series of running firefights with the advancing rebels, using their sniper rifles to good effect. A Russian forward air controller also started to call down air strikes, gaining the Syrian troops valuable time to get their defences organised. The commander of the Spetsnaz squad was later decorated with the Hero of Russian Federation, his country's highest medal for gallantry. President Putin reportedly demanded to present the medal personally to the officer in a Kremlin ceremony, after he heard that senior Russian commanders estimated the Spetsnaz team killed 300 rebels during the battle.

Thanks to the rear-guard action by the Spetsnaz team, government troops along the western edge of Aleppo city had rallied and were now putting up stiff resistance. Anti-tank missile teams on the roofs of buildings, including the Assad Military Academy, where General Saleh had his headquarters, picked off rebel armoured vehicles trying to push into the city. One squad of Syrian troops fought off the attack by forming a firing line behind a stone wall blocking entry to the military academy. The soldiers were filmed trading fire with rebels on the other side of a street.

More rebel reinforcements came forward. Two more vehicle-borne suicide bombs struck the government defences in the 1070 Housing Project in south-west Aleppo on 29th October, allowing more progress to be made in this contested district. The Nusra Front drivers of the converted BMP troop carriers made Jihadi martyrdom videos that were posted online in which they boasted that their "brothers" inside Aleppo would soon be liberated. These attacks involved BMP vehicles stashed with explosives in their rear compartments and up-armoured with huge steel plates to stop anti-tank missiles. One of the suicide bombs created a mushroom cloud several hundreds of metres high that could be seen across all of the city.

From 30th October, government reinforcements arrived in the west of the city, including units of the Tiger Force and Desert Hawk Brigade equipped with T-90 tanks, armed pick-up trucks, BMP armoured vehicles and 2S1 122mm self-propelled artillery. The tanks and gun vehicles were driven up to the edge of the build-up area controlled by the government troops and started to fire directly at rebel positions. Artillery observers and anti-tank guided-missile teams on top of high-rise buildings started to rain down fire on the woods and small villages to the west of the city. Huge explosions could be seen as vehicles and gun positions were hit by this fire. Russian jets were filmed taking part in these raids despite repeated claims by Moscow that its planes were not attacking targets in Aleppo.

After a pause, the opposition launched four more suicide vehicle borne-bomb attacks on 3rd November to spearhead more attacks on the southwest of Aleppo. The attacks made their deepest penetrations to date into government areas but Syrian troops held their ground and killed scores of fighters, as well as knocking out a number of BMP troop carriers that tried to move assault teams into the 3000 Housing Project. The streets and gardens around the housing project were soon littered with bodies of dozens of dead rebels.

In the days up to 4th November, there appears to have been little offensive activity by the estimated 8,000 opposition fighters besieged inside eastern Aleppo. There were no reports from pro-government or opposition media indicating major attacks to attempt to break out of the enclave. A single opposition T-55 tank was filmed being driven from a hide and then firing into a government-held district around the prominent Meriden Hotel on 30th October, but there appears to have been no concerted attempt to punch a breach through the government's inner siege lines and link up with the forces attacking from the outside. The Reuters news agency reported on 3rd November that opposition groups within the city had been fighting amongst themselves.

For a week, the rebels outside the city launched repeated attempts to break the government siege lines. This was the moment when the Syrian army had its hands full fighting off the rebel assault, but the defenders of the enclave made no serious moves to exploit this. The failure or unwillingness of the rebels inside the city to launch a break-out attempt sealed their fate. Eastern Aleppo would not be rescued.

During the last week of October, more Syrian troops were freed from duty around Damascus and were ordered to Aleppo. These included a 1,500 strong armoured brigade and elements of the Republican Guard Shudada Kafr Saghira Brigade, according to Syrian media reports. The troops appeared not to have been thrown straight into the fighting off the rebel counter-attack but were held back for the coming assault on eastern Aleppo.

Out in the Mediterranean, the Russian Navy was putting in place on the final moves before the assault on east Aleppo could begin. The Admiral Kuznetsov and her battle group sailed eastwards and passed the south coast of Crete on 2nd November, according to open source AIS tracking of the group's civilian-registered ocean going tug, the Nikolay Chiker. Subsequent tracking put the tug in a holding pattern south-east of Crete on 4th November.

Russia's only aircraft carrier was soon to be joined by the Kalibr cruise missile armed frigate Admiral Grigorovich, from the Black Sea Fleet, which was seen sailing through the Bosphorus into the Aegean Sea on the morning of 4th November. Analysis of open-source naval traffic through the Bosphorus Straits indicated that the Russian naval task group off Syria by then comprised six major and two minor warships, five support ships and three survey/intelligence-gathering vessels, in addition to the Admiral Kuznetsov.

Once the Russian ships had met up, the expanded battle group set sail for the Syrian coast. As the Russian battle group approached, Moscow notified the Cypriot aviation authorities that their warships and aircraft would be carrying out live "rocket test-firings" in a large block of sea and airspace stretching from near the Syrian territorial limit to some 50 kilometres from the eastern edge of Cyprus, between 10th and 22nd November. This Notice to Airmen, or NOTAM, warned civil and military aircraft to stay out of the exercise zone. On 11th November, the Russian Navy issued an additional NOTAM closing off several commercial air routes in the vicinity of their exercise area.

According to the commander of the carrier, Captain 1st Rank Sergey Artamonov, daily flights over Syria to familiarise his aircrew with "interaction" with Russian and Syrian forces began on 8th November. These appeared to be going smoothly until a Mikoyan MiG-29K combat jet operating from the Admiral Kuzentsov crashed in the eastern Mediterranean on 14th November. "An air accident involving a sea-based MiG-29K occurred as a result of an equipment fault during an approach for deck landing several kilometres away from the aircraft-carrying cruiser Admiral Kuznetsov," the Russian Ministry of Defence announced in a statement, quoted by the TASS news agency. "The pilot ejected himself from the aircraft and was taken to the Admiral Kuznetsov by a crew of the search and rescue service," the press release said. "His health is not in danger and he is ready to perform further tasks."

A Sukhoi Su-33 was lost on 3rd December after a similar incident with the Admiral Kuznetsov's arrestor wires. For several days the bulk of the carrier's air wing relocated ashore to Hmeinyan airbase until the arrestor-wire problems were resolved. This was not announced by Moscow but was revealed by commercial satellite imagery of base, which showed rows of Su-33s parked by the runway.

On the ground in Aleppo, units of the Tiger Force launched a series of limited offensives around the 1070 Housing Project to clear out the last pockets of rebel fighters still surviving who were clinging onto toeholds around the western fringe of the city. Once these were over, General Saleh started to re-organise his forces for the final offensive against the rebel enclave. The Tiger Force and the Desert Hawk Brigades were moved to the eastern side of the city ready for the offensive to begin.

The Russian air force and navy now started a two-week long operation against rebel forces on the western outskirts of Aleppo city to prevent a repeat of the October break-in offensive. Su-33s and MiG-29s began launching off the Admiral Kuznetsov to hit targets identified by Russian Forpost surveillance drones. The drones tracked vehicle movements in rebel-held territory looking for tanks, rocket launchers and any other rebel activity. The Russian intelligence-gathering operation in Syria was now far more advanced than it was at the start of Moscow's intervention in 2015, and Russian air planners in Syria were able to strike at what is known by the US military as "time-sensitive targets".

From analysis of Forpost video released by the Russian Ministry of Defence and social media posts by rebel groups it was possible to piece together one of these strikes against a group of rebels in a car in a village to the west of Aleppo. The video showed an air strike by a Russian Navy Su-33 against a car as it approached a bus station in the village. Comparison with commercial satellite imagery confirmed the location of the strike and the social-media posts put the rebel fighters in that location at the time of the strike. A video posted online showed the dead rebels at the location. The Su-33 lacked targeting pods with thermal imaging cameras so its pilots clearly needed to be guided to their targets by intelligence operatives monitoring the drone's video feed.

The Admiral Grigorovich now joined the battle, firing a number of Kalibr cruise missiles at targets to the south-west of Aleppo. Moscow also took the opportunity to unleash a salvo of land-attack missiles of the Bastion coastal-defence missile from a firing point near Tartus in Latakia province. This variant of the Bastion missile had never been used in action before.

A further ratcheting-up of the firepower being thrown at the rebels came when two Tupolev Tu-95 heavy bombers, supported by Ilyushin Il-78 air-to-air refuelling tanker aircraft, took off from an Arctic airbase and flew all the way down over the Eastern Atlantic, past the west coasts of Scotland and Ireland before heading into the Mediterranean. After flying through the Straits of Gibraltar and then past Sicily and Crete, the two bombers launched a handful of Kh-101 cruise missiles at targets to the west of Aleppo. Again, this was a first, as the Russian Long Range Aviation had never fired this type of missile from a Tu-95 in combat before. It appeared that the missile launch was a combat test of the weapon.

The bomber mission was treated very differently by the British government to the passage of the Admiral Kuznetsov through the English Channel the previous month. Britain's bombastic Defence Secretary, Sir Michael Fallon, was determined to avoid giving the Russians any more publicity and he ordered his ministry's press office to downplay the whole thing.

A Ministry of Defence spokesman in London denied that the bombers had been intercepted by RAF Typhoon fighters or that they had flown past Britain. When recordings of the RAF pilots intercepting the jets emerged on an online aircraft spotter-website, the ministry continued to deny the bombers had flown south past Britain. Next, a plane spotter website posted recordings of French Mirage and Portuguese F-16 fighters scrambling to intercept the Russian aircraft over the Atlantic and later off the Algarve. NATO then confirmed that the Russian planes had flown around the Iberian Peninsula. The Ministry of Defence in London at last confirmed that the reports of the Russian bombers' fight path into the Mediterranean were "factual". Apparently, Fallon had ordered the media blackout on the Russian bombers because he felt all the publicity that had been given the Admiral Kuznetsov had backfired and made the British government look weak.

For a two-week period, Russian jets and missiles hit a swathe of targets to the west and south-west of Aleppo to prevent rebel forces re-grouping to launch another attack to break the siege of the enclave in the city. The limited number of targets hit by the Russian strategic strikes – possibly less than 30 – indicates that they were intended to be psychological in nature. They were a demonstration of the overwhelming firepower available to back up the Syrian army attack on Aleppo and reinforced the message that the West was not going to intervene to help the rebels trapped in the city. The Russian air and missile attacks also boosted the morale of the Syrian troops who were soon to go in to action.

Under the cover of this operation, General Saleh reshuffled his units again to get them in to position for the final assault on the enclave. This time there would be no pause once a chunk of territory was captured. Operation Dawn of Victory would be pressed home until all the enclave was in government hands.

The Russian navy posted a new NOTAM with the Cypriot aviation authorities on 24th November, saying live "training flights and rocket test firings" in a large block of sea and airspace stretching from near the Syrian territorial limit to some 50 kilometres from the eastern edge of Cyprus, will continue until 27th December. This NOTAM said the closure of several commercial air routes in the vicinity of their exercise area would also remain in place until 27th December. A long period of combat was expected by the Russians.

Pro-government media reported that Syrian troops began a series of ground assaults on 18th November, apparently aimed at capturing discrete objectives around the eastern edge of the opposition controlled enclave. Video and still imagery posted online appeared to confirm government advances in the new cemetery, Tel al-Zuhar, Jabal Badro districts and the Old Sheikh Najjar industrial zone, with a number of opposition armoured vehicles being captured.

Government attacks were rebuffed on at least three occasions by opposition fighters defending the southern district of Sheikh Sa'eed. Palestinian militia units had also been attacking along the north eastern edge of the opposition enclave but made little headway.

Government troops made extensive use of fixed wing jet and attack-helicopter strikes, artillery, multiple-launch rockets, anti-tank guided missile and tank fire ahead of their ground assaults. The vast majority of this fire support was directed at front-line positions around the city to kill or traumatise any defenders. Debris from a SS-21 Tochka ballistic missile was also photographed inside the opposition enclave during this period. These attacks served to confuse rebel fighters about where the focal point of the Syrian offensive would come, and also denied them sleep to further undermine their ability to resist.

Units of the Syrian Arab Army's Tiger Force made the decisive breakthroughs on 25th and 26th November to completely capture the Hanano Housing Project, in north-east Aleppo, from opposition fighters. Video imagery of the attack showed Tiger Force T-72s leading columns of BMP armoured troop carriers up to the northern edge of the housing project. There only seemed to be a couple of hundred troops taking part in this attack. Assault troops dismounted from the vehicles and then moved into the built-up area.

There was no resistance from any rebel fighters. The front-line rebel trenches and bunkers had been abandoned. As the Tiger Force columns moved through the 1970s apartment blocks and wide streets the occasional sniper opened fire but Colonel Suheil al-Hassan's troops quickly silenced them with a few rounds from their tanks, BMPs and cannon-armed pick-up trucks.

Tiger Force officers were monitoring the advance on a video feed from Forpost drones in their headquarters and quickly realised the northern section of the enclave was not being defended in any co-ordinated manner. Colonel Hassan ordered his troops to keep advancing. By the end of the second day of the operation they had fully secured the Hanano Housing Project and were pushing into the narrow alleyways of the al Sakhour district.

A further government advance on 27th November, drove opposition fighters from the nearby Jebal Badro neighbourhood and brought Syrian troops to within one kilometre from their colleagues holding the western side of the Aleppo enclave. An attack further south by the Desert Hawks Brigade on Police Hill failed to penetrate the rebel defences.

The few rebel fighters that were left in the north of the enclave now fled south to avoid being trapped in a "mini pocket". This advance left the Syrian Arab Army in control of the Hallak, Bustan Al-Pasha, Inzarat and Haydariyah districts. On 28th November, the Syrian state news agency, SANA, announced the capture of the al-Sakhour district, completing the operation to drive opposition fighters from the north of their enclave. Syrian state-controlled media reports from the city, as well as social-media feeds from government soldiers, did not feature imagery of dead or captured opposition fighters, suggesting that most escaped and that they did not put up a fight.

As the government troops moved to set up defensive positions to secure their gains and re-position their assault units for the next phase of the operation, the civilian population of the north of the enclave started to emerge from the ruins of their homes. An estimated 8,000 took shelter in the nearby Kurdish enclave after YPG fighters joined the government operation on 28th November and occupied parts of Bustin al Pasha and Hallak districts. A further 18,000 were moved to refugee shelters set up by the government, the Syrian Red Crescent and Russian army in a nearby industrial zone. Warehouses were opened for families to sleep in and Russian army field kitchens fed the refugees, while Russian doctors and nurses provided medical assistance. Only a few civilians fled south with the retreating rebels.

After a series of meetings with his commanders and Russian advisors, General Saleh now switched the focus of his advance to the south, and the section of front-line directly adjacent to the Aleppo airport. The Tiger Force was again to lead the assault and it was moved to a jump-off position near to the Halwaniyah Youth Housing Project, a large complex of apartments in the eastern edge of the city. The attack on 30th November was fast-moving and violent. A Tiger Force T-72 tank and a couple of cannon-armed pick-up trucks drew up outside the housing project and started trading fire with a handful of rebel fighters in the upper levels of the buildings. Several BMP troop carriers then moved forward to deliver assault troops next to the apartments. The rebel fighters fled westwards back into the city, leaving the Tiger Force soldiers to pick over the debris and a handful of dead rebels.

In other battles on the southern edge of the rebel enclave, Republican Guard forces backed by a handful of T-72 tanks made a push into the southern suburb of Sheikh Sa'eed and achieved some success. An opposition counter-attack was quickly organised and this reversed many of the government advances in the district.

There appeared to be little sign of organised resistance in the central districts of Aleppo to the west of Halwaniyah, so a new Tiger Force attack was organised. It kicked off on 3rd December. Columns of Tiger Force infantry, backed by T-72 tanks and BMP troop carriers, weaved into the narrow streets of central Aleppo and met limited resistance in Karam al Jazmati and Karam al Myassar Districts until they reached a rebel stronghold around the National Eye Hospital. A deliberate attack had to be organised and this cleared the hospital and its grounds on 4th December. Tiger Force troops then moved to begin clearing the Old City quarter adjacent to Aleppo's historic citadel.

This advance was supported by heavy air strikes during 3rd December, with video imagery being posted online showing regular air attacks by Syrian and Russian aircraft. A Syria Arab Air Force (SyAAF) Su-22 was filmed popping flares over the eastern suburbs and later that day a Russian Aerospace Force Sukhoi Su-34 was recorded above city. This jet apparently dropped at least one bomb, although the Russian Ministry of Defence said that its aircraft had not attacked targets in the city since October. All these attacks appeared to be focused on front-line areas around the outer siege lines of the rebel enclaves.

Local media reported that a SyAAF Aero L-39ZA Albatross was lost in the early hours of 3rd December during a night-time sorties over the opposition held enclave in the east of Aleppo, its two crew killed after failing to eject. The aircraft was crashed over an opposition-held urban area between Aleppo Citadel and the National Eye Hospital after it was hit by ground fire.

There were small pockets of rebel fighters around the Old City and it took two days for Syrian troops to complete combing the district. A handful of dead rebels were photographed around the historic buildings but most fled southwards, leaving government forces in control of Aleppo's centre by 7th December. General Saleh made a triumphant visit to the Citadel walls to look down over the newly captured sections of the city.

The British, American and French governments attempted to introduce a resolution in the UN Security Council calling for a ceasefire on 5th December but the Russian and Chinese ambassadors vetoed the measure. The Syrian army would have a free run at capturing the remainder of the rebel enclave. By now more than half of it had been captured by government troops and the scene was set for the rest of the enclave to fall in a matter of days.

On 6th and 7th December, three important southern suburbs also came under attack. As the Old City was falling, the Desert Hawk Brigade renewed its assault on the Marjeh and Sheikh Lutfi districts in the southeast quarter of the enclave and pushed forward into several rebel-held areas. On 6th December, the Desert Hawk Brigade and the Syrian Marine unit renewed attacks on the Sheikh Lufti and Marjah suburbs in the south of the city, further reducing the area under opposition control. Neighbouring Sheikh Sa'eed was then attacked from the south. Over a four-day period, government troops advanced more than four kilometres westwards from the Aleppo ring road near the city's airport.

The rapid government advances prompted the opposition Leadership Council in Aleppo on 7th December to request a five-day humanitarian ceasefire to allow 500 wounded civilians and fighters to be evacuated to a zone controlled by Turkish-backed opposition forces to the north of the city. Syrian President Bashar al-Assad ruled out any ceasefire, just as his forces appear to be poised to capture the last remaining opposition held districts of Aleppo despite a last-minute announcement from Russia's foreign minister Sergei Lavrov on 8th December of a "suspension of combat operations" in the city.

All through the centre of the city, civilians were starting to emerge from their homes to greet the Syrian soldiers. Russian drones filmed thousands of people walking through the narrow alleys of the Old City looking for a way out. The Syrian government and Russian army started to guide them to pick-up points, where convoys of green-painted state transport company buses were waiting to take them to the refugee shelters outside the city. The images filmed from the drones showed long columns of people carrying suitcases, children and other possessions to out to pick-up points on the ring road around the city. The refugees were first directed to a series of reception centres in the Sheikh Najjar industrial zone, including one at Jibreen, where Syrian aid agencies, backed up by a Russian field hospital and field kitchens, were positioned to process them.

By 8th December, the size of the opposition enclave in Aleppo had shrunk by more than 75% since September, according to terrain analysis. At this stage, it now comprised a pocket no more than three kilometres across and four kilometres deep.

Government commanders now brought up new forces, including a unit of the 4th Mechanised Division equipped with T-90 tanks, the Syrian Marines Battalion as well as fighters and tanks from the Palestinian Liwa al Quds militia group, for their final attack. These units mounted a series of intense attacks starting on 9th December, backed by tanks firing at close range, artillery and rocket launchers, in the Sheikh Sa'eed and Karm al Da'da districts, as well as the area around Aleppo's Grand Mosque. After three days of heavy fighting the Syrian troops had cleared almost all of the eastern bank of the Queiq River, effectively putting the opposition forces in an untenable position in their rump enclave.

The final phase of the offensive that had began on 18th November culminated in a multi-pronged attack over 12th and 13th December which drove opposition fighters back into a 2.5-square-kilometre pocket along the western bank of the Queiq River.

Turkish and Russian diplomats brokered a ceasefire and evacuation deal on 13th December, but fighting broke out again on the following day, putting back the evacuation of the opposition contingent trapped in the enclave. After the United Nations accused pro-government forces of indiscriminate killings in areas they had just captured, diplomatic pressure mounted to get the evacuation deal back on track.

The first evacuation convoys from Aleppo to Idlib on 15th December moved more than 6,000 opposition supporters and their families, until the evacuation deal was suspended in a dispute over its terms the following day. The evacuations continued for four days until 22nd December when Syrian troops finally entered the last districts of eastern Aleppo. Apart from a handful of small incidents, reportedly involving pro-government Shia militia fighters, the evacuation went smoothly under the supervision of Russian troops, the Syrian Red Crescent and the International Committee of the Red Cross. Syrian troops remained disciplined throughout the evacuation and the rebels were able to leave with many of their weapons.

The Russian Centre for Reconciliation reported, on 15th December, that 108,076 civilians, including 47,183 children, had entered government-controlled territory since 27th November, with 3,033 fighters surrendering to government troops. The figures could not be verified but international media organisations in Aleppo also reported large population movements since the start of December and also broadcast reports from several refugee shelters, run by the government officials and Russian troops, containing thousands of refugees. In January 2017, the United Nations office in Syria confirmed that 110,000 people had sought refuge with Syrian government forces, compared to 34,000 who left with the rebel fighters to Idlib.

The start of the evacuation brought to an end to more than four years of resistance to the Damascus government in the north-west Syrian city, after a six-month-long offensive by Syrian army to capture the besieged opposition enclave in its eastern districts. The UN Human Rights Council's Independent International Commission of Inquiry on the Syrian Arab Republic into Battle of Aleppo reported in February 2017 that a few dozen men had been forcibly conscripted into the Syrian army and that a handful of execution style killings had taken place. Although the evacuations had taken place in terrible winter weather, hundreds of seriously ill patients had been moved by ambulance to hospital in Idlib and Turkey. Everyone who wanted to leave the enclave had been able to. Contrary to some predictions, a Srebrenica-style massacre did not taken place.

For the Russian and Syrian military, Operation Dawn of Victory was a significant tactical and operational success. General Saleh, his senior commanders and staff, assisted by their Russian advisors, had conducted a complex and multi-phased land, air and naval operation against an enemy in prepared positions inside an urban environment, amid a large civilian population. The operation led to hundreds of civilian casualties, which drew intense criticism from western governments, the international media and human rights organisations but the loss of life turned out to be nowhere near some of the claims made during the height of the battle. Ultimately, the civilian casualties were significantly less than during the US-led coalition forces operation to capture Mosul in Iraq, which was playing out at the same time as the Battle for Aleppo.

Not surprisingly the Syrian government hailed the opposition evacuation of Aleppo as a major victory. It restored government control to all of Syria's four major cities and forced the main group of rebel fighters in north-west Syria to retreat into the Idlib pocket. Many western observers focused on the retreat of the rebel fighters as being the main success for the government troops.

From the Syrian and Russian point of view, while this was an important event for them, the more important victory was in persuading the vast majority of the population to remain in government-controlled territory. In the battle for the hearts and minds of the Syrian population, the Damascus government had scored a major success. Although the western news media gave this aspect of the battle minimal coverage, for the Syrian government and the Russian military it was a vindication of their "reconciliation" strategy.

The majority of the population of Aleppo "voted with their feet" to back the Syrian government and not the rebels.

The collapse of opposition defences across the city started with a successful attack on the Hanano Housing Project. Subsequently, district after district in the north and centre of the city fell. Syrian commanders deliberately maintained the tempo of their advances to ensure opposition fighters were unable to re-build their defences. By exploiting their success, the Syrians kept the opposition on the back foot.

A large quantity of still and video imagery emerged during the battle – from opposition and government sources, as well as foreign news organisations. Analysis of this suggested that far fewer combatants were engaged in the battle – on both sides – than was previously estimated. The bulk of the fighting on the government side seemed to have been undertaken by the Tiger Force and the Desert Hawk Brigade. Signature vehicles, soldiers and commanders from these units appeared repeatedly at key events and locations, indicating they were always present at the important engagements. This suggested a small assault force of possibly less than 1,000 troops made the important breakthroughs, while larger contingents of militia fighters from the National Defence Forces, Palestinians, Iraqi, Afghan and Lebanese Shia groups were tasked to hold ground behind the assault units.

Imagery of government assault operations showed only a handful and tanks and armoured personnel carriers supporting attacks on large neighbourhoods, adding to the impression that the Syrians had not employed massed armoured forces for the operation. Opposition fighters inside the enclave also seemed to be a present in less strength than the 8,000 fighters claimed by the UN, and they proved to be far less organised and combat effective than had been expected.

The scale of the Russian involvement in the operation was not apparent at the time. In January 2017, the then commander of Russian Group of Forces in Syria, Colonel-General Andrei Kartapolov, revealed that the Admiral Kuzentsov's jets flew 420 sorties during the ship's cruise in the Mediterranean.

"Over the two months of their participation in combat operations, naval aviation pilots carried out 420 sorties, including 117 in night time. Actually, all flights were performed in complex weather conditions. A total of 1,252 terrorist facilities have been destroyed," Kartapolov said. "The strikes were delivered [from 8th November] against infrastructure facilities, the amassments of militants and military hardware, fire emplacements and strongholds of illegal armed formations. The tasks assigned to the aircraft carrier naval task force have been accomplished."

While the kinetic aspects of the Russian campaign were given a great deal of prominence, the involvement of Moscow's troops in less-visible aspects should not be neglected. Syrian government troops advancing in Aleppo received direct video feeds into their headquarters from Russian Forpost unmanned aerial vehicles orbiting over the city. Imagery appeared showing a Syrian army front-line headquarters in Aleppo equipped with at least two live video feeds, as well as a theatre wide display showing the position of aircraft across Syria.

The set-up of the Syrian Army's Tiger Force's so-called "special operations room" suggested that the Russian had set up a real-time downlink of imagery from a Forpost operating over Aleppo. Symbology on one of the video screens had in the past been linked to the Forpost.

A Syrian officer was pictured talking on multiple radios while monitoring the drone imagery of Aleppo. The Tiger Force had been in the vanguard of the Syrian offensive inside Aleppo over the preceding two months. On 10th December, the Russian Ministry of Defence released a video package to the RT network showing thermal imagery from a Forpost UAV showing columns of refugees moving through Aleppo's streets.

By western standards the Tiger Force's special operations room appeared to be rather primitive. The quality of the Forpost UAV imagery video displays were nowhere near as sharp or clear as those used with western UAV systems and there appeared to be limited means to manipulate video feeds. Given that the Russians had come late to the distributed-video-feeds game, this was not really surprising.

The rapid advance by the Syrian army through Aleppo would suggest that the rudimentary distribution of UAV video imagery was enough to give the Tiger Force a combat advantage. In particular, it appeared to give Tiger Force commanders the confidence to advance small units of troops boldly into the opposition-held enclave with minimal flank support. Thanks to their Russian "eyes in the sky", the Syrian troops could be confident that there was little risk of being attacked from unexpected directions. It is not clear how the video imagery was downloaded but the basic Searcher 2, on which the Forpost is based, is equipped with direct and beyond line of sight data links to allow the distribution of imagery to a variety of receivers.

The presence of a theatre-wide computer display showing the position of aircraft across Syria and neighbouring countries was also a new development. US-led forces had created so-called "recognised air pictures", or RAPs, for more than 20 years and they had become an important tool for the real-time command and control of airpower. This suggests the Russians had established a Syria-wide means to distribute their version of a RAP to front-line land commanders. This again gave Syrian commanders confidence that their operations would not be interrupted by US, Turkish or Israeli aircraft.

The Russian role in dealing with the 100,000 refugees who escaped to government-controlled territory from the east Aleppo enclave was a very important part of their campaign plan. From the evidence of some of the few aid workers and journalists who witnessed this humanitarian operation, it played an import role in winning the hearts and minds of the civilian population.

British journalist Vanessa Beeley visited the Jibreen refugee shelter and said the people there received hot food on a 24/7 basis from the Russian field kitchen. "They had been told by the people who held sway in the enclave that they would be killed by the 'Shia militia', a lie that had made them afraid to leave" she said. "The people said Jibreen was heaven compared to life in East Aleppo. They could just not believe how well they were being treated - the Russians were hugely appreciated"

Geopolitical events proved crucial in giving the Syrian government the confidence to execute their attack. US-Russia diplomacy broke down in the summer, so Syria's protectors in Moscow realised they would no longer face intense diplomatic pressure from Washington if they backed an all-out assault on Aleppo.

Political instability caused by the UK's Brexit referendum and the start of election campaigns in Italy, France and Germany hampered the formulation of effective policies towards Syria in Europe, while Saudi Arabia, the United Arab Emirates, Qatar and other Gulf Arabs were distracted by their intervention in Yemen and could not spare money or military resources to help their allies on the rebel side. In this geopolitical vacuum, the Syrian government and its supporters in Iran, Beirut and Moscow correctly sensed this was the time to "change the facts on the ground" in Aleppo.

Chapter 14
Boots on the Ground

Turkish ship watchers in Istanbul looking out at the Bosphorus on a December day saw the huge outline of the yellow-painted Russian Government chartered, roll-on roll-off transport Alexandr Tkachenko. They immediately spotted that something was different about today's Syria Express. The Aleksander Tkachenko's open top deck was full of more than a dozen green-painted Russian army vehicles, troop-carrying trucks, fuel tankers and command vehicles. These were not surplus cast-off Russian army vehicles destined for the Syrian military. This was a clear sign that Moscow was beefing up its presence in Syria. Days later, the Aleksander Tkachenko was spotted heading north through the Bosphorus. Then four days into 2017, she was seen again heading south with more Russian army vehicles on her top deck. Moscow's troop build-up was gathering momentum.

Later in January images started to be posted online by pro-Syria army bloggers showing surplus Russian army T-62 tanks and BMP infantry fighting vehicles on the dockside at the port of Tartus. Happy-looking Syrian soldiers could be seen in the images inspecting their new hardware, which would soon be spotted in action on the country's battlefields.

These deliveries of new military hardware to Syria were a signal that Moscow was determined to press ahead expanding its operations in the Middle Eastern country to give the Damascus government the chance to achieve a decisive military victory during 2017. President Putin wanted to end the war in Syria on his terms, over the coming year.

Even as the last green buses were completing their shuttle across the front lines around Aleppo, Moscow began to reap the political and diplomatic rewards for the battlefield successes of the Syrian army. Russia's military campaign was now set to evolve to meet the new circumstances created by success in Aleppo.

Russian diplomacy and military operations were clearly synchronised in the last weeks of 2016 and into 2017 with the objective of marginalising and isolating the rebels in Idlib and in the south of Syria from outside support. The idea was to lock them into ceasefires that would open the way for Damascus to begin reconciliation negotiations with communities and armed factions who were open to switching their allegiance. Particular efforts were put into speeding up the signing of reconciliation agreements with besieged enclaves to free up government troops for offensive operations elsewhere in the country. As government troops built up their strength, the pressure on rebel fighters in enclaves to surrender and agree to be evacuated grew. With little sign of any Western, Turkish or Gulf Arab intervention against Damascus, the morale in the besieged rebel enclaves was at rock bottom, making them more likely to rapidly vote with their feet or face the fate of east Aleppo. The momentum of the war was with Damascus and the Russians were aiming to capitalise on this.

While these efforts were ongoing, the bulk of the Syrian troops and supporting Russian airpower would be switched to taking back the central and eastern provinces of Syria from Islamic State. The Syrian military did not have the strength to carry out simultaneous offensives against the strong rebel forces in Idlib and Islamic State, so the inevitable showdown against the Idlib rebels would be "parked", while the main effort was switched to driving Islamic State out of Syria.

This was an urgent priority, as US-backed Kurdish forces were now making rapid advances in Northern Syria against Islamic State: unless government troops started their own offensives against Jihadis then pro-American groups could end up in control of vast swathes of Syria – including most of its oil and gas reserves. As the groups were accompanied by US special forces advisors, Syrian troops would not get Russian support to engage them for fear of sparking a shooting war with Washington. These pressures led to what in effect became a race to mop up as much Islamic State territory as possible.

Efforts by the Kremlin to cultivate Turkey's President Erdogan now paid dividends, boosting the top-level diplomatic strand of Moscow's strategy of neutralising the rebels in Idlib. Ankara broke ranks with Washington and the Gulf states and agreed to join a Russian- and Iranian-sponsored peace initiative. The defeated and demoralised rebels in Idlib and their political supporters based in the Turkish capital, Istanbul, had little choice but to do as Erdogan wanted. He controlled the border region connecting Idlib to the outside world so the leaders of many of the rebels based there quickly agreed to attend the new peace talks in Astana in Kazakhstan. Rebel fighters operating around Damascus and in southern Syria had also suffered a recent string of defeats: they followed suit and signed up to attend the new peace conference.

In the dying days of the Obama administration, there was no willingness in Washington to launch any rival initiative. The US was reduced to sending its ambassador to Kazakhstan along to the talks as an observer. Russia now appeared to be in the driving seat of Syrian diplomacy. The exclusion of the US – along with its allies, the UK and France - from the Aleppo evacuation negotiations and then the Astana peace talks was a telling sign of the Western powers' lack of influence on events on the ground inside Syria.

Moscow wanted to project a less "kinetic" image to the world to match its diplomatic focus on the Astrana peace conference. The Russian carrier battleground was ordered to head for home to show that Moscow was now talking peace. New high profile Russian commander was appointed to lead Moscow's forces in Syria as it drew down its naval forces in the eastern Mediterranean.

Colonel-General Andrei Kartapolov's appointment emerged after he hosted the Chief of the General Staff of the Syrian Armed Forces, Ali Abdullah Ayyoub, on a visit to the Admiral Kuznetsov and the nuclear-powered cruiser Pyotr Velikiy on 6th January 2017, prior to the ships' departure for their home base near Murmansk. Kartapolov was appointed to command the Russia's Group of Forces in Syria in December 2016 just as the operation against Aleppo was concluding. He replaced Lieutenant General Alexander Zhuravlev, who had led the Russian military mission in Syria since the previous July. Kartapolov moved temporarily to Damascus from his job as commander of the Western Military District. He was closely involved in the Russian intervention in Syria since it started in the summer of 2015, when he was head of the Russian general staff's main operational directorate. During the early days of the operation he routinely conducted briefings for the international media in Moscow. Unlike most of his counterparts, Colonel-General Kartapolov was a confident media and diplomatic performer, adding to the impression that Moscow was now enhancing its role in Syria. The general and his senior staff were soon being photographed on visits to Syrian units across the country. As well as finding out what was going on and the capabilities of Syrian units, these top Russian officers made a point of handing out medals to Syrian officers and soldiers involved in the Aleppo victory. Boosting the morale of their hosts ahead of the coming battles remained a top priority for senior Russians officers.

The size of the Black Sea Fleet's contingent of warships in the eastern Mediterranean also appeared to have been drawn down, with open-source tracking of shipping movements through the Bosphorus indicating that only one Kashin-class destroyer and two minesweepers remained on station off Syria by the middle of January 2017. The Kalibr cruise missile-armed frigate, Admiral Grigorovich, which fired its weapons during the Aleppo campaign in November, passed through the Bosphorus northbound on 18th December. The drawing down of naval forces confirmed that Moscow saw the Syria conflict as entering a new phase.

During the final days of December 2016, the purpose of the Russian army vehicles being shipped through the Bosphorous became apparent. The Russian media began broadcasting reports of a battalion of Russian military police en route to enhance security in Aleppo after the rebel-held enclave in the north west Syrian city fell to government forces. This troop deployment followed the dispatch of Russian military de-mining personnel and an Emergencies Ministry mobile hospital to Aleppo in late November and early December to assist the Syrian government in dealing with the humanitarian consequences of heavy fighting in the

city.
According to the Russian Ministry of Defence statements the military police unit, which comprised only professional contract soldiers, was to provide force protection for the Russian de-mining and medical personnel, as well as the officers of the Russian Centre for Reconciliation in the Syrian Arab Republic, which co-ordinated humanitarian relief operations and broker ceasefire deals between the government, local communities and opposition armed groups. Video released by the state-owned RT news network on 23rd December showed hundreds of military policemen preparing to deploy at an unidentified base in Chechnya, and other members of the unit arriving on Ilyushin Il-76 transport aircraft at Hmeinyan airbase in Latakia province.3 The Russian Ministry of Defence, in statement a reported by RT, said "the [military police] division has marched from Hmeinyan airbase to the city of Aleppo to perform duties as part of the Russian Centre for Reconciliation in the Syrian Arab Republic."

The Russian Defence Minister, Sergey Shoygu, was reported as telling President Vladimir Putin that the deployment of the military police battalion was needed to "ensure order" in the city. The Russian Government-chartered roll-on roll-off transport Alexandr Tkachenko was identified moving through the Straits of Bosphorus on 15th December and 4th January, carrying up to two dozen assorted military vehicles painted in the Russian military colours on each occasion, further confirming the build-up of Moscow's ground forces in Syria. The ship was reported as docking at Tartus in Syria on 17th December by open source maritime traffic monitoring, just before the military police personnel arrived by air.

The deployment of the military police battalion to Aleppo took the Russian military presence in the Syrian city to several hundred troops, although Moscow was keen to stress the non-combat role of the soldiers. The exact strength of the newly deployed unit was not disclosed by Moscow but Russian battalions usually comprise between 400 and 600 soldiers. When combined with the 200 de-mining personnel, the several dozen medical staff and the reconciliation centre officers, it most likely took the Russian presence in Aleppo to between 700 and 900 soldiers. This build-up of personnel in Aleppo showed greater resources were being deployed by Moscow to help bolster the efforts of the Damascus government's to support the thousands of civilians who had switched their allegiance to the government during the fall of eastern Aleppo.

It was also reported during the evacuation of eastern Aleppo that Iranian and Shia militia fighters refused to follow the orders of senior Russian officers and attempted to block the movement of rebels from the city. The arrival of more Russian military police "muscle" available to Moscow's men on the ground in Syria would have aided them in any future disputes with their "allies". In a media interview published later in the 2017 a member of the MP battalion revealed that the unit was in fact a special forces or Spetsnaz unit and had been issued with their red MP berets and MP arm bands just days before they flew to Syria. The enhanced Russian ground presence in Syria would allow more reconciliation operations to be undertaken simultaneously, dramatically speeding up the momentum of process. By the summer, the Russians would have four MP battalions in Syria to monitor the four de-escalation zones set up around Idlib, East Ghouta, Dara'a and the Rastan pocket. A rump contingent of Russian Aerospace Force strike jets also remained in Syria to continue to support the Damascus government, as well as the enhance ground force.

While Moscow was building up its presence on the ground, it was becoming apparent to senior Russian officers that the Syrian army would need to be expanded significantly if it was to launch more widespread offensive operations. Only a handful of Syrian army brigades were capable of conducting high tempo combat operations against well prepared opponents. A major drive was launched in November 2016 to form, train and equip more brigades that would be fight alongside battle hardened units, such as the Tiger Force of Suheil al-Hassan.

So work began to establish a formation which became known as the 5th Corps. It is sometimes referred to as the 5th Legion or 5th Attack Corps. Unlike the four pre-civil war Syrian Arab Army corps, the 5th Corps is not assigned a particular geographic area of operations. Russian advisors set up a network of training bases from late 2016 to begin setting up the first 5th Corps brigades and artillery units. Russia dispatched quantities of T-62 tanks, BMP infantry fighting vehicles, M-30 122mm howitzers and Ural trucks during late 2016 and early 2017 to equip the units of the 5th Corps. These are all relatively simple to operate and low maintenance items of equipment, indicating that the Syrian army was not ready to absorb and operate more sophisticated hardware.

Russian army trainers had been putting several thousands of Syria recruits through a rigorous training regime during the latter half of 2016. A smaller Russian trained Syrian special forces-type unit, dubbed the ISIS Hunters, was also formed at this time but the unit probably only contained just under 200 troops. The importance of the 5th Corps training project can be gauged from the fact the then chief of staff of the Russian Group of Forces in Syria, Lieutenant General Valery Asapov, was switched jobs to head up the effort. Dozens of Russian generals and colonels, backed up by scores of junior officers who actually ran the training classes for the Syrian soldiers, were assigned to the 5th Corps training team.

The first 5th Corps units were committed to the counter-attack to retake Palmyra in the spring of 2017. During the subsequent months up to five

5th Corps combat brigades and several artillery units appeared on battlefields across Syria. The performance of the 5th Corps units at first was mixed including suffering heavy casualties to Islamic State attacks around Palmyra but by the autumn of 2017 at least one brigade was committed to a prominent role in the attack to lift to the siege of Dier Ez Zor later in 2017.

Chapter 15
The New Enemy

As Russian and Syrian commanders contemplated the coming campaign they must have realised they would soon be facing their most skilled and determined opponents – the Caliphate Army, as the military arm of the Islamic State styled itself. While the brutal beheading of captured westerners, enslavement of women and sponsorship of terrorist attacks in European cities is well known, the organisation and capabilities of Islamic State's military forces in Syria have received less scrutiny. As Syrian and Kurdish forces rolled up the last Islamic State enclaves in during 2017 it became possible to piece together the inside story of its military arm.

The Caliphate Army's structure grew out of its origins in former Sunni insurgent groups that fought the American occupation in Iraq after the 2003 invasion. These groups contained a mix of Jihadi religious fanatics, former Saddam Hussain Ba'ath party loyalists and embittered Iraqi army officers. After US forces left Iraq in 2011. The Jihadis started to mobilise fighters on the border of Syria and mounted attacks against Iraqi government troops and cities. The outbreak of the Syrian civil war in 2011 gave them the chance to expand into the eastern regions of the country in a bid to establish their Caliphate. The Iraqi senior members of the organisation at this time grew to be the core leadership of the Caliphate Army.

Many observers were surprised at the dramatic increase in the size and capability of the Caliphate army from a few hundred men in 2011 to some 30,000 fighters at the peak of its powers in 2014. In Syria this was mainly due to its ability to co-opt or build alliances with groups of anti-Assad rebels and tribal fighters. Throughout 2013 and 2014, it progressively expanded across eastern and northern Syria by attracting or bullying other groups of fighters to join its cause. In the process it acquired all their weapons and military vehicles. After reaching a critical mass in early 2014 it was able launch a series of large-scale offensives that seized Mosul in Iraq, Raqqa in Syria and a swath of territory in eastern, central and north western Syria up to the eastern gates of Aleppo. This became the self-declared Caliphate in June 2014.

To defend the Caliphate, its military arm took on many of the trappings of a conventional army. It eventually contained several distinct type of units. The core leadership of the Caliphate Army operated from its capital city and this was home to its full-time or professional units. These were regularly featured in online Islamic State propaganda, which showed them spearheading attacks on Syrian army positions. These included a unit designated the Tank Battalion, which was equipped with several dozen T-55, T-62 and T-72 main battle tanks. There was an Artillery Battalion which controlled all its heavy artillery and multiple launch rocket systems. Assault operations were carried out by Platoons of Special Tasks who moved around Syria in columns of SUVs fitted with machine guns and anti-aircraft cannon or BMP armoured troop carriers. When foreign fighters started to arrive in the Caliphate in large numbers in 2014 and through 2015, the fittest and most motivated of them were directed to join Platoons of Special Tasks. These platoons would be augmented by heavy armour and artillery for specific missions, depending on the terrain and opponents to be faced. A fleet of low loaders moved the tanks, tracked vehicles and artillery between battle fronts. These professional units were kept fighting by a complex logistic operation that harvested abandoned armoured vehicles, artillery and ammunition from across Iraq and Syria. Small industrial sites across Iraq and Syria were put to work, machining metal into mortar and artillery shells.

Scavenging teams followed behind assault platoons to seize enemy equipment and then move it on low loaders to a former industrial site south of Tabqa airbase in Raqqa province, known as The Workshop. There the captured hardware was overhauled and returned to service. Heavily damaged vehicles were cannibalised for spare parts to keep the Caliphate Army's vehicles in working order. Improvised armour and weapons fits were also installed on many vehicles by the Workshop's staff, who also applied a numerical marking system to make it possible to determine if vehicles had been through their hands. More than 400 vehicles were eventually modified by the Workshop before it was captured by Syrian troops in the summer of 2017. The Workshop also specialised in modifying drones with bomb racks so they could be used as improvised bombers to strike with precision behind enemy lines.

The most distinctive product of the Workshop was the vehicle-borne suicide bomb or improvised explosive device (IED). These were SUVs, trucks or tracked armoured vehicles that were stuffed full of high explosives and protected by thick armour plate. Some even had video screens so the drivers could watch live images being broadcast from drones. This allowed the driver to head at high speed towards his target and dodge heavy enemy fire en route. They usually carried enough explosives to devastate a huge area and leave anyone unfortunate enough to be near the detonation shell-shocked and unable to resist follow-on ground assaults. Unlike the suicide bombs employed in Western Europe or Iraqi cities, the Islamic State suicide vehicle bombs on the battlefields of Iraq and Syria were employed alongside assault platoons to create tactical advantage. This was Islamic State's signature and gave it a battle-winning edge. When properly co-ordinated, the suicide vehicle bombs could smash open a defensive position and allow follow-on assault troops to overrun the stunned and wounded defenders.

The vast majority of the Caliphate Army's units were territorial defence groups formed from former anti-Assad militia groups and local tribal fighters. They were tasked with defending a specific location, under the direction of a senior Islamic State commander, known as an Emir, who was responsible to the leadership in Raqqa. These local groups often had very few heavy weapons beyond the ubiquitous SUVs armed with heavy machine guns. The relationship between local Islamic State units and the military command in Raqqa was little understood, but there have been persistent reports that "carrot and stick" tactics were employed to ensure their loyalty. Weapons and ammunitions were provided to loyal units but if the leaderships' rule was threatened they were ruthless in dispatching their professional forces to ensure loyalty. When a tribe in Dier Ez Zor province was deemed to be disloyal, many of its leaders and their families were hunted down and brutally killed.

When the tide of war turned against Islamic State in Syria during early 2016, the disposition of the Caliphate changed to meet the new circumstances. Moving large convoys of vehicles and troops around Syria became progressively more dangerous in the face of US and Russian air attacks so Caliphate Army units began to be re-deployed to bases just behind key front-lines to act as rapid reaction units.

Front-line sectors were mobilised for intensive defensive battles. Villages and towns were turned into strong points, protected by huge minefields and hundreds of IEDs. The defenders in turn dug deep tunnel complexes so they could have sanctuary from air, artillery and rocket attack. Almost every Islamic State-defended location was positioned around a tunnel complex. When Syrian and Kurdish fighters overran these positions in the summer of 2017, they found these tunnels had been dug several hundred metres underground and often had been fitted with electric light powered by generators. They were usually provided with satellite telephone and internet connections. Some had workshops to repair small arms. In a couple of cases these tunnels also included unmanned aerial vehicle repair shops.

The size of the Caliphate Army is a matter of considerable debate. In 2015, the US military estimated it as being 30,000 strong but in early 2016 they claimed to have killed 26,000 Islamic State fighters during the previous 18 months. By late 2016, the US military were claiming the size of the Caliphate Army in Iraq and Syria was down to 20,000.

Given the size of the area that the Caliphate Army had to defend it seems highly likely that most of its front-line positions across Iraq and Syria could have been occupied by a force that had taken such heavy losses. Defensive positions were built around key villages, hilltop positions or distinctive geographical lines such as river banks. On the outskirts of these positions, small detachments of fighters manned observation posts and controlled command-operated mines or IEDs. Their job was to slow enemy advances and give warning so reaction forces could be mobilised to launch counter attacks or engage the enemy with artillery, tanks or guided weapons.

These tactics were modified according to the terrain. In the lush agricultural terrain of North West Syria around Aleppo, Islamic State defensive positions were based around strong points in villages which dominate the wide agricultural drainage ditches that criss-cross the region. In the desert regions of central and eastern Syria, Islamic State defensive positions were based around high peaks and ridges that dominated key roads. An outer crust of minefields was complimented by a series of small positions with a handful of fighters in them, watching for any enemy activity. These observers would call up artillery, tanks, guided-missile teams and drone bombers to engage enemy columns.

Positioned just behind the front-line were small reaction forces, based inside large industrial buildings or hidden from aerial surveillance in woods and equipped with a several dozen highly motivated fighters with armed SUVs or BMP troop carriers. Invariably these reaction forces had a number of suicide vehicle bombs, primed and ready to go. If the enemy captured a key piece of terrain then the suicide vehicle bomb would be released with an assault force following close behind. The impact of these rapid surprise counter attacks could be catastrophic and lead to routs, as shellshocked government troops fled for safety.

At a defence conference in Moscow in August 2017, Colonel General Igor Korobov, Head of the Russian General Staff's Main Department, detailed the impact of Islamic State "bee swarm" tactics, carrying out chaotic shelling assaults and surprise attacks on Syrian government units, which involved small but well-trained groups. "Terrorists are capable of quickly changing tactics, shifting from guerrilla assaults to frontal attacks and vice versa," said Korobov. "Their groups that are fighting government troops and militia units are quite small, so the militants rely heavily on surprise attacks aimed at intimidating and demoralizing their adversaries."

The use of suicide vehicle bombs reinforced Western media perceptions that Islamic State fighters all wanted to go down fighting in pursuit of martyrdom. This image was sharpened further by the behaviour of the Islamic State garrison trapped in Mosul, which certainly fought to almost the last man. However, experience in Syria suggests that the bulk of the Caliphate Army had no intention of holding positions to the last man, just for the sake of it. Time and again it would withdraw rather than have their units surrounded. Russian and Syrian commanders learnt a lot about fighting Islamic State during the battles around Kweires Airbase to the east of Aleppo in November 2015 and the advance on Palmyra in March 2016. The start of their campaign would not be launched on their terms. Islamic State struck first and re-captured Palmyra in December 2016 in a daring surprise attack.

Chapter 16
Back to Palmyra

While the Battle for Aleppo was reaching its denouement in December 2016, Syrian government forces suffered a significant setback when Islamic State fighters launched a surprise attack on the desert city of Palmyra.

Ever since the summer of 2016, the Syrian High Command and the Russian military had scaled back operations in the central desert to concentrate resources on the Aleppo campaign. After making some gains pushing eastwards in a bid to break the siege of Dier Ez Zor, the Syrian troops ran into heavy resistance from Islamic State fighters. Crucially, the Syrians appeared to lack the manpower and resources to capture the peaks and ridge lines that overlooked the main road that ran from Palmyra through Arak and Sukhnah, to Dier Ez Zor. Without control of the dominating high ground, any troops on the road below would be vulnerable to artillery fire and raids from Islamic State contingents on the mountains.

The Syrian force at Palmyra set up a security perimeter around the city and relied, on Russian attack helicopters, guided by a small team of Russian special forces forward air controllers, to patrol the desert to warn of Islamic State attacks. A small compound was set up by the Russians inside Palmyra city for the forward air controllers, with a communications team to work with the Syrian army headquarters in the city and a security unit of Naval Infantry to escort visiting VIPs to the ancient ruins. The base itself in turn was run by a group of private security contractors. There were less than 100 Russians in Palmyra in late 2016.

The Syrian army garrison in the Palmyra region was probably a little over 2,000 troops. Most of them were sent out into the desert and on to ridges to man a series of check points. A small rapid-reaction force with tanks and armoured vehicles was based inside Palmyra airbase, ready to respond to major threats to the city.

During the summer and into the autumn of 2016, Islamic State combat groups started to probe the Syrian defences with increasing determination. Russian Mil Mi-28 and Kamov Ka-52 attack helicopters, forward-deployed at Shayrat airbase to the east of Homs city, were usually able to see off the Islamic State raids on the outer line of check points. Occasionally, the Russians called in fast jets or the bigger Tupolev Tu-22M3 heavy bombers to deal with large concentrations of Jihadi fighters.

During November and December, Islamic State forces in Mosul, in Iraq, and Raqqa, in northern Syria, came under intense pressure. Iraqi troops pushed into the heart of Mosul, forcing leaders of the group to begin relocating to Syria to re-establish military headquarters, weapons factories, supply lines, training and recruitment centres. At the same time, Kurdish-led fighters of the Syrian Democratic Front pushed towards Raqqa from the north, with US air support.

Senior Islamic State leaders wanted possibly to gain more strategic space in Syria to compensate for lost territory in Iraq. A new offensive in Syria also held out the possibility of capturing more Syria army arms depots to replenish lost stockpiles of tanks, artillery, rockets and small-arms ammunition. The target of the new Islamic State offensive would be Palmyra and the Syrian T-4 airbase at Tiyas, both in eastern Homs province, and the city of Dier Ez Zor, where a 4,000-strong Syrian garrison was holding out some 150 kilometres behind Islamic State lines to protect the city's 100,000 civilian population.

Syrian-based media reported, after Palmyra fell, that 4,000 Islamic State fighters had been involved in the attack that took the city. The reports had a feel of self-justification, to try to make excuses for the loss of such an important prize. How the city fell is more straightforward.

The bad weather hampered Russian and Syrian air reconnaissance over the central desert region, allowing Islamic State combat groups to mass close to Syrian front-lines to the east, north and west of Palmyra. The majority of Russia's Forpost surveillance drones were also heavily committed to the Aleppo battle so there was little spare capacity for them to patrol around Palmyra.

The first Islamic State attacks involved huge vehicle borne suicide bombers striking at the large Syrian checkpoint at the grain silos on the main road towards Arak. Assault troops followed behind the suicide bombers, sending the surviving defenders fleeing into the centre of city. This was a classic Jihadi tactic, which was designed to break open Syrian defences and paralyse any effective counter-attacks. Other attacks were launched along the strategic ridge line to north of Palmyra, and westwards towards T-4 airbase.

With an Islamic State column advancing along the main road into Palmyra city, the small Syrian garrison and its Russian advisors decided that they could not form an effective defence line before the Jihadis got inside the city. The 200 or so defenders jumped in any vehicles they could find and fled westward to T-4 airbase. The Syrians left around a dozen tanks and other armoured vehicles in perfect working order in their base at the airport, as well as a large stockpile of ammunition. Islamic State filmed propaganda videos inside the abandoned Russian base – it looked like the Russians had left hot meals on their mess hall tables. Syrian troops across the region soon joined the retreat to the safety of T-4 airbase.

Syrian President Bashar al-Assad blamed American support of rebel groups in Syria for the loss of Palmyra but the commander of the US-led Combined Joint Task Force-Operation Inherent Resolve, US Army

Lieutenant General Stephen Townsend, said the Syrian military had spread itself too thin to mass forces for the Aleppo operation. "Because ISIS has not been able to retake ground in Iraq or succeed in any attacks on US, coalition, or Iraqi forces, they saw this weak spot and had a little bit of a victory", he said.

The huge T-4 airbase was the Syrian army's defensive bastion in the centre of the country. As well as being home to more than a dozen Su-22 bombers, Aero L-39 light strike jets and Mi-24 attack helicopters, the base was protected by a ground-defence battalion with its own tanks, howitzers and ZSU-23-4 anti-aircraft guns. These latter weapons could be turned against ground targets in the open desert to deadly effect. Around the base was a huge ring of sand berms or ramparts and pre-dug firing bunkers for tanks and artillery pieces.

Columns of Islamic State armed pick-up trucks, backed by T-72 tanks and 130mm artillery pieces, pursued the retreating Syrians across the desert towards T-4. It seemed as if there was little to stop the Jihadi advance.

The airbase defence force was mobilised to man the sand ramparts around the base and wait for reinforcements from Damascus to save the day. The first wave of Jihadi attacks were repulsed between 13th and 15th December but the Islamic State onslaught was not over. Jihadi mobile columns pushed down from the mountains to the north of the airbase to threaten the road to Homs city. While to the east of T-4, more columns swept in from the desert and then hooked back up to surround the Syrian airbase to strike at the Homs road from the south. A contingent of the 800th Republican Guard Regiment then arrived from Aleppo to bolster the defences of T-4, joining the air force troops holding the line around the airbase.

A series of dramatic videos appeared online at this time. Islamic State pick up trucks pushed almost up to the berm line and the outline of the airbase's hangers can be clearly seen on the horizon. On the government side, pictures emerged showing tanks and anti-tank guided-missile teams firing from the berms at the attackers. It looked as if the fate of the airbase rested in the timely arrival of the reinforcements to allow the Syrians to hold the line. A new Russian special forces team arrived to bolster the forward air controllers who had escaped from Palmyra to co-ordinate close air support. This was a wild battle with both sides desperate to win. The Jihadis made repeated attempts to storm the airbase, using night time and bad weather to cover their advances.

By the turn of the year, the Islamic State offensive had run out of steam and the Syrian High Command began planning a major offensive to drive back the Jihadis and re-take Palmyra. The task of leading the counter-offensive would fall to newly formed Syrian units, which had benefited from training by Russian advisors and deliveries of new T-62M tanks,

BMP troops carriers, M-30 152mm howitzers and trucks from Russian army stocks. At the heart of this build up was a formation dubbed the 5th Corps. For the Palmyra operation its 1st Brigade and an artillery battalion was sent to T-4 airbase with an estimated 1,000 troops. A smaller Russian-trained Syrian special forces-type unit, dubbed the ISIS Hunters, was also dispatched to T-4.

To complete the attack force, the Russians dispatched some of their own artillery to T-4 including a battery of 2A65 MSTA-B 152mm field guns and the TOS-1A thermobaric-explosive-tipped multiple rocket launchers. A group of senior Russian officers also arrived at T-4 to help co-ordinate the upcoming operation.

Even before the Syrian counter-offensive began, Islamic State opened a new offensive against the Syrian garrison at Dier Ez Zor. The Syrian outpost controlled a series of key road junctions and bridges that hindered Islamic State communications between its capital in Raqqa and its territory in Iraq. Hard-pressed Islamic State commanders also saw the Syrian garrison as a potential source of arms and ammunition to replace material lost in the increasingly desperate fighting around Mosul in Iraq. Islamic State gunners first fired anti-tank guided-missiles to knock out the last two L-39 fighters at Dier Ez Zor airbase to deprive the Syrian garrison of its immediate close air support. A surprise ground offensive followed that cut the road between the airbase and the main Syrian garrison in the city. Heavy fighting then raged as both sides duelled for control of this road. The Syrian hold on the and the city both looked precarious. As well as being home to more than 100,000 civilians and 4,000 Syrian troops and militiamen who would be a risk of being massacred if Islamic State overran the city, Dier Ez Zor was a crucial government bastion in eastern Syria. It was a potential jumping-off point for government troops to launch a major operation to re-establish Syrian sovereignty in swathes of eastern Syria held by Islamic State.

In a sign of the seriousness of the situation, the Russian Aerospace Force mobilised its heavy bombers to strike back and relieve the pressure on the Syrian garrison. The first raid, by six Tu-22M3s, took place on 21st January, with each bomber unloading a stick of between 12 and 24 FAB-250-270 unguided "iron" bombs. Further raids were revealed by the Moscow Ministry of Defence on 23rd, 24th and 30th January, each involving six Tu-22M3s flying from Mozdok airbase in southern Russia. The strikes involved surveillance support from Russian Forpost drones, according to analysis of video imagery of the strikes released by the Russian state-owned news network, RT. One sequence of video released on 30th January showed a strike on a former army barracks and storage complex to the north of the Dier Ez Zor. The participation of Forpost UAVs in these operations suggested that the Russians had moved a launch-and-recover element, as well as ground control stations, into central Syria to control the drones, or were operating at long-range beyond-line-of-sight data link from the main Russian airbase in Latakia province.

Another sequence of video shows three Tu-22M3 strikes on industrial sites to the east of Dier Ez Zor, which the Russians claimed were being used as "ammunition and explosives plants and warehouses". This video featured different Symbology, similar to that used in the cockpit displays of Su-30M or Su-35S fighters suggesting it was recorded by one of the Russian escort fighters.

Russian and Syrian air commanders had also embarked on innovative measures to bring reinforcements and supplies into the besieged city. Syria-based media reported that an airbridge had been set up to Dier Ez Zor city via Qamishli airport, in the far north-east of Syria. The Al Masdar News agency, which had close links to the Syrian military, reported that Syrian and Russian Ilyushin Il-76s first flew the reinforcement and supplies to Qamishli, where they were cross-loaded onto Mil Mi-17 helicopters for the flight into the enclave. It published a photograph on 22nd January showing scores of Syrian paratroopers from 104th Airborne Brigade crammed in the hold of an Il-76 heading to Qamishli.

The increasing importance of Qamishli airport to the air bridge into Dier Ez Zor was a recognition that helicopter flights over Islamic State-controlled central Syria were dangerous and difficult operations. Central Syria's high mountains degraded helicopter performance significantly. From Qamishli, Syrian helicopter pilots could easily fly down the Nahr Jaghjagh and Nahr Khabar valleys into the besieged enclave.

On 17th February, Russian air force also continued to strike at Islamic State elsewhere in Syria, with Tupolev Tu-95 long range bombers launching Raduga Design Bureau's Kh-101 cruise missiles at a target near the Syrian city of Raqqa, which the Islamic State group claimed as the capital of its caliphate. The strike was announced by the Russian Ministry of Defence on 17th February and it released video clips of the raid, showing one of the conventionally armed Kh-101 stealth cruise missile being released from a Tu-95 bomber and then a building exploding. The TASS news agency said, "the targets included militant camps and training centres as well as a command centre of one of the major Islamic State units."

Analysis of the Russian Ministry of Defence video imagery, showed that one of the targets attacked was a large three-or-four storey building in the town of Al Aassadiah, five kilometres north of Raqqa city. According to local media reports, this town was only five kilometres to the west of a prison and industrial complexes captured by Kurdish-led militia forces of the Syrian Democratic Front (SDF) the day after the missile strike. Although the Russian video showed the target building exploding and a large part of its outer wall collapsing, the wider impact of the strike could not be discerned. The advocacy group, "Raqqa Is Being Slaughtered Silently", reported on 17th February that a Russian air strike in the "Tishreen Farm North Raqqa" area killed 14 civilians, although it is not clear if they were referring to the same attack. This attack was the sixth strike by Russian Long Range Aviation on targets in eastern Syria in a month.

It is unclear how many aircraft or missiles were employed in this Raqqa raid, with the video released by the Russian Ministry of Defence only showing one missile being launched and one target being hit. The TASS news agency suggested more than one aircraft was involved when it said "bombers" had participated in the strike. The missiles appeared to have been launched from over eastern Syria rather than the Mediterranean because of the presence in the video of a Sukhoi Su-30 or Su-35 aircraft. The terrain below the bombers also appeared to be a flat desert region, consistent with eastern Syria.

While the additional air support appeared to stabilise the situation around Dier Ez Zor, Russian and Syrian commanders were still determined to launch a wide-ranging ground offensive to clear Islamic State from the central desert region. This was to re-take Palmyra and then open a ground route to Dier Ez Zor. The region was also home to most Syria's oil and gas reserves which were seen as the key to rebuilding the country after the war and ensuring the survival of the Damascus government in the long term.

Syrian troops backed by Russian attack helicopters, began their offensive at the end of January with the initial aim of driving back the Islamic fighters from the berms around T-4 airbase. At least four Syrian armoured columns moved out into the desert on different axes to clear as much ground as possible. Lieutenant General Sergey Rudskoy, chief of the Russian General Staff's main operations directorate, was reported by the TASS news agency as telling a news briefing in Moscow on 7th February that Syrian troops had advanced 25 kilometres from T-4 airbase with the help of Russian air support. Still and video imagery of Syrian operations in the central desert region, published by news and social media, confirmed the participation of Russian Aerospace Force Mil Mi-28 and Kamov Ka-52 attack helicopters as well as Syrian Mi-35s and fixed wing jets.

"On the way to Palmyra, the Russian air group-supported Syrian army has considerably expanded the area under its control near [T-4]," Rudskoy said. "A total of 783 square kilometres has been retaken from the terrorists. The Syrian army has moved 25 kilometres eastwards to taken the El-Beida [desert]."The commanding heights along the road have been put under control. A greater part of the way towards Palmyra has been covered."

To the south of T-4 airbase, imagery showed Syrian columns clearing the Tiyas crossroads and then pushing south towards al-Hayr al-Gharbi castle, which was claimed captured on 1st February. Another Syrian column captured Bir Abu Jarbou village on the same day, in a drive to secure a key ridge that dominated the approach to Palmyra from the south west.

Footage filmed by a Syrian news crew showed Mi-28s attacking an Islamic State position in the al Beida district some 25 kilometres west of Palmyra on 6th February. Other film from this location showed Syrian troops approaching the Hayyan gas and oil field to the north east of T-4. Although the US Department of Defence twice denied in February 2017 that there was any co-operation with Russian and Syrian military operations against Islamic State, the US-led coalition appeared to be intervening against the Jihadi defenders of Palmyra. According the coalition's strike reports, an Islamic State tank was attacked in the town on 4th February and, two days later, nine coalition strikes "destroyed 17 heavy equipment vehicles, 11 vehicles, four dump trucks, three front-end loaders, three [trucks converted into suicide bombs] and two tanks near Palmyra."

It appeared that the Damascus government had committed between two and three thousand troops backed by significant numbers of tanks, armoured vehicles, artillery and rocket launchers, to its Palmyra operation. These forces appeared to have been grouped into independent combined arms columns of around 400 to 500 troops, mixing tanks, BMP and BTR-82A troop carriers, artillery, BM-21 rocket launchers and cannon-armed trucks to allow them to move rapidly across the region's open desert terrain.

The central desert region was an area where the Syrian army's tanks and artillery, as well as support from Russian attack helicopters, gave it obvious tactical advantages. Islamic State tanks and other vehicles were very vulnerable to Syrian tanks and anti-tank guided weapons. Dug-in Islamic State infantry, however, appeared to have been more of a problem for the Syrian government troops, who had to use heavy artillery and rocket barrages to clear them.

A reported surprise counter-attack against the Syrian troops at the Hayyan Petroleum Company site on 7th February showed the Jihadi groups continued to posse a dangerous threat. Islamic State's use of vehicle-born suicide bombers also continued to be an effective way to breach Syrian fixed defensive positions.

Russia suffered its biggest loss in a single improvised explosive device attack since the start of its intervention in Syria on 20th February when four of its soldiers were killed. The personnel, described as "military advisors", were lost when a Syrian army convoy they were accompanying was struck on the road between Homs city and T-4.

The vehicle was blown up as a vehicle column of the Syrian troops was moving from the T-4 military airbase towards Homs, the Russian Ministry of Defence was reported as saying on 20th February by the state-owned TASS news agency.

"On February 16, 2017, four Russian servicemen were killed in the Syrian Arab Republic as their vehicle hit a remote-controlled bomb," said the ministry. "The Syrian troops' vehicle column, that included a vehicle with Russian military advisers, was moving from the area of the Tiyas aerodrome towards the city of Homs." Another two Russian military advisers were wounded in the blast, the ministry added.

In March, the defence ministry confirmed that a Russian Ground Forces major general had been severely injured in an improvised explosive device (IED) attack neat T-4 the previous month, losing both his legs and an eye. The officer, Major General Peter Milyuhin, was one of two survivors of the attack. He was the head of the combat-training staff of the Western Military District and was reported to be working on the staff of the Commander of Russian Group of Forces in Syria, Colonel-General Andrei Kartapolov. After being initially treated at a Russian military hospital in Syria, he was evacuated back to Russia.

Up to this incident, the Russian Ministry of Defence had confirmed deaths of 25 regular military personnel in Syria since the start of Moscow's intervention in September 2015, with the majority being lost in aircraft shoot-downs and indirect-fire attacks on bases. The deaths in Syria of more than dozen Russian private military contractors or personnel linked to special forces and intelligence agencies were also reported by the Russian media or non-governmental organisations but not confirmed by the Russian Ministry of Defence. The 16th February incident was the largest loss of Russian life in a single IED incident since the start of the Russian intervention, although a handful of Russians had been killed individually in landmine or IED incidents.

During the final two weeks of February, Syrian and Russian forces inched closer to Palmyra. Syria's state news agency, SANA, announced the capture of the UNESCO World Heritage city, home to many ancient archaeological sites that had been deliberately destroyed and damaged during Islamic State's rule, on 2nd March. Video broadcast by the Russian state-owned news network RT on 2nd March showed Syrian troops positioned in the 13th Century Fakhr-al-Din al-Ma'ani Castle, situated on top of a ridge that overlooks the modern settlement of Tadmur and the city's archaeological district.

A column of Syrian troops with around a dozen tanks, BMP troop carriers and other vehicles was filmed by RT entering the city from the south, while three large smoke plumes could be seen rising from Palmyra's airport where fighting was reportedly still taking place. Syrian troops told RT's reporter that improvised explosive devices had been left in the castle and other parts of the city. SANA reported that the Islamic State fighters had fled the city late on 2nd March.

Video imagery released by the Syrian military over the previous seven days showed the widespread use of Russian Mil Mi-28 and Kamov Ka-52 attack helicopters to support the advance. A Syrian air force Aerospatiale Gazelle observation helicopter was also filmed flying in the forward combat zone.

The Syrian advance had been supported by extensive artillery and rocket systems. At least one battery of seven M-30 122mm howitzers and four BM-21 multiple launch rocket systems were seen at a fire position close to the Palmyra Triangle on 1st March. Two days earlier a TOS-1A thermobaric rocket launcher was filmed driving towards the front-line at the Palmyra Triangle area, just outside the city. Russian soldiers were filmed operating the TOS-1As in Syria over the preceding year but it could not be determined who was operating the system seen near Palmyra.

Syrian media reported that the main units participating in the battle included the newly formed 5th Corps, elements of the 18th Tank Division, as well as National Defence Force militia units including the Military Shield Forces, al-Badia regiment and Shaitat tribesmen. Russian special forces and forward air controllers were operating in support of the Syrian army as well.

Islamic State fighters attempted to stage a conventional defence of Palmyra, including trying to hold the Hayyan ridge, by deploying T-72 tanks, improvised rocket launchers and 120mm mortars. A video released by the Islamic State-linked Amaq news agency 28th February showed Jihadi tanks and mortar crews engaging Syrian positions on the main road from Homs on the western approaches to Palmyra.

Aircraft of the US-led coalition also appeared to have assisted the Syrian advance by staging more than 20 air strikes on Islamic State forces around Palmyra after 20th February, including targeting six tanks and more than 30 vehicles. Spokesmen for the US-led coalition over the previous month continued to deny that any co-operation was taking place with the Russian Aerospace Force over Syria, only confirming the "deconfliction" of aircraft movements was taking place.

The Syrian assault on Palmyra reversed almost all the gains made by Islamic State since they took the city in a surprise attack in December 2016. Palmyra's fall came seven days after the loss of al Bab, in northwest Syria, to Turkish-led forces, a rapid Kurdish-led militia advance to the north east of Raqqa, and sustained Iraqi progress to clear the western half of Mosul. The outer ramparts of the Islamic State caliphate in Syria and Iraq were being squeezed hard by a combination of Turkish, Iraqi, Syrian and Kurdish ground forces, backed by US-coalition, Russian, Syrian and Turkish air power.

The resistance offered by Islamic State forces appeared to be reducing in intensity, with Jihadi troops increasingly often retreating when faced by overwhelming force. The Jihadis had also staged fewer counter-attacks against exposed flanks of Syrian, Kurdish or Iraqi ground forces. It seemed the end game for the Islamic State's caliphate was unfolding. In the aftermath of the successful assault on Palmyra, Russia's defence ministry announced the death of another of its soldiers during the fighting. Twenty four year-old Artyum Gorbynov was killed as he was protecting a group of Russian military advisors outside Palmyra on 2nd March.

Russian special forces played a prominent role in the operation to capture Palmyra between the 1st and 3rd of March. A news report broadcast by journalists embedded with the small special forces team showed the Russian soldiers engaging an Islamic State vehicle-borne suicide bomber with a 9K113 Konkurs anti-tank guided missile. The team, who operated from a GAZ Tigr armoured utility vehicle, also were shown directing air strikes by Mil Mi-28 attack helicopters on the edge of Palmyra airbase.

"Contract soldier Artyum Gorbynov was conducting a mission in the Syrian Arab Republic to protect a group of Russian military advisors. Gorbynov died on 2nd March in the area of Palmyra, rebuffing an attempt by a group of Islamic State militants to attack positions of Syrian troops, where Russian military advisers were at that moment," said the defence ministry.

Beyond his status as a professional or contract soldier, the ministry released no details of Gorbynov's military service or unit. Media reports claimed he was a private assigned to the 96th Separate Intelligence or Reconnaissance Brigade.

The recapture of Palmyra was a major test of the 5th Corps of the Syrian army. Thanks to Russian advisors and equipment, the 5th Corps units committed to the Palmyra attack performed well, although they did suffer several casualties due to inexperience on a number of occasions. The role of Russian special forces advisors and forward air controllers proved pivotal during the final phases of the battle for Palmyra, suggesting Moscow's men were "the glue" that held together the disparate Syrian units across the central desert front.

Interestingly, Islamic State fighters across the desert front opted to retreat rather than fight to the death when they were cornered. The Jihadi columns around Palmyra put up heavy resistance and tried to fight a conventional defence with tanks, artillery and other heavy weapons. This was a one-sided fight when faced with Russian and coalition air power. The outcome of the third Battle for Palmyra suggested that Islamic State's days controlling central Syria were numbered.

Chapter 17
Race to Raqqa

On 24th February, the head of US Central Command flew into the heart of Syria on board a US Air Force Special Operations Command (AFSOC) Bell-Boeing CV-22 Osprey tilt-rotor aircraft. The American general and his command team strode out of the Osprey on a dirt runway some 60 miles north of Raqqa, the capital of the Islamic State's so-called Caliphate. He was soon huddled in a meeting with senior Kurdish commanders of the YPG militia groups to plan the next phase of the war. Later during his visit, which was filmed by a US news network, General Joe Votel went to inspect militia recruits undergoing training. The militia fighters said they expected in a matter of days to be on the front lines which were now less than 10 miles from the northern outskirts of Raqqa. The American news team reported that in a few days US military cargo aircraft were expected to begin landing at the airstrip to deliver new supplies of arms and ammunition to the Kurdish fighters and their allies in the Syrian Democratic Front (SDF).

General Votel's mission into Syria was a graphic illustration that the war against the Islamic State was entering a new phase as Kurdish-led militia fighters, backed by US special forces advisors on the ground and US-led coalition air strikes, were closing in for the final assault on Raqqa. This phase of the conflict against Islamic State was fraught with military, political and diplomatic complexity. Only five days after General Votel's visit to the Kurdish base, Turkish strike jets and artillery had begun hitting YPG positions at Manbij, some 30 miles away from the site of the Kurdish headquarters.

As General Votel was meeting his Kurdish allies, further to the east columns of SDF militia fighters were making rapid advances towards the Euphrates valley. In a week-long offensive, dubbed Operation Euphrates Wrath, fast moving militia columns stormed more than 60 villages and retook more than 1,762 km2 of territory. Advancing with the militia fighters were small teams of US and coalition special forces who were acting as joint terminal attack co-ordinating (JTACs) or forward air controllers (FACs). Whenever the militia ran into resistance from Islamic State fighters, the coalition JTACs would get on their satellite radios and summon up a coalition strike jet. Crucially, the JTACs had locator beacons so their positions showed up on huge computerised map displays at the US Combined Air Operations Centre (CAOC) at al Udeid airbase in the Gulf state of Qatar. This meant the pilots of any inbound strike jets could be warned of the location of friendly forces. Armed with this critical safety information, the pilots and JTACs were then able to co-ordinate how to put precision-guided ordnance on target.

On the ground, the militia forces which lacked heavy artillery or tanks would pull up their SUVs to watch the air strikes go in. As bomb after bomb pulverised their enemies with pinpoint precision, the militia fighters would cheer. Then they would pile back into their vehicles and take up the advance again. These tactics worked superbly against the demoralised and disorganised Islamic State fighters sent to hold the 100-mile long desert front to the east of Raqqa. By the end of February, the SDF alliance was less than five kilometre from the Euphrates river and was poised to cut the last road route from Raqqa to Islamic State held territory in Iraq.

Over the past two years the US had gradually increased its contingent of special forces advisors on the ground in Syria helping anti-Islamic State militia groups across the north of the country. By early 2017, some 500 US personnel were in the country. The majority were what were termed Tier 2 units of advisory teams and JTACs from the US Army's Special Forces or Green Berets and the US Navy SEALs. They were backed up by medical, psychological warfare, engineering experts and command teams. One of these experts, a US Navy bomb disposal operative, was killed in a road-side bomb blast in November 2016. Contrary to many reports, the famous Delta Force of the Joint Special Operations Command or JSOC was not on the ground in Syria. They were held at a secret base in Iraq ready to launch raids when high value Islamic State targets, such as senior leaders or drone experts, were identified by intelligence.

To sustain the US advisors in Syria, AFSOC dispatched many of its assets to the region. This was a classic AFSOC mission – getting US personnel into remote and sensitive locations without being noticed or intercepted. The Turkish attitude to the Kurdish YPG militia was a major complicating factor for American commanders. Ankara considered the YPG to be an extension of the PKK groups which operated inside Turkey and was considered a terrorist group by the Turks. So any logistic support for US special forces operating with the YPG in northern Syria had to be run out of Iraq. There were only two precarious road routes into Syria from Iraq, across war-damaged bridges and skirting front line zones. This meant that AFSOC's CV-22s were the best way to quickly get people and equipment into northern Syria. AFSOC's CV-22s, as well as US Army Boeing MH-47G Chinooks of the 160th Special Operations Aviation Regiment (SOAR), were reportedly based at Irbil International Airport, in Iraq's Kurdish region, to provide air transport into northern Syria.

During the start of the US mission in northern Syria, the CV-22s and MH-47Gs mostly flew at night to avoid Islamic State man-portable surface-to-air missile threats. But as the SDF expanded the territory it controlled, the AFSOC and 160th SOAR aviators started to fly during daytime. As a result photographs and videos of the American helicopters started to be posted online by local people.

A network of small airstrips had been opened across northern Syria by YPG and SDF engineers working under the direction of AFSOC air field operation experts and there were reports of fixed-wing transports flying into Syria but no pictures emerged of these aircraft in the early days of the intervention. The most likely suspects for these missions were AFSOC Lockheed Martin MC-130 Combat Talon transports, Dornier C-146A Wolfhound utility aircraft or the U-28 variant of the Pilatus PC-12. A contingent of AH-130U Spooky gunship aircraft were also in the Middle East and were on call to provide close air support for US special forces and their allies. The AFSOC psychological warfare Lockheed Martin EC-130J Commando Solo were also deployed to the Middle East, broadcasting propaganda to undermine Islamic State morale.

The Turkish-Kurdish political rift created a very peculiar situation because the US special forces troops were also advising a rival rebel group called the Free Syrian Army (FSA), who were operating in northern Syria under the banner of the Turkish-led Operation Euphrates Shield. The Turkish Army and FSA entered North West Syria in August 2016 after a spate of Islamic State-linked terrorist attacks in Turkey but suffered heavy casualties at the hands of Islamic State fighters. US advisors and JTACs accompanied the Euphrates Shield forces into Syria to co-ordinate air support in a very confused tactical situation.

Turkey, however, had allowed the US Air Force to open a combat search-and-rescue (CSAR) site at Diyabikir airbase to support the ongoing coalition air strikes into Syria. This site housed a detachment of Sikorsky HH-60G Pave Hawks and Lockheed Martin HC-130J Combat Shadow air-to-air refuelling tankers, as well as a field hospital. These helicopters and aircraft were reported to be part of the 1st Expeditionary Rescue Wing that had been set up to co-ordinate coalition CSAR operations and forces across Iraq and Syria. As well as being ready to recover downed airmen, the CSAR forces at Diyabikir were well placed to bring out to safety any wounded or injured special forces operatives in Syria that needed urgent evacuation.

When the Russian Aerospace Force began its air operations inside Syria in September 2015 the Russian and Americans set up a hotline to deconflict their aircraft. At first this was little more than the US and Russia exchanging the satellite telephone numbers of the US-led CAOC in Qatar and the Russian air operations centre at Hmeinyan airbase in Latakia. This had since evolved to the use of video conferencing. Each day Russian and American officers exchanged details on where their aircraft would be operating so blocks of air space could be cleared of each other's aircraft. There had been a handful of near-miss incidents involving US and Russian aircraft since 2015 but it appears that they were genuine accidents rather than deliberate provocations.

The looming battle for Raqqa resulted in Syrian, Turkish, Kurdish and other rebel groups conducting ground operations in close proximity to each other creating a new order of complexity for air commanders and aircrew. Political differences meant it was difficult for these forces to co-operate or even communicate with each other. The accidental bombing of Syrian soldiers near the besieged enclave of Dier Ez Zor by a large package of US, UK, Danish and Australian jets in September 2016 caused a major diplomatic incident and showed what could happen if ground forces in sensitive regions were accidentally bombed.

In North West Syria, around the towns of al Bab and Dier Hafir increasingly confused fighting was taking place to drive out Islamic State fighters from the region. The issue of ground forces de-confliction was highlighted by an incident on 1st March, which saw Russian and Syrian aircraft bombing FSA fighters inside Syria in a series of strikes that came within three miles of a US advisory team. US Army Lieutenant General Stephen Townsend, overall commander of US-led Combined Joint Task Force-Operation Inherent Resolve, said during a news briefing that the US forces were "advising at command echelons a little bit farther back" and observed the air strikes. When it became apparent that the strikes were hitting FSA positions, the US officers made "some quick calls" to Russia through the established communication channels and Russia stopped the bombing. Islamic State forces had previously held the villages before FSA forces moved in. "And so we worked out an arrangement, a de-confliction," Townsend said. "This is something that goes on daily in the air. Not every day on the ground, but daily in the air there's a de-confliction arrangement with the Russians." The FSA forces did suffer casualties in the strike, Townsend said. The US military in February 2017 proposed a higher level of co-ordination between US and Russian senior officers to better de-conflict air strikes on ground targets to prevent the accidental targeting of ground units. Strikes by Iraqi Air Force Lockheed Martin F-16 Vipers into eastern Syria – reportedly with the permission of Damascus - in late February showed that the complexity of the air operations in Syria was growing.

Fast moving developments on several fronts in early 2017 saw beleaguered Islamic State fighters penned into a shrinking enclave in the western part of the Iraqi city of Mosul; Kurdish-led Syrian Democratic Front (SDF) militia fighters reached the Euphrates river to cut the last direct road route from Raqqa to Iraq; Syrian government troops, backed by Russian airpower, recaptured Palmyra and made rapid advances to the east of Aleppo along the Euphrates valley; a surprise US-led air assault operation seized Tabqa dam to the west of Raqqa on 22nd March and four days later US-backed SDF forces captured Tabqa airbase and trapped Islamic State fighters inside Tabqa town. On top of this, the Pentagon confirmed that it had dispatched 400 US Marines, backed by a detachment of BAE Systems M777 155mm field guns and Boeing

AH-64 Apache attack helicopters, into Syria to support the SDF as they approach Raqqa. It also emerged that some 2,500 additional US paratroopers of the 82nd Airborne Division would be heading to Kuwait to be available for future operations across Iraq and Syria. Within a few weeks the SDF and their US allies had effectively trapped the Islamic State garrison inside the capital of the Caliphate.

The rapid advance of the US-backed SDF was having an impact among Russian and Syrian officers in Damascus. Their fears about the Kurds and their US allies occupying and not giving up large chunks of eastern and northern Syria were being realised. The Syrian army would need to step up the pace of its advance.

Chapter 18
Tiger Force Advances

It looked like a classic Tiger Force assault operation. BM-21 rocket launchers, D-20 152m howitzers and T-55 tanks fired salvo after salvo on the Islamic State front line trenches. Infantry assault teams then moved forward to begin clearing Jihadi strong points from a string villages south of al Bab. Further scenes in the video clip filmed by a crew from the Russian ANNA network with the Tiger Force showed that the Islamic State defence proved half-hearted, with the bulk of the Jihadis retreating and only a handful of snipers remaining behind to slow up the Syrian advance.

The ANNA crew stayed with the Syrian troops through the advance. On a daily basis they reported vehicle-borne suicide bombers being sent towards the Syrian lines in a bid to further delay their advance. Video imagery from the period showed several heavily armoured pick-up trucks being stopped by Syrian tank and missile fire. Occasionally, the vehicles got through and killed Syrian soldiers in forward check points.

This was the front-line of the Syrian army's newest offensive. It soon became a three-sided race - between Syrian, Turkish and Kurdish forces - to win control of as much territory as possible as the Jihadi group collapsed across northern Syria. Whoever controlled the most territory would have a better position at any eventual peace talks.

Each party had very different agendas. For the Damascus government controlling territory was a sign of legitimacy and authority, so the more territory it could capture the better. Although the Russians and Turks had patched up their differences, Syria's President Assad remained deeply suspicious of President Erdogan's long-term agenda. In August 2016, after a spate of Jihadi bombings inside Turkey, Ankara had backed Free Syrian Army rebels in northern Aleppo. Turkey then sent troops to dislodge Islamic State fighters from the border region. Fearing the Turkish troops would never leave after the war, the Syrians were determined to ensure they were penned into as small an enclave as possible.

The coming operation would see the Syrians make dramatic and strategically significant advances to wrong foot the US and its allies. Neither Moscow nor Washington would back attacks on their opponent's local allies because Russian or American advisors could be present with them. The fear was that the death of US or Russian soldiers would spark a shooting war. So whichever side was able to capture land first had the advantage and would not be able to be evicted. The Syrians appeared to recognise this new reality and became masters at working it to their advantage.

The Kurdish People's Protection Units or YPG had carved out a semi-independent mini state across northern Syria, including enclaves in Aleppo city, the Afrin pocket and a whole swathe of territory stretching from the Euphrates river to the Iraqi border. The Kurds had joined the US sponsored Syrian Democratic Forces (SDF) alliance and participated in an offensive against the capital of the Islamic State caliphate, Raqqa. Turkey's President Erdogan loathed the YPG and he was determined to limit the territory they controlled inside Syria by ensuring that his allies, the Free Syrian Army, could secure the dominant position in the northern Syrian by capturing Raqqa.

In this scenario, the interests of the YPG and the Syrian government came into alignment. They began to co-ordinate their operations to neutralise a large group of Islamic State fighters based in the city of al Bab. These fanatical fighters had held off Turkish troops and pro-Ankara rebels of the Free Syrian Army for more than two months. The Syrians and the YPG appeared to enter into a loose alliance to link up behind Al Bab to prevent the Turkish-led forces pushing eastwards into the Euphrates valley and opening a route to Raqqa.

In an added level of geopolitical complexity, both the Russians and the United States tentatively supported the Syrian and YPG operation. The Americans had a long-established alliance with the YPG which was beginning to reap dividends, and had brought Kurdish and SDF fighters to within striking distance of Raqqa. The Turkish move into the Euphrates valley threatened to disrupt the US-Kurdish alliance, and American military commanders did not rate the Free Syrian Army as an effective fighting force that stood a chance of taking Raqqa from Islamic State. The Russians, meanwhile saw the situation as a chance to put the Syrian army into a position to strike at Raqqa. This would give Damascus and Moscow a say in the final operation to take the Islamic State capital, and ensure a potentially better position in the diplomatic end-game in Syria. The public-relations impact of Syrian and Russian forces being involved in the liquidation of the Islamic State caliphate's capital were too good to be missed.

Not surprisingly, this important mission was entrusted to Colonel Suheil al-Hassan and his Tiger Force. Several of his regiments were concentrated north of Aleppo in late January and the Russian army moved up special forces operatives to co-ordinate air support for them. Russian mine-clearing sappers with force protection from the Military Police Battalion in Aleppo were also dispatched to help the Tiger Force clear captured villages of improvised explosive devices left behind by retreating Islamic State fighters.

The fight for al Bab set the tone for the next two months of fighting in North West Syria, with the Syrians and Kurdish YPG pushing northwards and westwards respectively. The Turkish-backed FSA rebels pushed southwards and eastward.

At first Islamic State resistance was fanatical. They knocked out several heavily armoured Turkish Leopard tanks and captured some troop carriers. The Syrians and Kurds concentrated on trying to close the escape route behind the Islamic State. Just when it looked as if the Tiger Force and YPG would be successful, the Jihadis mounted a rapid escape through to the east in the last week in February.

The race now began, as Syrian troops and the YPG worked in unofficial alliance to link up and prevent the FSA reaching the Euphrates. This would effectively close down the option of the Turks and their allies entering the Euphrates valley and being able to strike toward Raqqa. While neither the Syrians nor the Kurds wanted the other to have the lead in the battle for Raqqa, they both had a common interest in making sure the Turks were kept out.

Despite the political rivalry, the Russian, Turkish and US air forces had put in place de-confliction measures to make sure their aircraft did not end up being in the same piece of sky at the same time. This was to prevent mid-air collisions and their aircraft accidentally opening fire on each other. The Russians spoke to the Turks and Americans on behalf of the Syrians, the US Air Force represented its coalition allies in the three way de-confliction exercise, which was conducted over a telephone conference call each day. The US and Russians had set up this hot line between the respective air operations centres in Qatar and Syria in September 2015 but in the opening days of 2017 as the complexity of the battlefield in North West Syria grew, they stepped up the level of co-ordination and brought in the Turks.

Russian and Turkish aircraft carried out their first de-conflicted air strikes in North-West Syria on 18th January as part of intensifying attacks on Islamic State forces defending al Bab. According to Sergey Rudskoy, chief of the Main Operational Directorate of the Russian General Staff, some 36 targets were hit around the town by aircraft from both countries' air forces.

"The air operation, agreed with the Syrian government, involved nine warplanes of the Russian Aerospace Force, including four Sukhoi Su-24M, four Sukhoi Su-25 aircraft and one Sukhoi Su-34 bomber, as well as four F-16 and four F-4 fighters of Turkey's Air Force," he said at a media briefing in Moscow on 18th January. According to Rudskoy, all the targets were previously fixed by the two general staffs and their air force commands. "In the past two days, a reconnaissance mission involving unmanned aircraft and cosmic [space-based] reconnaissance equipment was carried out in order to help fix the targets," he said. The strikes had by then "already proven highly effective," Rudskoy said.

The Turkish armed forces played down the co-operation with Russia and did not describe the strikes as "joint". In its own statement, the Turks said their jets hit targets on three occasions during the morning and afternoon on 18th January. British Panavia Tornado GR4 jets carried out an attack during the day and US armed unmanned aerial vehicles flew a reconnaissance mission, according to the Turkish statement. It added that: "Russian warplanes also hit Daesh [Islamic State] targets in southern al Bab under the agreement signed by Turkey and Russia on 12th January allowing them to coordinate air operations in war-torn Syria."

UK military sources also played down the level of co-operation with Russia, with a senior Royal Air Force officer saying on 19th January that only "deconfliction" of aircraft took place between the US-led coalition, the Turks and Russians. "This was deconflicted as usual but we were not involved in any joint or coordinated operation," said the officer.

In the first week of March, the Tiger Force launched a two-pronged offensive from its positions around Kweires Airbase. While one axis aimed due east toward the Euphrates, another Tiger Force contingent struck north to link up with the YPG. In a matter of days, Suheil al-Hassan's troops had linked up with the YPG north of the town of Dier Hafir. The Turks were furious and started bombarding YPG positions around Manbij. This in turn made the Americans concerned that the up-coming offensive against Raqqa would be stalled because the Kurds would divert their troops to confront the Turks, who were still nominally a major US ally and NATO member. Just as the situation was threatening to get out of hand, the Russians played a blinder.

In secret talks with the Kurds, the Russians offered to escort contingents of Syrian troops and border guards into YPG territory to set up a buffer zone between them and the Turks. Within hours the Russian MP Battalion in Aleppo was on the move northwards putting Moscow's boots on the ground in one of the most strategic pieces of real estate in Syria.

The Americans immediately saw the danger to their alliance with the Kurds and were determined not to let Moscow take on the role of protector of the YPG around Manbij. So after some arm-twisting with the YPG leadership, a column of around 100 American troops in HUMVEE and Striker armoured troop carriers headed to Manbij to establish what was termed a "joint security zone" between the Kurds and Turks to be patrolled by US and Russian troops. The crisis was averted but it showed that both Moscow and Washington were locked into a race for influence across Syria.

As this drama was unfolding in the upper Euphrates valley, a new bout of fighting broke out along the southern edge of the Idlib pocket between rebel fighters and government troops. A string of government villages in the north of Hama province fell to rebel fighters. The Syrian High Command in Damascus recalled Colonel al-Hassan and part of his Tiger Force to launch a counter attack. Many of the Tiger Force soldiers came from the region and could be relied upon to fight to defend their home villages and relatives with some vigour.

On 4th April, the town of Khan Shaykhun, a few kilometres behind the rebel front line was the scene of an incident that became a major international controversy. The White Helmet rescue organisation began posting graphic videos of what they said was a gas attack by government aircraft. The daughter of the new US President, Donald Trump, saw television news reports of the attack and reportedly demanded that her father do something about it.

Over the next two days the US government declared that the Syrians were behind the attack, which various reports said had left between 58 and 100 civilians dead. The US, British, French and Turkish governments blamed the Damascus government. The Russians squared up behind the Syrians and claimed rebel chemical weapons stored in the town had been released after being hit by a government air strike. President Trump decided to launch a retaliatory missile strike on the airbase, where the Syrian aircraft it said were involved in the gas attack had taken off from.

Late on the evening of 6th April, a US officer telephoned the Russian Aerospace Force command post at Hmeinyan airbase to warn them that more than 50 US Navy Tomahawk Land Attack Missiles (TLAM) would soon be heading towards Shayrat airbase in central Syria. The Americans wanted to give the Russians the chance to evacuate their attack helicopters and support personnel who were operating at the base in support of Syrian troops fighting Islamic State around Palmyra.

After a series of telephone conversations with their helicopter units at Shayrat, the Russian air command managed to issue them with orders to take off for safety. Before leaving the Russians warned their Syrian allies that an attack was coming and all the personnel at the base were able to take cover. Early on the morning of the 7th April, 59 TLAMs fired from the USS Ross and USS Porter, cruising in the Eastern Mediterranean, impacted around the base, destroying at least 11 of its 22 hardened aircraft shelters (HAS) and several other support facilities. A couple of hours after the attack the Russians sent up a Forpost unmanned aerial vehicle to inspect the damage. Video footage from the drone was released to the media later that morning and showed several fires still burning across the base. Later in the morning, Russian and Syrian journalists were allowed on the base to film the damage. Among the smouldering HAS, four or five Sukhoi Su-22 and three MiG-23 fighter bombers could be seen burnt out or damaged.

The available imagery also suggested that large parts of the airfield were not targeted and at least two Su-22s were seen undamaged. The two main runways were not directly attacked, although several images suggested that missile debris and other material was scattered over them. Two missiles appeared to hit one taxi way just in front of a HAS and one runway showed signs of shrapnel damage. This damage required little work to clean up. A Russian television crew, when leaving the airbase, filmed a Kub or SA-6 surface-to-air missile battery beside the site's main gate and this showed four missile launcher vehicles and one P-15 radar that were undamaged.

The US Navy TLAM strike caused considerable damage to Shayrat airbase but this did not appear to be enough to put the site fully out of operation. Local media reports from 8th April suggested at least two Su-22 strikes were launched from the base on that day. This seemed to confirm that aim of the US strike was not to systematically destroy the base but to send a message to the Syrian Government about the use of chemical weapons.

The Khan Shaykhun incident and the subsequent missile attack generated much diplomatic and media controversy. The Organisation for the Prohibition of Chemical Weapons (OPCW) launched an investigation that subsequently pointed to a "Sarin nerve gas-like" substance being used in the incident. Several non-government organisations made similar claims. There were also dissenting voices, including former UN weapons inspector Scott Ritter, who criticised the OPCW investigation for relying almost solely on chemical samples and other evidence provided by the White Helmets and groups linked to the rebels who controlled the Idlib pocket.

The British, French and US governments used the United Nations Security Council to lambast the Russians for protecting the Syrians, by using their veto to prevent action being taken against Damascus. The British UN Ambassador, Matthew Rycroft, announced during the 12th April session that samples from Khan Shaykhun had been analysed by British scientists and had "tested positive for Sarin or a Sarin-like substance". When this author used the Freedom of Information Act to see a copy of the reports by the scientists at the British chemical weapons research centre at Porton Down, the Foreign and Commonwealth Office in August 2017 refused to "confirm nor deny" that such reports actually existed. It seemed that events had moved on.

In the end, all the fury and rage over the Khan Shaykhun incident did not impact on events within Syria. The US and its allies did not change their policy of concentrating on defeating Islamic State. There would be no concerted western military action against the Damascus government.

Chapter 19
Operation Dawn

According to some accounts, the Tupolev Tu-95 is a "lumbering Cold War dinosaur". A Russian Aerospace Force Sukhoi Su-30 fighter pilot was filming the giant bomber with a video camera in July 2017. The vast expanse of the eastern Syrian desert filled the frame until the fighter pilot zoomed in on the silver-painted bomber, with a huge red star on its tail. Then the Tupolev's bomb bay doors opened and a white-painted metal pipe dropped out. For several seconds it just fell before two wings deployed and its rocket motor kicked in. Then the Kh-101 stealth cruise missile powered away, leaving the Tu-95 and the gaggle of escorting Sukhoi fighters far behind.

Hundreds of miles to the west Russian Forpost unmanned aerial vehicles were circling over the targets, waiting to record the missile strikes for damage analysis. Three missiles were filmed hitting farm buildings in the eastern districts of Hama province. In one of the video sequence, the Kh-101 could be clearly seen as it punched through the roof of a flat-roofed building. Russian air commanders in their operations centre at Hmeinyan airbase in western Syria watched the missile strike live on a giant plasma screen television. They were considered so successful that within a few minutes the Russian Ministry of Defence's public relations department in Moscow had been emailed digital video footage so it could be re-packaged into a You Tube clip to be uploaded on the ministry's Twitter feed.

This was 21st Century warfare, Russian style. A 1950s-vintage Soviet designed nuclear bomber had been modified to fire satellite-guided cruise missiles, against targets detected by Israeli-designed drones hundreds of miles away. Within minutes the video footage of the missile strikes had been uploaded onto the internet, using US-sourced social media platforms as part of a propaganda campaign to convince the world that Moscow was doing more to fight Islamic State that the United States and its coalition.

The summer of 2017 would see Russian involvement in the Syria conflict reach new levels of intensity as Moscow provided critical support to enable the Syrian army to launch an unprecedented series of co-ordinated offensives aimed at recapturing the centre and east of the country. Russian officers had built up more than 18 months' experience of supporting Syrian offensives, combining close air support, long-range missile strikes, artillery and rocket attacks and helicopter gunship raids under the control of teams of special forces operatives on the front-line with Syrian troops. At the same time, Russian officers had mastered the darks arts of so-called "soft power" to win over local people and tribal fighters to the cause of the Damascus government.

Until the summer of 2017, Russian officers in Syria had generally only supported Syrian offensive operations on narrow and well defined parts of the battlefield, such as the 2016 Battle for Aleppo and the re-taking of Palmyra in the spring of 2017. Over the coming months the Russians would become more ambitious and support a multi-axis advance across the length and breadth of the Syria desert region, from the Euphrates valley in the north down to the Jordanian and Iraqi borders. This was a highly ambitious undertaking that was aimed at establishing Syrian government control of the entire centre and east of the country. The bulk of this region was dominated by battle-hardened Islamic State fighters, but a significant chunk in the south was also control by militia groups allied to the United States, Jordan and Britain.

The campaign to re-take Palmyra and then the rebel offensive out of the Idlib province meant the Syrians were not ready to begin their major offensive until early May 2017. To get them ready to go, the Russians also expanded the footprint of their special forces and advisors. Social-media imagery showed they had teams working in the headquarters of the Tiger Force in the Euphrates valley. Advisors and trainers were positioned with units of the 5th Corps in eastern Hama, along with a battery of Russian 152mm howitzers. The large contingent of Russian special forces operatives, advisors and trainers who had helped recapture Palmyra remained with the Syrian 18th Division in the desert to the east of iconic city and were reinforced with a detachment of Russian BM-27 multiple-launch rockets, backed up by the bulk of the Russian attack helicopters in Syria.

The final element of the attack force was provided by Iranian-led and advised -Shia militia fighters and Palestinian units, which were re-positioned from south of Aleppo onto the southern desert axis. Iran's armed drone contingent was also re-positioned to support this drive. Russian staff officers were sent to the headquarters of the Syrian 1st Armoured Division south of Damascus to co-ordinate air support for the new offensive.

During the first months of 2017, the number of Russian Military Police battalions in Syria was ramped up to four units to allow a presence to be established in the fringes of each of the so-called de-escalation zones in Idlib, East Ghouta, Dara'a and the Rustan pocket north of Homs. This deployment of more than 1,000 Russian soldiers in turn allowed the Syrians to pull out troops from these sectors to join the desert offensive. Russian air capability had also been expanded in time for the offensive with the return of a detachment of Sukhoi Su-25SM "Rook" ground-attack jets to Syria, as well as the deployment of more Sukhoi Su-34 precision strike jets. The Rooks had been pulled out from Hmeinyan airbase a year earlier as part of President Putin's "the war is over" diplomatic offensive. While the Su-25 squadron had its maintenance base at Hmeinyan, a forward arming and refuelling point was set up at the giant Syrian airbase at T-4, to the west of Palmyra, to enable the Rooks to spend more time on station over the central desert battlefield.

The Shayrat airbase missile attack meant Russian air commanders were acutely aware of the potential for more confrontations with the Americans as Syrian troops advanced into areas close to where US military advisers were based. Daily flights were mounted over the centre of the country by Beriev A-50 airborne radar and control aircraft to expand radar and communication coverage.

To give Russian commanders precision-strike capabilities, the Black Sea Fleet put in place a rota of ship and submarine deployments to ensure that vessels equipped with the Kalibr cruise missile were always on station within range of Syria during the summer of 2017. The Russian Aerospace Force's Long Range Aviation also kept several of its bombers on alert to strike at Syria.

The Russian effort in Syria was joined together by a huge communications network. Speaking at a defence conference in Moscow in August 2017, Lieutenant General Khalil Arslanov, head of the Main Directorate for Communications of the Russian Armed Forces revealed that it had to massively expand its communications network for the Syria operation. "The land satellite network has tripled, relay satellites' capacity has increased, antenna systems for military and dual-use communications satellites have been readjusted, and the leased resource has been expanded," he said. "Hand-held and mobile satellite terminals were widely used in Syria."

A new aggressive commander of the Group of Russian Forces in Syria had arrived in April, just in time to oversee the new offensive in the east of the country. Colonel General Sergei Surovikin had a reputation in the Russian army for being an officer who drove his troop's hard and got things done. When he was a divisional commander, one of his officers shot himself dead in front of the command staff after receiving a dressing down from the general. As a junior officer he had also been linked to coup plotters against Russia's first democratically elected president, Boris Yeltsin, in 1991.

Operation Dawn 1, as the first phase of the Syrian offensive was codenamed, was set to kick off in May 2017. At the start it seemed like a series of disconnected small-scale operations across separate axes but as it gained momentum in June and July, the strategic implications became clearer.

Euphrates Valley Axis
This main axis of advance for the Colonel Suheil al-Hassan's Tiger Force, which returned to the strategic region in early May after being diverted to Hama province to counter a rebel offensive out of the Idlib

pocket.

Opposing the Tiger Force were the remnants of several Jihadi groups that had defected to Islamic State in 2014 from less radical groups. After throwing their lot in with Islamic State these fighters had tried to drive both the Syrian army and moderate rebels from Aleppo province. These fighters were predominately Syrians and they had cross sword with the Tiger Force and its commander on several occasions. Their main defensive tactic was the use of extensive minefields and IEDs to create protective shields around a series of village strong points. There were small groups of fanatical foreign fighters with them and the Jihadis had many willing suicide bombers in their ranks. Time and again the Tiger Force had out-manoeuvred these Islamic State fighters but instead of staying put and fighting to the last man, they retreated rather than be encircled. Since January, the Jihadis had been retreating across the Dier Hafir plain. They were tired and their morale had taken several knocks. It is difficult to assess numbers but the Islamic State fighters probably only numbered several hundred men. As they retreated, they ended up having to defend longer sections of front, with fewer fighters. The Islamic State front was very brittle. This weakness would be at the heart of the Tiger Force's coming offensive.

Video imagery of the Tiger Force offensives during May showed very violent bombardments of Islamic State front-lines and then the Syrian troops advancing into empty villages. The Jihadis appeared not to be able to put up any co-ordinated resistance.

Syrian troops re-captured Jirrah airbase and faced a brief counter attack by two suicide bomber trucks and a drone fitted with improvised bombs. The Syrians held their ground and the Jihadis begun to retreat, every time the Tiger Force looked like it was going to trap them. By the end of May, the Tiger Force had re-taken Maskanah, the last major town in Aleppo province, and had crossed the administrative border into Raqqa province. They were now approaching Tabqa airbase, which had fallen to Kurdish YPG fighters during April. The race was now on to secure control of the south bank of the Euphrates from the US-backed YPG and its Syrian Democratic Forces allies. YPG control of Tabqa seemed to give them the upper hand and they looked like they could easily block all the west-east roads in Raqqa province to keep the Syrian army out of the middle Euphrates valley.

In one of their first such moves, the Syrians moved fast to head off the US-backed allies. The Tiger Force headed into the desert to bypass the YPG on 13th June. Five days later they had captured the strategic crossroads town of Resafa. They then kept going eastward until they reached the Euphrates in early July. There were scattered groups of Islamic State fighters in villages but organised resistance from Jihadis seemed to have ceased. The Kurds were blocked from moving southwards.

Russian commanders regarded the Tiger Force as the Syrian army's most reliable units so they did not see the need to provide it with significant assistance during the first phase of the Euphrates valley offensive. This changed after the Syrian entry into Raqqa province. Officers from the Russian reconciliation centre joined up with the Tiger Force to begin recruiting a militia from tribes in the south of the province who had previously been loyal to Islamic State. This became another arena of competition with the Americans, who were also trying to recruit these tribes to the SDF. The rapid arrival of the Tiger Force in Raqqa province interrupted American plans and by early July, the Russians had managed to persuade several hundred tribal fighters to throw in their lot with the Damascus government. The fighting quality of these men left a lot to be desired but it was a major political success for the Russians.

This was a period of considerable tension with the US, as the Tiger Force columns by-passed the YPG positions at Tabqa. Russian and US officers used their telephone link to de-conflicted air support for their respective allies on a daily basis. With the Syrian troops and Kurdish fighters only a few hundred metres apart, the system broke down on 18th June. The Syrians called up one of their Sukhoi Su-22M4 strike jets to hit what they thought was an Islamic State controlled village south of Tabqa. It turned out to be a Kurdish held village and US advisors called up a US Navy Boeing F/A-18E Super Hornet to intercept the Syrian jet. The US jet promptly shot down the Sukhoi.

US laws enacted after the Russian occupation of Crimea in 2014 prohibits direct military co-operation with Russian forces – only de-confliction - and Washington was still refusing to co-operate with the Damascus government. However, American and Russian commanders in the Middle East recognised that there could be more incidents in the confused battlefield along the Euphrates valley unless improved links could be established between their allies. The answer was for the Kurds to act as the link with the Syrians on the ground. In early July, the veteran British journalist Robert Fisk visited the Tiger Force forward headquarters in Resafa and found a Kurdish officer working side- by-side with a Russian Aerospace Force colonel. A way had been found to co-ordinate the fight against Islamic State in the Euphrates valley.

The Jihadis were not completely beaten. As the Tiger Force tried to move along the Euphrates in the last days of July they took the town of Shina. Ten Islamic State suicide bomb trucks were launched against the Syrian troops around the town, catching them by surprise and killing more than 50 soldiers. At the nearby Rumeylah oil field another six Syrian soldiers were killed and 15 wounded in further suicide attack.

Hama Province Axis
The next major grouping of Islamic State fighters in Syria was based

around the mountain stronghold of Uqayribat in the far east of Hama province. This was a wild region that dominated central Syria, from Hama city in the west and to the south where it overlooked Palmyra. It also contained several gas fields and gas- production facilities.

The Islamic State used its bases in this mountainous region to launch raids on the narrow road from Hama city to Aleppo, fire rockets at Salimaniyah city and a nearby gas-production facility, as well as raiding the Tiyas-Palmyra road. There were probably no more than 900 hardcore Islamic State fighters and a similar number of tribal allies in the region but its rugged terrain meant they could hold off superior number of Syrian troops by controlling a few key approach roads up narrow valleys. These Islamic State fighters were some of the most determined in Syria and they had been responsible for a series of audacious raids on the Hama-Ithiyia support road to Aleppo, which involved columns of heavily armed pick-up trucks driving through the night to set up ambushes metres from the side the road. An Islamic State video from early 2017 showed one of these ambushes destroying several tank transporters on the road.

Syrian regular and militia troops struck eastwards from Salimaniyah in May but the attack got bogged down very quickly. A Russian artillery battery was dispatched to beef up the assault in June, along with the Syrian Desert Hawks brigade. The attack was a fiasco. Scores of Desert Hawk soldiers were killed and dozens of armoured vehicles destroyed by Islamic State missile teams. It was such a disaster that Russian officers advising the Syrians recommended that the Desert Hawk militia be disbanded and its soldiers be sent to join the Russian-advised 5th Corps. The Desert Hawk's flamboyant commander, the self-appointed "Colonel" Mohammed Jaber, relocated to Moscow to return to his business activities.

The Russians tried to jump start the Syrian offensive against Uqayribat in late June with a Kalibr cruise missile strike and then in early July Tupolev Tu-95 long-range bombers also fired Kh-101 cruise missiles at targets around the town. Little head way was made.

The Southern Desert Front

The Syrian government had been driven from almost all of its southern border with Jordan and Iraq in 2013 and 2014 by a combination of US-backed militias in the west and Islamic State in the east. US, British and Norwegian special forces had set up a base in 2015 at Al Tanf, just inside Syria, near the point where the Jordanian and Iraqi borders meet. They had recruited a couple of hundred fighters, who they dubbed the New Syrian Army, in a bid to stop Islamic State moving westwards along the Syrian-Jordanian border. To the West, other US-armed and -trained militias had staged an on-off war with the Syrian army. Hardly anyone lived in this barren desert region and the various militias operating in it probably numbered only a few hundred fighters.

In early 2017, the US-backed militia at Al Tanf began an offensive to try to drive Islamic State back to the Euphrates. This involved several columns of armed pick-up trucks driving into the desert to try to find and engage isolated forward Jihadi positions and pinpoint them for US air strikes. This was billed by the US as the southern front against Islamic State, which would lead to the capture of their stronghold in the middle Euphrates valley at Abu Kamal.

In Damascus, this was viewed with alarm as it would eventually see a whole swath of territory along the Jordanian and Iraqi borders come under the control of US-backed militias. The New Syrian Army travelled with US advisors in their columns so the Russians would not allow direct attacks on them in case it led to a shooting war with America.

The southern prong of Operation Dawn was designed to counter this threat. Several columns of tanks, armoured vehicles and armed pick-up trucks were positioned along the southern edge of the eastern Qalamoun mountain range to sweep down into the desert region. The western axis scored early success against the US-armed militia in Suwayda province, prompting retreats when the rebels came under threat of encirclement.

In the desert of eastern Damascus province, the Syrian columns drove back the outposts of the New Syrian Army and they approached Al Tanf in early June. The US declared a 50-kilometre "de-confliction zone" around the base and said they would strike at any ground force that approached.

Several Shia militia groups had been moved from Aleppo to join the desert offensive, along with their Iranian advisors, and they were provided with top cover from Iranian Shahed-129 armed drones. The Russians flew daily Sukhoi Su-30 and Su-35 fighters patrols over the desert front to protect their own advisors working with the Syrian columns.

The Russians, Syrians and Iranians were pushing to see what reaction they would get from the Americans. When an advanced Syrian column got within 25 miles of Al Tanf the US bombed it twice, on 6th and 18th May. The Syrians kept advancing and called up a Shahed-129 drone to attack a New Syrian Army column on 8th June. Russian Sukhois circled overhead. When the Iranian drone fired a missile that exploded a few metres from a US special forces Hummer truck the Americans responded. This was the first time US troops had come under enemy air attack since the Korean war in the 1950s. A US Air Force McDonnell Douglas F-15E Strike Eagle lined up behind the Iranian drone and shot it down with a heat-seeking missile. A pair of Russian Sukhois on patrol nearby did not interfere. Moscow was not going to start a war for the sake of an Iranian drone. Other ways would be found to neutralise the US-backed militia at Al Tanf.

When the Syrian state news agency, SANA, announced on 10th June that its troops had reached the Iraqi border to the east of Al Tanf it became clear that Damascus had just ordered its troops to bypass the US-declared "de-confliction zone", rendering the Al Tanf base an irrelevance. The Damascus Ministry of Defence later released video footage of the operation showing more than 20 assorted military vehicles moving across the desert toward Iraq, with air support from an Aerospatiale Gazelle helicopter. At least one T-90 main battle tank and BMP infantry fighting vehicles were filmed in the column. Two bulldozers, including one with an armoured cab, were filmed building up sand ramparts to protect the armoured vehicles and anti-tank missile teams, equipped with 9M113 Konkurs and 9M14 Malyutka missile systems. Dozens of Syrian soldiers could be seen manning the new position. From the footage it did not appear that they had linked up with Iraqi troops or meet any resistance from pro-US fighters or Islamic State forces.

"Units of the Syrian Arab Army, in cooperation with the allied forces, completed on Friday evening the first stage of the military operations in the Syrian Badia [desert] and were able to reach the border with the friendly Iraq northeast of al-Tanf," the Syrian Arab Army General Command said in a statement on 10th June. In Moscow the day before in a Russian Ministry of Defence briefing, the Syrian advance was marked on a situation map, which indicated the Syrian troops had reached positions some 60 kilometres to the north-east of the US base al Tanf.

Arak-Sukhnah Axis
Syrian troops, with strong Russian backing, had retaken Palmyra in early March and continued to push eastwards along the main road to Arak and Sukhnah. The Islamic State defenders of Palmyra had retreated eastwards and took up positions on the hills dominating this road, forcing the Syrians to stage a series of assaults to clear them out.

Russian special forces teams and advisors with the 800th Republican Guard Regiment and 5th Corps were in action on a daily basis calling down Russian attack helicopter strikes, artillery and rocket barrages on the Jihadi positions. This was a slow and time-consuming business. By early June, they had cleared the hills around Arak and then swept into the town. In late July, the key road junction town of Sukhanh came under attack. Russian officers from their reconciliation centre had also been at work in eastern Homs to recruit tribal fighters to the Syrian cause. They were grouped into a force that the Damascus dubbed the Euphrates Hawks. Syrian officers claimed more than 4,000 fighters had rallied to their cause. This was probably an over estimation and from imagery of their fighters operating on the Sukhnah front in this period it would seem that the Euphrates Hawks only mustered a couple of hundred fighters. The Islamic State fighters around Sukhnah fought hard with tanks, artillery and rocket launchers. They were mainly foreign fighters and had established a network of tunnels and underground fighting positions in the hills overlooking the town. It took the Syrians and their Russian allies until early August to pry them out of Sukhnah.

In the first week of August, the Syrian army was poised to launch the final phase of Operation Dawn to sweep down into the Euphrates valley and break the siege of Dier Ez Zor.

Chapter 20
Lifting the Siege of Dier Ez Zor

In the dusk the Russian special forces commander could be seen briefing a parade of Syrian soldiers. They looked a scruffy bunch. Each Syrian had a different uniform and combat equipment but all the 50 or so men looked like hardened killers.

In the background, a pair of Russian Kamov Ka-52 Alligator attack helicopters were spinning up their co-axial rotor blades. With the pep-talk over, the Syrian soldiers doubled over to three Mil Mi-17 helicopters which had their rear clam-shell doors removed to speed the fighters exit when they landed near their objective. Watching the scene at the remote desert airbase was the commander of the Syrian Tiger Force, Colonel Suheil al-Hassan.

In a series of videos of the operation released by the Russian and Syrian military, three Syrian air force Mi-17s could be seen lifting off first and then the Russian Ka-52s followed them into the night. Subsequent night-vision goggle imagery then showed the assault force disembarking from the Mi-17s near buildings in a desert location. Gun-camera imagery from the Ka-52s was also included in the video package, showing missile engagements against three vehicles.

The Syrian news agency, SANA, reported the next day that the airborne assault operation led to the capture of the towns of Khirbet Makman and al-Kadir, on the borders of Raqqa and Homs provinces. It said the raid took place 21 kilometres behind Islamic State lines and was followed by a ground assault, which linked up with the helicopter-landed troops. The video imagery showed the remains of three abandoned SUVs, including one fitted with an anti-aircraft cannon, being inspected by Syrian troops on the day after the raid. A group of more than 40 Syrian troops were shown in the video. The body of one dead Islamic State fighter was seen in the film.

The Russian news agency, TASS, reported a statement released by the Moscow Ministry of Defence on 14th August, confirming the role of Russian helicopters in the assault. "Russian military advisers took direct part in the preparation of the operation and control over it," said the ministry. Before the operation, Russian Ka-52 helicopters hit a force of the Islamic State near the village of Al-Kadir, the ministry said, adding that the helicopters directed fire by Syria's multiple rocker launchers. "The helicopters, equipped with night-vision instruments, effectively directed rocket fire and destroyed the terrorists' armour and armed vehicles," it said.

This remarkable operation showed the extent of Russian involvement in the final phase of the Operation Dawn series of offensives in eastern Syria. While Russian air support, directed by forward air controllers on the ground, had been routine in the Syrian campaign since the spring of 2016, the operation to lift the siege of Dier Ez Zor and then clear Islamic State from the middle Euphrates valley would see an unprecedented level of Russian direct participation on the battlefield.

The joint Syrian-Russian helicopter operation on 11th-12th August was the opening move of an ambitious offensive that would clear out Islamic State fighters from central and eastern Syria in a matter of weeks. The first phases of Operation Dawn over the previous three months had brought Syrian troops into position to strike and more reinforcements had been moved up to reinforce the attack force from the Damascus region. Two brigades of the elite 4th Mechanised Division had been positioned around Ithiya in the far north-east of Hama province. At least one Republican Guard brigade and the ISIS Hunters special forces unit had been positioned to the north of Palmyra. These forces were to strike south and north respectively to form a pocket of Islamic State fighters in eastern Hama around the town of Uqayribat.

To the east, several Tiger Force regiments and the 124th Regiment of the Republican Guards, backed by locally recruited tribes, were grouped south of Resafa ready to strike towards Sukhnah. In the eastern district of Homs, the 800th Republican Guards Regiment, units of the 5th Corps and more tribal fighters were ready to attack northwards from Sukhnah to link up with the Tiger Force. On this central axis, a Russian 152mm MSTA-B howitzer battery and BM-27 rocket launchers were close to the front to support the attack.

Commercial satellite imagery detected at least four Russian Sukhoi Su-25SM Rook close-air-support jets at T-4 airbase to the west of Palmyra, along with Russian Mil Mi-24/35 and Mi-28 attack helicopters. At Palmyra's own airbase, a Syrian air force squadron of nine Aero L-39 Alabatros light-attack jets were also detected. These helicopters and jets would be in action on an hourly basis once the offensive got underway.

While the Islamic State group in Hama province had given its Syrian opponents a hard time over the past three months, its colleagues in Raqqa and Homs provinces had suffered a steady stream of casualties and equipment losses. Some 2,000 Islamic State fighters were trapped in Raqqa city by US-aided militia fighters from the Syrian Democratic Front and the Kurdish YPG. Raqqa was also the nerve centre of the Islamic State military logistics and equipment repair organisation so its isolation meant Jihadi fighters elsewhere in Syria had limited ability to replenish their losses and ammunition supplies. Many Islamic State units were reduced to launching raids on remote Syrian outposts to try to capture arms and ammunition.

To support the Syrian ground offensive, Russian air power was surged to ensure strike jets were in the air around the clock. Russian Beriev A-50 AWACS radar surveillance jets flew daily sorties from Hmeinyan airbase to co-ordinate the air support effort. Russian Forpost unmanned aerial vehicles were dispatched to watch the battlefields of eastern Syria around the clock and the artillery group on the ground near Sukhnah was provided with an Orlan 10 detachment to help it find targets.

Russian strike aircraft surged their sortie rate to 60 or 70 a day, Colonel General Sergei Rudskoy, Chief of the Main Operational Directorate of the General Staff of the Russian Armed Forces, said on 21st August. "Within the last five days, Russian aircraft have performed 316 flights and 819 strikes," he said. "This month, aviation of the Russian Aerospace Forces has carried out 990 combat flights and 2,518 aviation strikes."

The Russian-Syrian heli-borne landing was the cue for the four assault groups to begin closing the pincers. The advance by the Tiger Force and the 800th Republican Guard Regiment was carried out against almost no resistance. Video imagery posted online by government sources on 19th August, showed the commander of the Tiger Force, Colonel Suheil al-Hassan, directing operations by armoured and mechanised forces across the desert from an Aerospatiale Gazelle observation helicopter.

There were a few isolated Islamic State outposts in the way of the Syrian advance but the two strike forces manoeuvred around them in the desert before linking up on 24th August. When the Tiger Force encountered resistance, they employed overwhelming firepower. In one video clip from this time, the Tiger Force artillery can clearly be seen firing airburst sub-munition-dispensing shells above their targets.

The concentration of Tiger Force units south of Rasafa for the offensive meant the garrisoning of the Euphrates valley was left to a unit of the 5th Corps and tribal fighters. These troops were caught by a surprise attack near Ghanem Ali by an Islamic State mobile column led by suicide truck bombers that scattered hundreds of them into the desert and left 100 dead. More than 50 Syrian soldiers swam the Euphrates to seek safety in Kurdish lines. The Amaq news agency broadcast imagery showing Islamic State fighters recovering one T-55 tank, half a dozen howitzers and anti-aircraft guns, several trucks and a huge stash of ammunition.

The multi-pronged Syrian advance prompted an unprecedented series of retreats by Islamic State fighters in north-east Hama province and in south-east Raqqa as they tried to avoid being caught in the impending trap. These retreats allowed the 4th Division pushing south and the troops driving north from Palmyra to link up, forming a second pocket within a pocket.

As this manoeuvring on the ground was taking place, Russian strike jets began hitting the Islamic State convoys as they tried to escape encirclement. Roads across the battlefield were soon littered with the burned-out carcases of dozens tanks, lorries and pick-up trucks. There were few Islamic State positions to overrun: the Jihadis did not appear to have prepared the area for systemic defence. The exception was a large tunnel complex built into the mountain in the desert outside the town of Tabya, which was later uncovered by Syrian troops. This was not a fighting position but a bolt-hole for senior leaders to hide from aerial surveillance and air strikes.

By the end of August, the Islamic State defensive lines in central Syria had been shattered. More Syrian troops had struck eastwards from Salamiyah to further pressurise the trapped Islamic State fighters. It took more than six weeks of methodical advances to finally clear the pockets of Islamic State resistance, with Syrian troops having to attack village by village. Uqayribat fell in early September and Syrian troops found a tank-repair shop and a network of underground tunnels around the town. Even though the Damascus government declared the region clear of Jihadis on 4th October, fighting continued for several days. Controversy surrounded whether the Syrians did a deal to allow the last several hundred Islamic State fighters to evacuate to the Idlib pocket. The Syrians owned up to allowing a so-called humanitarian evacuation of the families of the Jihadi fighters. Pictures emerged online of a convoy of trucks, cars and buses moving north out of Islamic State-held territory on 9th and 10th October. When these alleged "civilians" took over a string of villages in the Idlib pocket and started fighting with Nusra Front fighters it became clear that they had used the "humanitarian" evacuation as a cover for their escape. Its seems highly likely the Damascus government approved their evacuation to rid itself of these hardcore Jihadis and save its soldiers having to continue fighting them. This followed on evacuation followed on from a deal in August by the Syrians and Lebanese Hizbullah leadership for 400 Islamic State fighter to be bused under s safe passage deal from Arsal on the Lebanon border to Dier Ez Zor.

Further to the east, the Syrians and their Russian allies were pressing their advantage to begin the operation to break the three-year-old siege of Dier Ez Zor. While the 800th Regiment and 5th Corps began to advance directly along the Sukhnah-Dier Ez Zor highway, the Tiger Force struck out into the desert. Its advance was mostly unopposed and, by 4th September they were only a few kilometres from the Dier Ez Zor garrison's most westerly position, inside the 137th Brigade base.

To the south, Russian advisors, artillery and attack helicopters were leading the Syrian ground advance. The Russian soldiers were filmed by the RT news networks on several occasions during the first days of September engaging targets with anti-tank missiles near the town of Kabawjib as they helped the 800th Regiment and 5th Corps advance. The Russian frigate, Admiral Essen, fired three cruise missiles at targets in the final villages along the road to Dier Ez Zor on 5th September to help them advance.

Islamic State mortar fire was blamed for the deaths of two Russian soldiers on 4th September, according to a statement from the Moscow defence ministry, reported by the TASS news agency. It said the servicemen were escorting a road convoy of the Russian Centre for Reconciliation of the Warring Parties personnel.

"The motor convoy came under mortar shelling by Islamic State terrorists in the province of Dier Ez Zor. As a result of shelling, one serviceman was killed and another one was badly wounded," the ministry said. "The wounded serviceman was promptly taken to hospital but died of deadly wounds, despite efforts taken by medics."

This all came to a climax on 5th September when the lead mine clearing tank of the Tiger Force cleared a path through the mine field to the 137th Brigade base. Scores of Syrian and Russian journalists were on hand to film the historic link up and witness the Syrian commander of besieged garrison, Brigadier General Issam Zahreddine, embracing the first Tiger Force soldiers. For the photo-opportunity the Russian soldiers kept a low profile – this was to be a Syrian victory.

Even as the televised celebrations were taking place inside 137th Brigade base, Syrian and Russian commanders were making preparations for the next phase of the operation. Syrian engineers followed behind the Tiger Force to widen and improve the improvised road through the minefield to allow humanitarian aid convoys to bring food to the 100,000 civilians trapped in Dier Ez Zor city and to speed the delivery of more ammunition and other supplies for the army garrison. The 800th Regiment had yet to fully clear the main road into Dier Ez Zor so until then the desert road was the only route into the city. A set of photographs emerged of a large Syrian army supply convoy moving down the desert road and intriguingly this included a column of Russian-made PMP bridge/ferry units, as well as at least two Soviet-era PTS-M amphibious vehicles and several BMK water boats. It is unclear when the Syrian army took delivery of the bridging equipment but records from the Cold War era make no mention of the Syrians receiving any of this highly specialist kit from the Soviet Union. This suggests the bridging equipment was from Russian army stocks and it arrived a few weeks before on the Syria Express shipping route. The Russians were clearly planning ahead for the Syrians to cross the Euphrates.

The Syrian army did not rest after the Tiger Force pushed through to 137th Base and the following day it began an operation to break through to Dier Ez Zor airbase, which had been isolated for several months from the main Syrian garrison in the city. A contingent of around 50 Lebanese Hizbullah fighters joined the final breakthrough operation on 9th September. Russian Su-25SM carried out several low-level rocket attacks on the final positions, while Tiger Force tanks gave covering fire. Then the Syrian soldiers and Hizbullah fighters simply walked through the bomb and shell scarred landscape to make the link-up.

A large contingent of Tiger Force troops, supported by 5th Corps troops, were also sent north along the western bank of the Euphrates to clear it of Jihadis. They met resistance at several villages but deployed heavy artillery and air strikes from L-39 strike jets to clear them out until the Islamic State fighter staged a last stand at Ma'adan on 24th September. Footage from Russian journalists who travelled with the Tiger Force showed the town had suffered heavy damage and there were a couple of destroyed tanks and vehicles on the outskirts. However, news and social-media imagery from inside the town did not show more than a handful of dead bodies. The Islamic State fighters had got away over the Euphrates.

As the Syrian troops broke through to Dier Ez Zor city, on the eastern bank of the Euphrates the Kurdish YPG and their allies started their own offensive, with US air support, to clear Islamic State from positions down to the Iraqi border. This region contained several large oil and gas fields and the Damascus government was keen to make sure than their troops - not the US-backed SDF -captured them.

The size of the SDF advance was revealed when the Russians on 24th September released a set of 12 satellite images showing the positions of US Special Forces and SDF vehicles in the east of Dier Ez Zor. The images showed the US and SDF forces arrayed in six main fighting positions and compounds astride the main road south from al-Hasakah to Dier Ez Zor city. This included some 25 Hummers, around 50 armed pick-up trucks, five Cougar mine-protected vehicles, 10 mini buses and one heavy-equipment transporter. Three of the Cougars were based in a defended compound that contained communications equipment, suggesting this was a command post for US advisors. The Cougars were routinely used by US advisors in SDF territory. The number of vehicles suggested a combined force of between 400 and 500 US and SDF personnel were involved in the operation in Dier Ez Zor province. The tension between the Moscow and US boiled over on 16th September when the Americans accused the Russians of bombing a SDF position on the eastern bank of the Euphrates, close to Dier Ez Zor city, which injured several Kurdish fighters.

The operation to cross the Euphrates now began, with Syrian troops striking out from Dier Ez Zor airbase to capture a stretch of river bank a few kilometres away. Russian television journalists filmed General Zahreddine organising the night time operation on 18th September which saw the bridging column rushed forward to the river bank as soon as reports came in from the assault troops that the bridging site was secure. The PTS-M amphibious vehicles carried the first assault troops of the 4th Division across the river and then the PMP ferries were launched into the river to begin ferrying T-55 tanks, MT-LB armoured troop carriers and armed pick-up trucks across. This was the first combat assault river crossing ever carried out by the Syrian army in its history, which made it all the more remarkable.

Analysis of the video imagery broadcast on the Russia 1 and Russia 24 networks, as well as still images posted on social media, indicated the crossing point was 10 kilometres south of Dier Ez Zor city, near to the villages of Sabhah and Marrat. At the same time, the Syrian state news agency, SANA, reported that government troops had launched another amphibious operation to seize Sakr island, directly across the Euphrates from Dier Ez Zor city.

The urgency of building up the bridgehead was not lost of Russian Lieutenant-General Valery Asapov, who was the senior advisor with the Syrian 5th Corps. Russian journalists filmed him at the bridging site helping to load ferries with vehicles and supplies.

No doubt Islamic State commanders realized the danger posed by the Syrian bridgehead and they mobilized their fighters to surround the bridging site. In one of the most bizarre incidents of the Syrian war, the Islamic State drone bomber squadron was sent to attack the bridging site. The Jihadi news agency Amaq subsequently released a video of one of its drones dropping a mortar bomb on a Syrian PMP ferry on 20th September. It hit the ferry but none of the crew appeared to be killed or injured. On 24th September the Russian Ministry of Defence announced that General Asapov and a senior Russian colonel had been killed in a mortar attack in Dier Ez Zor. There is a strong suspicion that they were killed in one of the drone strikes on the bridging site.

In the face of fanatical Islamic State resistance, the Russians realized that the Syrians needed to speed up the movement of troops and supplies across the Euphrates. A proper bridge was needed. Moscow responded by dispatching a Russian army bridging unit and its equipment to Syria by air. A video of at least two PMM-2M amphibious bridge/ferry vehicles being unloaded from a giant Russian Aerospace Force Antonov An-124-100 Ruslan strategic airlifter at Hmeinyan airbase in Syria was released by the Free Syria News blog on 24th September. Other images appeared at the same time of a convoy of bridging equipment moving in a convoy escorted by Russian BTR armoured troop carriers through the desert to Dier Ez Zor. Russian army engineers then set to work building a MARM road bridge over the Euphrates for their Syrian allies. This soon came under Islamic State drone attack.

Video footage broadcast by Moscow-based Channel 1 on 25th September showed smoke generators in action around the bridge in a bid to hide the crossing site from Islamic State surveillance. A Russian army engineer officer was interviewed at the scene describing the work of his soldiers to build the bridge over the Euphrates to help Syrian troops expand their bridgehead on the eastern bank of the river.

The Head of the Russian Defence Ministry's Road Service, Vladimir

Burovtsev, was quoted by the TASS news agency, saying "unmanned aerial vehicles were used [against the troops building the bridge]. Explosive substances and grenades were falling on us from the air during the installation work. However, we have no losses. No [soldiers were] injured or affected. Everything was erected in the set terms."

Burovtsev said the bridge was 210 metres long and took the Russian engineers two days to build. At the bridging site, which analysis of the video imagery indicated was at the same location used by the Syrian army on 18th September to make their initial crossing of the Euphrates, Russian troops were also seen using the PMM-2M self-propelled amphibious ferries to assist in the crossing operation.

The dispatching of the bridging equipment to the Euphrates was only part of a ramping-up in deliveries of vehicles, equipment and ammunition to Syria during the autumn of 2017. At a conference in Moscow in November 2017, the Russian defence minister Sergei Shoygu said around 2,000 tons of cargo was being delivered to Syria by air and sea on a daily basis, co-ordinated by the National Centre for State Defence Control. The Turkish ship-watchers in Istanbul reported five Russian landing ships moving south through the Bosphorus in October, as well as a large chartered roll-on roll-off ship, the Alexander Tkachenko, which was photographed with her top deck crammed full of green-painted trucks. A set of photographs was posted online showing that the ship's cargo decks were also full of military vehicles, including utility vehicles, trucks and T-72 tanks. A commercial satellite photograph of Tartus on 21st October showed the Russian Ropucha-class landing ship, the Tsezar Kunikov, berthed in the port and more than 20 large trucks parked down the dock awaiting to be loaded. These included several low loaders ready to move large items of cargo.

Across eastern Syria, Islamic State now embarked on a series of raids against both government troops and US-supported Syrian Democratic Forces (SDF) fighters to try to slow down and turn back their advances. The biggest raids against Syrian troops took place on 28th September with a series of attacks by mobile columns in sports-utility vehicles, backed by BMP armoured vehicles, against the main road linking Arak in Homs province with Dier Ez Zor city. Small settlements along the road were briefly captured and the town of Sukhnah partially surrounded until Syrian reserve units counter-attacked and re-opened the road. The raiders overran Syrian checkpoints and ambushed military vehicles on the road killing dozen soldiers, including 14 Lebanese Hizbullah personnel, and capturing two Russian private security contractors.

To the east of the Euphrates, Islamic State fighters also appear to have launched raids on Kurdish-led SDF forces to the east of the Euphrates. Imagery was released by the Islamic State news agency Amaq on 24th September showing a claimed ambush on an SDF convoy on Al-Khirafi Highway in rural Hasakah province. Further imagery was released by Amaq showing another raid by Islamic State on SDF fighters based near the Jafra oil field on 12th October, including fighting across railway tracks near the facility. All these attacks showed Islamic State vehicle columns, carrying scores of fighters, moving across open desert terrain to deliver dozens of assault troops close to their objective and then taking their opponents by surprise. The bodies of several SDF fighters were shown in the imagery.

At the same time as the Islamic State column was striking at the Tadmur-Arak-Dier Ez Zor road, a group of Jihadi fighters appeared more than 100 kilometres behind Syrian lines to seize the town of Qaraytayn in Homs province. Unlike in the other attacks, the Islamic State fighters appeared to have chosen to try to hold the town in the face of a Syrian operation to set up a cordon around it. It was unclear exactly how the Jihadi column entered the town. Initial Syrian reports claimed "sleeper cells" and "reconciled" former Jihadis relocated to the town from the Arsal pocket on the Syria-Lebanese border were behind the attack. Subsequently, Amaq posted a series of images of columns of Islamic State vehicles heading towards the town and a video showing balaclava-wearing fighters in the town under air attack from a Syrian Sukhoi Su-22 bomber.

The adoption of mobile raiding tactics by the rump Islamic State forces in Syria suggested that they were looking for a way to avoid sharing the fate of their counter-parts in Raqqa, Mosul and the Hawija pocket in Iraq who suffered massive losses to Iraqi or SDF forces after being trapped in pincer moves.

In perhaps the most audacious Islamic State unconventional military operation during the raids against the Arak-Dier Ez Zor road, the Jihadi drone unit was sent to attack the Syrian army main arms depot in Dier Ez Zor city sports stadium on 8th October. A video published by Amaq showed the drone dropping bombs on the stadium and their huge explosions ripping it apart. Imagery posted online by Syrian civilians showed a huge column of smoke rising over the city.

As the battle was unfolding in the Euphrates valley, resistance was ending in the former capital of Islamic State's self-declared Caliphate in Raqqa. It concluded with a ceasefire agreement being struck between the Jihadis and the Kurdish-led Syrian Democratic Forces (SDF) in the city on 14th October. According to the US special forces commander in Syria, US Army Major General James Jarrard, the SDF forces had suffered 434 killed and 905 wounded fighting within Raqqa city since June. These heavy loses made the Kurdish commanders reluctant to suffer any more casualties finishing off the last Islamic State fighters, who were expected to fight to the death, taking hundreds of Kurds with them. So a deal was struck. The 250 remaining fighters, along with more than

3,500 family members, civilian supporters and hostages, were loaded on to local trucks and buses before being driven across north-eastern Syria to be dropped off in the desert close to Islamic State front-line positions near the Omar oil field.

To support the continuing Syrian ground operation across eastern Syria, the Russian military moved to set up a forward base inside Dier Ez Zor city. Commercial satellite imagery from 1st November showed the base inside the city's former police academy, which revealed road blocks at the compound's main gate and more than 20 military vehicles inside including BTR troop carriers, Tigr armoured utility vehicles and large transport trucks. This suggested several hundred troops were operating at the base. The Russian Ministry of Defence had already announced the deployment of a 175-strong de-mining team to Dier Ez Zor and the bridging unit. Russian journalists regularly visited the city and their reports showed several senior Russian officers working with Syrian troops and inspecting what was happening. In a tour de force of information warfare, the Russian army flew a contingent of western journalists around Syria by helicopter, including taking them to a former Islamic State tank repair depot at Uqayribat and then to Dier Ez Zor to see Russian troops delivering humanitarian aid to the citizens of the city. The population all seemed happy to have been rescued by the Syrian and Russian armies.

The final phases of the Dier Ez Zor operation started to unfold in October after the Islamic State raids had been contained. The 17th Division inside Dier Ez Zor city, co-ordinated with units of the 4th Mechanised Division and 5th Corps on the east bank of the Euphrates, in a methodical drive to isolate the last Islamic State fighters inside the city. The 4th Division and 5th Corps then swung north to move up the eastern bank of the Euphrates. The race to capture the Omar oil fields ahead of the SDF was put on hold. It appeared that the Islamic State raids had unsettled Syrian commanders and they wanted to tighten their noose around the remaining Jihadi positions to avoid any more battlefield surprises.

A delegation of Russian officers set out from Dier Ez Zor on 19th October to meet their counter-parts in the YPG at the Conoco oil refinery complex on the eastern bank of the Euphrates. This followed a meeting in Qamishli between the Russians, Syrians and Kurds earlier in the month. The aim was to better co-ordinate their operations and set firmer de-confliction lines as both Syrian and YPG units pushed south along the Euphrates valley towards Abu Kamal. From this point on, friction on the ground between the Syrians and YPG eased considerably, although the Russians and Americans continued to trade rhetorical blows about who was doing the most to fight Islamic State.

In the first week of October, the Tiger Force's Tarmah Regiment, supported by 5th Corps units and a Russian 152mm MSTA-B artillery battery began an encircling operation aimed at capturing the Islamic State's alternative capital at Mayadeen, some 40 kilometres south of Dier Ez Zor on the western bank of the Euphrates. The Syrian column swung 20 kilometres out into the desert and then appeared on the western fringes of the city. Syrian and Russian artillery and rocket crews set up a fire base on a hill overlooking the city, while Tiger Force infantry infiltrated down into the urban area down several gullies. A Russian mobile command-post vehicle could be seen in video imagery of the fire base.

A huge barrage of artillery and rockets, backed with strikes by Russian Su-24Ms and Syrian L-39s, peppered Islamic State positions around the historic Mayadeen citadel, the market and several industrial sites. Over two days, the Tiger Force first cleared the western approaches and then captured the citadel. Colonel Suheil al-Hassan arrived to choreograph the final assault from an observation post on top of the citadel. When its infantry entered the city on 14th October, they met little organised resistance. There were a few dead Islamic State fighters in the streets but the population had long fled. It appeared that the Jihadis had decided to disappear into the desert.

In their haste to escape, the Islamic State fighters left behind one of their largest caches of arms and equipment, which the Tiger Force put on display to Syrian and Russian media. This included more than 1,000 assorted small arms and machine guns, as well as RPG-29 anti-tank weapons, rocket propelled grenades, night vision equipment and five trucks loaded with munitions.

At least six different types of drones were on display including more than 20 hobby drones, which appeared to be Chinese-manufactured DJI Phantom derivatives. One larger hobby drone appeared to be fitted with improvised bomb racks. The imagery showed what appeared to be four indigenous Islamic State drone designs, including one delta wing drone and two conventional take- off and landing drones. These included one part-completed drone that had an estimated fuselage length of two metres. Three hand-launched drones with cameras and payload bays were also on display.

Two T-55 tanks and a T-62 tank bearing the markings of the Islamic State armoured vehicle Workshop south of Raqqa were put on display, along with a Hummer vehicle, a M-46 130mm howitzer, two D-20 152mm howitzers, a truck- mounted 122mm D-20 howitzer and a disassembled, US-made, M-198 155mm howitzer.

A couple of days later, the commander of the Russian forces in Syria, Colonel General Sergei Surovikin, flew into Mayadeen by helicopter to see the arms haul for himself, accompanied by a posse of Russian journalists. Surovikin and Suheil al-Hassan then took the journalists to visit the joint Russian-Syrian command post that had co-ordinated the attack and view a selection of drone "greatest hits" videos from the battle, showing air strikes and artillery fire blasting building after building.

In the aftermath of the successful Mayadeen assault, two parallel operations were launched to finish off the last Islamic State strongholds in the east of Dier Ez Zor city and Abu Kamal. The Tiger Force Taha Regiment was sent to join the Dier Ez Zor assault, which escalated in intensity in the last days of October.

This operation was very violent, with intense artillery and air support hitting the Islamic State positions throughout their enclave. Behind the firepower, the Tiger Force moved forward in their tanks and armoured vehicles, led by armoured bulldozers to clear the earth ramparts built by the Jihadis to block streets throughout their enclave. Syrian air force L-39s were filmed over the city dropping scores of bombs on a daily basis.

Unlike in Mayadeen, the bulk of the Jihadis in the enclave appeared at first to want make a fight of it and it took nearly two weeks for the Syrians to fully clear the city on the western bank of the Euphrates. By 3rd November, the Jihadis final defence line was cleared in the city. Then the Syrians brought up a T-55 bridging tank to allow the Tiger Force assault troops to move onto Kati Island in the middle of the Euphrates. Picking through the ruins of the devastated Islamic State enclave, Russian journalists filmed several dead fighters and dozens of abandoned or destroyed vehicles, including suicide bomb trucks. The Syrian troops reported that many of their enemies had fled across the Euphrates the night before the enclave fell. The Russian ANNA news network filmed the body of a dead fighter floating in the Euphrates that seemed to support the theory that the Jihadis had staged a panic withdrawal.

Over the next three days the Syrians began collecting the abandoned Jihadi hardware and showed it off to the media. The booty included six working T-55 and T-62 tanks and thousands of AK-47 and M-16 assault rifles in pristine condition, as well as several hobby drones.

The final coup de grace against the last Islamic State stronghold in Syria would fall to the Syrian, Hizbullah and Shia militia force that was positioned just outside the T-2 oil-pumping station in the desert some 60 kilometres to the west of Abu Kamal. This front had been static for several weeks but during October it had been reinforced by the T-90 tanks and 2S1 122mm self-propelled guns of the Syrian 4th Mechanised Division, a column of Hizbullah with T-55 tanks, BMP troop carriers, BM-21 rocket launchers and armed pick-up trucks, as well as a contingent of the Afghan Shia Fatemiyoun militia brigade.

Arrayed against them were several Islamic State fighting units, positioned behind earth works or berm fortifications on top of a dominating hill around T-2. There were probably a few hundred fighters blocking the Syria advance and they included several determined would-be suicide bombers equipped with trucks packed with explosives.

The Syrian advance was methodical and ruthless. Artillery and rocket launchers pounded Jihadi berm lines before infantry advanced to clear them out, led by armoured bulldozers to smash through the defender's mine fields. Pro-Syrian and Hizbullah news crews followed the advance and filmed some remarkable footage of Islamic State suicide trucks making forays out of their positions and then being hit by tank fire or guided anti-tank missiles.

This wing of the advance received strong support from the Iranian Revolutionary Guards Corps who had advisors and forward air controllers on the ground with the advancing columns. Hizbullah's media wing released video reports containing imagery from Iranian Shahed-129 armed drones attacking what it said were Islamic State infantry and pick-up trucks fighting from berm lines.

Further air support was provided by the Syrian L-39 light strike jets flying from their forward operating site at Palmyra . This squadron was manned by some of the most highly trained and experienced Syrian pilots and over the previous two months they had been filmed making dramatic low-level strikes along the Euphrates valley.

The advance on Abu Kamal was co-ordinated with the Iraqi army to the east, who simultaneously launched an offensive towards the border city of Al Qaim along the southern bank of the Euphrates creating a pincer movement against the Jihadis.

As all these ground manoeuvres were unfolding, the Russian air force and navy joined the fray, hitting Islamic State targets in eastern Syria over five consecutive days as fighting intensified around the last major pocket of Jihadi fighters in the country. This would be the most intense period of strategic air and missile attacks since the major four-day-long bombing and missile offensive in November 2015, after the loss of the Russian airliner over Egypt. To make this possible, the Russian Aerospace Force's Long Range Aviation branch had re-activated its temporary Tupolev Tu-22M3 squadron at Mozdok in North Ossetia with six bombers.

A combination of submarine-launched Kalibr cruise missiles and Tu-22M3 long-range bomber strikes hit a series of targets around Abu Kamal from 31st October. The first attack involved Kalibr missiles fired from the Kilo class submarine Veliki Novgorod, in the Mediterranean, on 31st October. "Three missiles wiped out command centres, a fortified stronghold and its manpower and armoured vehicles, and a large weapons depot near Abu Kamal," said a Russian Ministry of Defence statement.

On the following day, six Tu-22M3 long-range bombers of the Russian Aerospace Forces flew south from Mozdok over Iran and Iraq to hit targets near Abu Kamal using dumb, or iron bombs. Moscow's defence ministry said the bombers hit "strongholds, ammunition and armament depots of insurgents."

On 2nd November, six more Tu-22M3 bombers carried out further attacks on more Islamic State strongholds and ammunition depots around Abu Kamal. A day later, six more Tu-22M3 sorties were launched against Abu Kamal, along with a further six Kalibr cruise missiles fired from the Kilo class submarine, the Kolpino, in the eastern Mediterranean. The missiles and bombs were said to have hit Islamic State "fortifications, weapons and ammunition depots, manpower and command centres". Sukhoi Su-24 and Su-34 strike aircraft, flying from within Syria, also joined this operation. The strike operation continued on 4th November with a further mission by the Tu-22M3 force, which hit "armament and ammunition depots, and ISIS command centres" in Abu Kamal.

The Russian Ministry of Defence never published any drone imagery of the impact of the Tu-22M3 strikes so it is difficult to assess whether they found their intended targets or what damaged they cause. From Russian imagery of the aircraft taking part in the raids, it seems that each Tu-22M3 dropped a stick of six 500lb or 229kg unguided bombs. It would seem that the Russian were aiming to put 36 bombs in a small area to shock and disorientate any Islamic State fighters caught in the bomb zone. Social-media footage from on the ground during one of the Russian bomber strikes showed a line of bombs detonating in close proximity and creating huge smoke clouds. This effect and the lack of resistance to the Syrian and Hizbullah advance towards Abu Kamal suggests the Tu-22M3 strikes had the intended impact.

Over the first week of November, the Syrian, Hizbullah and Shia militia columns relentlessly blasted their way past the outgunned and outnumbered Islamic State defence lines until they were positioned a few kilometres outside Abu Kamal. The Syrian state news agency, SANA, announced the capture of Abu Kamal on 9th November and said government troops and their allies had also "established control over wide areas on the Syrian-Iraqi borders and ensured the security of the roads between the two brotherly countries [of Iraq and Syria]".

The Syrian army command said that the city had fallen after its troops had engaged "in fierce battles in which large numbers of terrorists were killed including ISIS leaders." It said army units "are still pursuing ISIS terrorists who fled away in different directions to eliminate the rest of the terrorists' dens in al-Badia (desert) after destroying their positions and equipment."

The statement said that "continuous co-ordination between the Syrian and Iraqi armies has played a big role in clearing large swathes of the border area."

Video imagery released by Hizbullah's media organization on 9th November showed columns of Syrian and Hizbullah T-55 tanks, BMP armoured vehicles and armed pick-up trucks approaching the north-western outskirts of Abu Kamal. A distinctive radio tower in the western edge of the town could be seen in the video. The assault troops did not appear to come under any type of fire as they moved into the western suburbs of the town.

The claims of victory from SANA, however, proved premature, and within hours, Jihadi anti-tank missile teams were picking off Hizbullah vehicles on the outskirts of Abu Kamal, stalling the assault operation. The Syrians and Hizbullah brought up heavy 122mm and 152mm artillery as well as BM-21 rocket launchers to bombard the town. In imagery of this fire base, several Russian command-post vehicles and a satellite-communications antenna could be seen in video filmed by a BBC News team indicating that Russian officers were instrumental in pulling together the various surveillance, artillery and air assets committed to the operation to take Abu Kamal. Russia's Tu-22M3 squadron was called into action again, flying three big strike missions against the town on 15th, 17th and 18th November. By 18th November, Hizbullah posted the first imagery from inside Abu Kamal suggesting it had at last fallen. Islamic State could still strike back, despite the heavy pressure it was under. On 13th November a squad of Russian-speaking suicide bombers bluffed their way past the Syrian guards at Dier Ez Zor airbase and reached the flight-line. They detonated their bombs, destroying or badly damaging four L-39 strike jets.

The final fall of Abu Kamal signalled the end of Islamic State's control of urban areas in Syria and Iraq and the end of conventional combat operations against the Jihadi group. In October 2017, the US military was estimating that between 3,000 and 7,000 Islamic State fighters remained around Abu Kamal but they did not appear to have fought to the last man in the town, preferring to flee into the desert to the north and east. The Islamic State's remaining fighters and leaders went on the run in small groups. Some made a last stand in a string of small towns along the Euphrates, between Mayadeen and Abu Kamal, into December but by the end of 2017 the Jihadi fighters had ceased to put up any organised resistance.

Chapter 21
Russia's War in Syria Assessed

In October 2017 US-backed allies finally captured Raqqa - the so-called capital of the Islamic State – after a four-month-long siege. A few weeks before, Russian-supported Syrian troops broke the Jihadi group's three-year- long siege of the eastern city of Dier Ez Zor. Islamic State fighters seemed in full retreat across Syria. The Jihadi enclave inside Dier Ez Zor city finally fell on 3rd November and on 9th November the Syrian army and its allies began the assault on the group's last urban strong-hold, Abu Kamal.

Moscow at last had good news to celebrate from Syria. The Russian President flew to Syria on 11th December to declare victory. A beaming Vladimir Putin told his soldiers on the tarmac at Hmeinyan airbase, "in just over two years, Russia's armed forces and the Syrian army have defeated the most battle-hardened group of international terrorists. The conditions for a political solution under the auspices of the United Nations have been created."

Putin then announced that many of the soldiers and airmen would be returning home, declaring, "The Motherland awaits you." It was a huge publicity stunt. Only a third of the Russian aircraft at the base would return home and Moscow's remaining troops and jets continued to support on-going Syrian operations into 2018.

Yet only two years before, the situation had been very different. Syria's President Bashar al-Assad's depleted armed forces were in retreat across the country in the face of advances by both Islamic State and an alliance of anti-government rebel groups.

For Moscow, intervention in Syria came with none of the political complications faced by the Americans, who struggled to reconcile their desire to fight the Jihadis of Islamic State with their previous preoccupation with deposing President Assad. Putin viewed Assad as a long-established Russian ally and he was not going to allow the Syrian leader and his government to fall victim to what Moscow dubbed "another US-sponsored regime-change operation". The overthrow of Libyan leader Muammar Gaddafi in 2011 and the fall of Ukrainian President Viktor Yanukovych in 2014, added to Putin's resolve to back Russia's friend-in-need in Damascus.

Putin dispatched air, naval and specialist ground units to Syria in September 2015 and organised a coalition of allies across the Middle East to back Russian intervention. Iran and Lebanon's Hizbullah both sent military advisors and ground troops, as well as mobilising and training Shia militia fighters from across the Middle East to fight in Syria. Iraq's government - nominally a US ally - also agreed to open its airspace to Russia aircraft and cruise missile strikes. Within Syria, the Russians made no distinction between Islamic State and so-called "moderate rebels". They were all trying to overthrow the Assad government and needed to be defeated.

The Russians had to build up a coalition of local allies within Syria. Russian officers and advisors were attached to every major Syrian Arab Army headquarters. Special forces operatives and forward air controllers were sent into the field with Syrian units during major operations to co-ordinate air and other support. Joint headquarters also had to be established to bring together Syrian, Russian, Iranian, Hizbullah and other allied contingents.

Moscow's operation saw jets and helicopters based inside Syria flying 34,000 sorties by the end of 2017. It also involved the employment of strategic bombers of the Russian Aerospace Force's Long Range Aviation, cruise missile firing submarines, surface warships and embarked strike aircraft on the Russian navy's only aircraft carrier, the Admiral Kuznetsov. The co-ordination of strategic assets required high level work across almost every branch of the Russian armed forces.

To co-ordinate and control all its military operations in Syria, the Russians set up a headquarters in Damascus headed by a Colonel General-ranked officer, which is equivalent to a western four-star officer. He controlled a number of force elements. The largest and most prominent was the Russian Air Group at Hmeinyan airbase, which operated fast jets including Sukhoi Su-24M bombers, Su-34 multi-role strike jets, Su-25SM ground attack aircraft, Su-30SM and Su-35S fighters. The air groups also boasted Forpost unmanned aerial vehicles, derived from the Israel Aircraft Industries Searcher 2 product, Tupolev Tu-214 multi-sensor surveillance aircraft, Il-20M signals-intelligence aircraft and Beriev A-50 airborne radar and command aircraft. A contingent of Russian attack helicopters, including Mil Mi-28s, Mi-24/35s and Kamov Ka-52s are also based in Syria at a number of forward operating locations close to battle fronts. An air operations centre was set up at Hmeinyan airbase to control all Russian air operations in Syria, as well as co-ordinating long-range cruise missile strikes into the country launched from aircraft, ships and submarines. In response to the loss of a Su-24 to a Turkish F-16 in November 2015, the Russians made the first deployment of S-400 strategic anti-aircraft missiles to Syria, although they were not used in action.

The Russian Ground Forces played a major role in the Syria operations. The Spetsnaz or special forces received considerable prominence for their work as forward air controllers and battlefield advisors with Syria troops. An artillery group equipped with 2S65 MSTA-B 152mm towed howitzers, BM-27 Uragan multiple-launch rocket systems, TOS-1A thermobaric-warhead-tipped rocket launchers and Urlan-10 hand-launched mini unmanned aerial vehicles operated on several Syrian battlefields.

Shore-based Bastion anti-ship missiles also saw action in the land attack mode in 2016. KBM 9K720 Iskander theatre ballistic missiles were spotted at Hmeinyan airbase in early 2016 but no reports have emerged of them being fired in anger. KBP Instrument Design Bureau Pantsir-S1 point air defence systems were also deployed to Syria.

One of the most innovative units was the Russian Centre of Reconciliation of Warring Parties in the Syrian Arab Republic, which was heavily involved in negotiating cease fires, organising the evacuation of rebel fighters and trying to persuade tribal fighters to join the government army. Four battalions of military police were eventually sent to Syria to act as force protection for the reconciliation centre personnel operating throughout the country. A Russian training mission also worked with the Syrian army, building up several new units including the 5th Corps during 2016 and 2017.

Russia's intervention in Syria saw many combat firsts, with many pieces of hardware getting their operational debut. These included the Novator Design Bureau Kalibr ship and submarine-launched cruise missiles, Raduga Design Bureau Kh-55 and Kh-101 air-launched cruise missiles, Tupolev Tu-95 and Tu-160 Strategic bombers, Su-30, Su-34 and Su-35 tactical fighters, the Su-57 5th generation stealth aircraft, Ka-52 and Mi-28 attack helicopters, Su-33 carrier-borne strike fighters and the Admiral Kuznetsov aircraft carrier.

While the deployment of big so-called "double digit" Russian S-300 and S-400 SAMs attracted considerable attention they have yet to be used in anger in Syria. In August 2017 the Russian military claimed their Pantsir S-1 systems had shot down 12 hostile unmanned aerial vehicles in Syria. GAZ Tigr light armoured utility and Kamaz Typhoon mine protected ambush resistant (MRAP) were used extensively in Syria. A significant first for the Russian army was the airlifting of MARM road-bridge and PMM-2M sets to Syria to build a bridge across the Euphrates in September 2017, while under attack from bombs dropped from Islamic State hobby drones.

This surge in operational deployment of high-end equipment to Syria boosted Russian arms sales around the world, with orders from Algeria, India, China, Iran and Indonesia flowing to Moscow.

When comparing the performance of American and Russian in hardware in Syria the issue of precision needs to be addressed. The US-led coalition placed great stress on its precision-strike operations, from both manned aircraft and General Atomics MQ-1/9 Predator/Reaper unmanned aerial vehicles, as a means to reduce civilian casualties to an absolute minimum. This no civilian casualty approach has characterised US-led air operations throughout the Syrian campaign. The widespread employment of MQ-1s and MQ-9s to provide persistent surveillance of Islamic State territory also allowed the US-led coalition to identify, track and then strike at high-value targets, including several individuals accused of being involved in the planning and execution of terrorist attacks in Western Europe.

The Russians made repeated claims that they had also struck at Islamic State and other rebel leadership targets in Syria but Russian fast jet aircraft do not appear to have made extensive use of precision guided munitions. Out of their workhorse strike jets – the Su-24, Su-25 and Su-34 – only the Su-34 routinely seemed to employ precision guided weapons. The older Su-24s and Su-25s rely on "dumb" bombs, albeit guided by recently upgraded bombing computers using the Russian GLONASS system that is comparable to the US Global Positioning Satellite (GPS) system. At least one Su-24 was photographed using a hand-held GPS receiver mounted on its cockpit dashboard. While western laser or GPS-guided weapons routine achieve accuracy measures in a couple of metres CEP or circular error of probability, the bombing computers used on the most up-to-date variants of the Su-24 or Su-25 have a CEP of between 10 and 25 metres, according Russian aerospace sources and analysis of bomb damage assessment videos from Syria released by the Moscow Ministry of Defence. While this level of accuracy provides a useful capability against large buildings, artillery positions, convoys of soft-skinned vehicles in the open it is more problematic when employed against high-value targets, such as individual people or vehicles. There are also widespread reports of civilian casualties from Russian air attacks in Syria.

The Russians, however, brought a degree of precision to their air campaign in Syria by the widespread use of Forpost unmanned aerial vehicles to monitor targets for air strikes. A kill chain established by Russian air commanders who pipe the video imagery from Forpost tactical UAVs into their operations centre at Hmeinyan airbase. Senior officers then made engagement decisions and issued attack orders to pilots. The Russian kill chain was far in advance of that used by the US and its allies in the 1991 Iraq war and the 1999 Kosovo conflict. It some respects the Russian command system was even in advance of the US counterpart in the 2003 invasion of Iraq. While the Russian kill chain appears not as sophisticated or mature as that operated by its contemporary western counterparts, it was undoubtedly effective and provided Moscow's air commanders with a distinct battlefield advantage that played an important part in many battlefield successes in Syria.

While the successes of Moscow's military were lauded by the Russian government and media, the operation in Syria highlighted many shortcomings. The Russians appear to have been dependent on the Forpost drone but they did not have many of them. The repeated ability of Islamic State fighters to appear out of the desert and surprise Syrian outposts, suggests that the Russians had yet to field a wide-area surveillance system such as the US E-8 JSTARS or the British Sentinel R.1 airborne stand-off radar aircraft. The size of the Russian contingent in Syria and its structure was limited by the reluctance of Moscow to deploy conscript soldiers. The need to constantly rotate contract or professional soldiers to Syria, as well as in eastern Ukraine, meant there were never enough of them to go around. This in turn prompted Moscow to turn to private military contractors to fill the ranks of its training teams working with Syrian army units. The Russian Aerospace Force never appears to have deployed more than 40 tactical jets to Syria at any point during the campaign, suggesting it suffered from resource constraints. Moscow did not make an open ended, unlimited commitment of military forces.

At a tactical and operational level, Moscow can claim its military achieved important objectives in the face of predictions of failure. US President Obama famously predicted that the Russian intervention in Syria would end in failure and bog Moscow's troops down in a Vietnam-style quagmire. The Russians, however, now point to the successes of their Syrian allies in driving rebel fighters from Eastern Aleppo in December 2016 and breaking the siege of Dier Ez Zor in September 2017. A few weeks later the commander of Russian forces in Syria, Colonel General Sergey Surovikin, was present to watch Syrian troops storm the town of Mayadeen, which served as the Islamic State's alternative capital after Raqqa was besieged in June 2017.

The cost of this intervention has been high by western standards but nowhere near those incurred in the Georgian war of 2008, where Russia lost more than 150 troops killed in action, or the Chechen conflicts in the 1990s that left more than 10,000 Russian soldiers dead. The Russians have owned up to losing more than 40 service personnel in combat or accidents in Syria, along with the loss of four aircraft and six helicopters up to the end of 2017.

Moscow's intervention in Syria has had a profound impact on western military officers who observed it first hand in the Middle East. While London, Paris and Washington routinely lambast the Russians for the civilian casualties caused by their air strikes and support for the Damascus government, in private many British and US officers are less judgemental. Some express admiration for the audacity and daring of the Russian campaign. "It just goes to show what you can do when you are not been second guessed by the bureaucracy we have," commented one British army officer who served in Middle East in 2017.

Such comments don't fit in with the strategic communications narrative, espoused by US-led coalition so few serving western military officers have little meaningful to say in public about the Russian intervention. This started to thaw in January 2018 when British Air Commodore Johnny Stringer gave a briefing on his tour as UK's Air Component Commander in the Middle East in the year up to October 2017. One of his main points was that Russian information operations during its intervention in Syria have often left US-led coalition countries struggling to respond.

He said overcautious civilian and military leaders had regularly left the Russians and other actors in control of the "information space" in the Syria-Iraq theatre. "Dignified silences will be filled by other people," he said. "If we are not willing to operate [in the information space] we will cede it to other people."

Stringer said Russian operations in Syria were "fascinating" and described how they carried out sophisticated messaging that rapidly changed. The Russian Ministry of Defence repeatedly uploaded YouTube video clips of long-range bomber strikes, unmanned aerial vehicle operations, and Kalibr cruise missiles being launched from naval vessels to give the impression they were militarily equivalent to the West, but Stringer said the reality was that 90% of Russian airstrikes in Syria involved unguided weapons.

Stringer said Russian information operations were highly nuanced to win over audiences, with 80% of the output being factually correct, but the remaining 20% ranged from "the opaque to inaccurate". "They want people to give them the benefit of the doubt", he said. "The Russians think that people are suffering from compassion fatigue and that the ends justify the means."

He also described the cyber and electronic warfare environment in Syria as "vibrant", noting that satellite imagery of the main Russian airbase in western Syria showed several electronic warfare systems had been deployed there over the past two and half years.

"Since the 1990s we [in the West] thought we had the sole rights to the electro-magnetic spectrum," he said. "The electro-magnetic environment never went away. Everyone now plays in that environment."

Western armed forces and governments struggled at times to deal with the information operations of the Russians and other actors in the Syria-Iraq theatre. "This is a difficult space to get your arms around – traditional military education is not suited to it," Stringer said.

Many US and British officers working in coalition headquarters in the Middle just could not get their minds round the fact that the Russian officer who they dealt with professionally on a daily basis to de-conflict air operations over Syria had completely different values and attitudes.

Stringer recalled disbelief in the coalition air headquarters in Qatar when the Russians released satellite imagery of US special forces positions in eastern Syria in September 2017. "There was a shaking of heads and people were saying "how could they do this to us"," he said. "Some of my colleagues were outraged, saying "that's not fair". But you have just got to get over it."

Countering Russian information operation it appears requires a whole new mindset and understanding of the "new rules of the game".

The strategic impacts of the Russian intervention are still unfolding. So by the end of 2017 it would seem that Moscow has gained more than Washington. President Assad's government seems more secure than ever. His army has regained control over all of Syria's major cities, nearly three quarters of its population and looks set to regain the majority of its territory in the near future. The moderate rebels are in disarray and preoccupied with defending their last enclaves rather than advancing on Damascus. Russia is dominating the Astana peace process, which is the most active set of negotiations to resolve the conflict. Moscow has re-emerged as major player in the Middle East region and is set to have significant military bases in Syria for the foreseeable future. Russian companies are playing a large role in rebuilding Syria's post war economy and are gaining extensive access to the country's oil and gas reserves in its desert regions and under the eastern Mediterranean. President Putin will no doubt be happy that his Syrian adventure has paid off.

The Syrian intervention told the world a lot about the Russian armed forces. The the most interesting takeaway is that the senior leadership of the Russian armed forces have regained their self-confidence and, perhaps more importantly, their self-respect. During Soviet times, the famous World War Two STAVKA, or headquarters of Main Command of the Armed Forces of the USSR, was rightly credited with masterminding the Red Army's victory over Nazi Germany. The collapse of the Soviet Union and the bungled wars in Chechnya in the 1990s severely damaged the reputation of Russian generals.

While the war in Syria is no way comparable to World War Two, Russia's intervention has been carried out with professionalism and some élan. Russian generals crafted a complex and multifaceted campaign plan that drew in many diverse components in the midst of a confusing and fast-moving battlefield. The Russians also showed an ability to learn from their mistakes and adjust their plans when unexpected events occurred. Repeatedly, the Russians and their Syrian allies surprised and out-manoeuvred their battlefield opponents and their US-led rivals. The January 2016 offensive north of Aleppo, the June 2017 advance to the Iraqi border and the crossing of the Euphrates in September 2017 were all daring and dramatic battlefield moves. On top of this, the actual Russian deployment in September 2015 was a text-book exercise in strategic surprise. Russia will be a formidable rival in future international crisis. At the heart of the Russian success has been their far better understanding of Syria compared to the US and its allies. Moscow's men had a head start from the days of their old Soviet-era alliance with the country, but their commanders on the ground soon realised that the morale and motivation of their opponents was in many cases weak and that this could be exploited. The US and its western allies, particularly Britain and France, became locked into the mindset that Assad and his government was a Saddam Hussein-style "Republic of Fear" and that Syria's people were just waiting for the right moment to rise up in revolt. This might have been the case in 2011 or 2012 but by 2016 the dynamics of the war had changed.

In the end the majority of Syria's population, along with the rump of its army, rallied to the Damascus government's cause. While Russia's troops contributed to several battlefield victories, perhaps their most important role was psychological – by its intervention, Moscow created a political and military dynamic that sent the message that Assad was going to win. This boosted the morale of government troops to keep them fighting after years of defeats and setbacks, while Assad's opponents realised that no outside powers were going to help them and that their revolution was doomed. In 21st Century conflicts, being able to understand this aspect of warfare is a critical war-winning skill. The Russians seem to have it in spades. They also appear to be willing to take risks to achieve psychological advantage on the battlefield.

When the former UK defence secretary Michael Fallon famously dubbed the Russian aircraft carrier, the Admiral Kuznetsov, the "ship of shame" because of its role in the 2016 Battle for Aleppo, his ranting highlighted the bankruptcy of western policy in Syria. Fallon was prepared to moralize and pontificate but in the end he was not willing to lift a finger to translate his outrage into action. Not surprisingly, the people of Syria could see that western backing for the rebel cause was cynical and ultimately hollow. No matter how many times western leaders complained at the United Nations in New York about Russian jets bombing civilians or the war crimes of Assad, on the ground the Syrian population could see that the rebels were a lost cause. A swift victory for the Damascus government was seen by many Syrians as the best way to bring the agony of the civil war to an end and avoid the country being overrun by Jihadis. In the end, the US, Britain and France ended up as observers of the Syrian conflict and were unable to shape events in their favour. But politicians in Washington, London and Paris could feel good about themselves for being morally superior to the "cynical" Russians, who were accused of acting as if the "ends justified the means" and not having any moral scruples.

Despite the warm glow of success, the Russian intervention in Syria also highlighted some other trends. First of all, much of Russia's military hardware is still old and the country is struggling to find money to replace it in significant quantities. Western technology, such as the Forpost drones, was instrumental to the Russian success in Syria. Russia was reluctant to deploy its conscript soldiers to Syria, indicating that Putin and other Russian leaders will be unwilling to use the country's mainly conscript ground forces in future foreign adventures. One notable feature of their Syrian intervention was a strong reluctance on the part of the Russians to get into a shooting war with the US, Turkey or Israel. This suggests that Moscow is not inevitably set on starting a military conflict with the West in the Middle East, the Baltic States or elsewhere. Putin has little interest in starting World War Three. His interests are limited to protecting his allies and gaining economic advantage. In areas where western troops were deployed in Syria, Russian forces kept well away from them. Russia proved that it will exploit power vacuums but did not want to bring the current international world order down. Putin's Russia might crave the respect and power of the old Soviet Union but it is not a Communist revolutionary state bent on global conflict.

Appendix I
Order of Battle
Group of Russian Forces in Syrian Arab Republic, 2015-2017

In early 2016, some 5,000 Russian military personnel were in Syria. By end of 2017 this had grown to nearly 6,000 personnel. Most these personnel served between three and four month tours of duty in Syria. The President Putin said in December 2017 that some 48,000 Russian personnel served in Syria between 2015 and the end of 2017.

Headquarters Group of Russian Forces in Syrian Arab Republic (GRFS) Based in Damascus, most likely inside the Russian Embassy compound. Commanded by a colonel general or lieutenant general ranked officer.

Commanders of Group of Russian Forces in Syria
•Aug 15-Jul 16   Colonel General Alexander Dvornikov (formerly the deputy commander of Central Military District, then promoted to commander Southern Military District)
•Jul 16-Dec 16 Lieutenant General Alexander Zhuravlev (former GRFS Chief of Staff up to Jul 16)
•Dec 16-Apr 17 Colonel General Andrei Kartapolov (former Chief of the Main Operational Directorate of the General Staff, them promoted commander Western Military District)
•Apr 17 - Dec 17 Colonel General Sergei Surovikin. (Commander Eastern Military District)
•Dec 17- ?? Colonel General Alexander Zhuravlev (for second time, also commander Eastern Military District)
Chiefs of Staff Group of Russian Forces in Syria
•Sept 16 to Jul 17 Lieutenant General Alexander Zhuravlev
•?? -Nov 17 Lieutenant General Alexander Lapin (promoted to command Central Military District)

Centre for Reconciliation of Warring Parties in Syrian Arab Republic
Located Hmeinyan in Latakia province, under the command of lieutenant general. Some 200 personnel are reported assigned to the centre. It has established forward operating bases in Aleppo, Homs and Dier Ez Zor provinces. It has also co-ordinated the deployment of Russian mine clearing and medical units across Syria.

Commanders Centre for Reconciliation of Opposing Sides in Syrian Arab Republic
•Jan 16-Jul 16? Lieutenant General Sergei Kuralenko (former commander intelligence centre with Iraq and Iran in Baghdad)
•Jul 16-Dec 16 Lieutenant General Vladimir Savchenko
•Nov 17 Lieutenant-General Sergei Kuralenko
Chief of Staff Centre for Reconciliation of Opposing Sides in Syria Arab Republic
•Late 2017 Major General Yevgeny Poplavsky (met leader of YPG in Dier Ez

Zor in December 2017)

Aerospace and Missile Defence Group

It operates one S-300 and two S-400 surface-to-air missile systems, as well as detachments of Pantsir-S1 point defence systems. S-400 and Pantsir-S1 have been located at Hmeinyan airbase since November 2015. A second S-400/Pantsir site was set up at Masya in Hama province in the summer of 2017. A S-300 Syria was deployed to Syria in October 2016 and it was since been identified at a site near Tarus naval base. Pantsir-S1 teams have also been identified deployed to Palmyra and Kweires airbase.

Artillery Group

A brigade-sized artillery group has been deployed in Syria since September 2015, comprising sub-units equipped with the MSTA-B 2A65 towed 152mm howitzer, TOS-1A thermobaric multiple launch rocket launchers, BM-30/9K58 Smerch multiple launch rocket system and Orlan-10 mini unmanned aerial vehicle. A detachment of 9K720 Iskander theatre ballistic missiles have been based at Hmeinyan airbase since early 2016. Artillery units identified as deployed troops to Syria include the 120th and 291st Artillery Brigades. The TOS-1A have been operated by the 29th NBC Regiment.

Security Detachment

This is located at Hmeinyan and is based around a infantry battalion, supported by a detachment of T-90 tanks and BTR armoured vehicles. These units have been provided by the 18th, 21st, 27th, 28th, 34th, 74th and 136th Motor Rifle Brigades, as well as the 7th Tank Brigade.

Military Police Battalions

Four military police battalons deployed to various locations around Syria to support the activities of the Reconciliation Centre. The first unit, of Chechen MPs, deployed to Aleppo in December 2016. During 2017 this was expanded to four battalions, each of around 400 troops, based in de-escalation zones in Idlib province, Homs province, the Damascus region and southern Syria. Units have been drawn from MP units recruited from the Caucasus region, including Dagestan and Ingushetia. One unit was withdrawn in December 2017

Special Forces Group

This provides teams of combat advisors and forward air controllers to operate with front line Syrian units. Drawn from units of the Special Forces of the Main Directorate of the General Staff of the Russian Armed Forces, known as the Spetsnaz GRU. Units identified as provide personnel to work in Syria include the 3rd Guards, 9th,22nd and 346th Spetsnaz Reconnaissance Brigades.

Training Mission to Syria Arab Army

This is headed by a lieutenant general ranked officer and comprises several training teams based in Syrian garrisons and advisory teams who work with Syrian army units in the field. Russian private military companies also assist in this work.

Commanders Training Mission to Syria Arab Army

• Summer 2016 Major General Sergey Sevryukov (worked with Ba'ath Bri-

gades in Aleppo summer 2016, then takes over Command 5th Corps)
•?? To Feb 17 Major General Peter Milyuhin (wounded near T-4 by IED)
•Feb 17 to Aug 17 Lt Gen Valery Asapov (former chief of staff to Centre for Reconciliation then commander 5th Corps, killed in action in Dier Ez Zor Sept 17)

Air Force Group in Syrian Arab Republic

Operated mainly from Hmeinyan airbase in Latakia province, where the Russian air operations centre is also located. Commanded by a major general. Forward operating bases for aircraft and helicopters have been established at Shayrat, T-4, Palmyra, Kweires and Dier Ez Zor airbases.

Unless marked all units are based forward based at Hmeinyan airbase, Syria. The personnel from the units rotated to Syria for three to four months at a time.

Sukhoi Su-24M strike aircraft
4th Centre for Combat Application and Crew Training, Lipestk
11th Composite Aviation Regiment, Marinovk
37th Composite Regiment, Gvardeyskoy
98th Separate Mixed Aviation Regiment,Monchegorsk
277th Bomb Aviation Regiment (Su-24M2), Komosomolsk-an-Amor
455th Bomber Aviation Regiment, Voronezh
559th Bomber Aviation Regiment,Morozovsk
6980th (ex 2nd Composite Aviation Regiment), Chelyabinsk/Shagol
Sukhoi Su-25SM ground attack aircraft (forward based at Palmyra, T-4 and Dier ez Zor)
18th Guards Red Banner Assault Aviation Regiment, Chernigovka
37th Composite Aviation Regiment, Gvardeyskoye
266th Assault Aviation Regiment, Step
368th Assault Aviation Regiment Su-25SM/SM3), Budyannovsk
960th Assault Aviation Regiment (Su-25SM/SM3), Primosko Akhtarsk
999th , Kant
Su-30SM fighter aircraft
3rd Guards Fighter Aviation Regiment, Krymsk
14th Fighter Aviation Regiment, Khalino
22nd Fighter Aviation Regiment, Tsentralnaya Uglovaya
23rd Fighter Aviation Regiment, Dzengi
31st Guards Fighter Regiment, Millerovo
120th Mixed Aviation Regiment, Domma
929th V.P. Chkalova State Flight Test Centre, Akhtubinsk
Sukhoi Su-34 strike aircraft
47th Separate Mixed Aviation Regiment, Buturlinovka
257th Independent Composite Aviation Regiment, Khabarovsk Krai
277th Bomber Aviation Regiment, Komosomolsk-an-Amor
559th Separate Bomber Aviation Regiment, Morozovsk
Sukhoi Su-35S fighter aircraft
22nd Fighter Aviation Regiment, Tsentralnaya Uglovaya
23rd Fighter Aviation Regiment, Dzengi
159th Composite Aviation Regiment, Besovets
A-50 radar surveillance and command aircraft

144th Airborne Early Warning Aviation Regiment, Ivanovo
Tupolev Tu-22M-3 long range bomber
6950th (ex Red Banner Naval Missile Carrying Aviation Group), Olenegorsk (forward based at Mozdok)
52nd Heavy Bomber Aviation Regiment, Shaykovko (forward based at Mozdok)
6952nd (ex 200th Heavy Bomber Aviation Regiment), Belaya/Irkursk (forward based at Mozdok)
Tupolev Tu-95 bomber
6950th (ex184th Heavy Bomber Aviation Regiment) (home based at Engels)
Tupolev Tu-160 bomber
6950th (ex 121st Heavy Bomber Aviation Regiment) (home based at Engels)
MiG-29SMT multi-role fighter
116th Fighter Aviation Combat Employment Centre, Astrakhan (Sept to Dec 2017)
Ilyushin Il-20M signals intelligence aircraft
535th Independent Composite Transport Aviation Regiment, Rostov-on-Don (forward based at Hmeinyan airbase and Damascus International Airport)
Ilyushin Il-22PP signals intelligence aircraft
117th Independent Composite Transport Aviation Regiment, Orenburg (forward based at Hmeinyan airbase and Damascus International Airport)
Tupolev Tu-214R multi-sensor surveillance aircraft
RuAF?/Kazan Aircraft Production Company, Kazan
Forpost unmanned aerial vehicle
368th Assault Aviation Regiment, Budyannovsk

Russian Navy

Black Sea Fleet Contingent

The Black Sea Fleet is responsible for providing naval support to the Russian Group of Forces in Syria, as well as for the operation and security of the Russian naval base at Tartus in Syria. Force protection elements include a detachment of the 11th Independent Coastal Missile-Artillery Brigade K-300P Bastion-P anti-ship/land attack missile system based in the hills above Tartus. In September 2015, a battalion group of the 810th Naval Infantry Brigade deployed to Tartus. It deployed force protection teams to Aleppo and Palmyra. Contingents from the 61st and 336th Naval Infantry Brigades have since rotated into Syria.

Russian Navy Black Sea Fleet Deployments to Syria
(Dates refer to north/south bound transits through Bosphorous)
Moskova(Slava-class Cruiser) 25/9/15 to 8/1/16
Smetlivyy (Kashin-class Destroyer) 19/09/2015 to 27/12/15, 07/03/2016 to 9/6/16, 29/10/16 to 5/3/17, 22/05/2017 to 2/6/17
Ladnyy (Krivak-class frigate) 24/09/2015 to 7/10/15, 06/05/2016 to 9/6/16
Pytlivyy (Krivak-class frigate) 26/05/2016 to 2/7/16, 6/8/16 to 26/11/16, 22/7/17 to 3/8/17, 12/9/17 to 14/9/17
Admiral Grigorovich (Admiral Grigorovich-class frigate) 25/09/2016 to 16/10/16, 4/11/16 to 18/12/16, 02/03/2017 to 29/3/17, 7/4/17 to 11/7/17,

25/9/17 to 3/10/17, 2/12/17 to ??

Admiral Essen (Admiral Grigorovich-class frigate) 10/07/2017 to 21/9/17

Kovrovets (Natya I class Minesweeper) 14/02/2016 to 27/5/16, 27/12/16 to 2/5/17

Ivan Golubets (Natya I Minesweeper) 03/11/2017 to ??

Valentin Pikul (Natya I Minesweeper) 14/05/2016 to 17/8/16, 24/03/2017 to 7/8/17

Mirazh (Nanuchka-III Guided Missile Corvette)16/11/16 to ??, 05/10/2016 to 20/11/16

Zeleni Dol (Buyan-M Guided Missile Corvette)14/02/2016 to 13/4/16, 12/8/16 to 16/9/16,5/10/16 to?

Serpuhov (Buyan-M Guided Missile Corvette) 31/03/2018, 12/8/16 to 16/9/16, 5/10/16 to ??

R-109 (Tarantul-III Missile Boat) 24/09/2016 to ??

Ivanovets (Tarantul-III Missile Boat) 13/06/2016 to 19/10/16

Veliky Novgorod (Improved Kilo Submarine) Sept to Nov 17

Rostov-on-Don (Improved Kilo Submarine) Nov to Dec 16

Kolpino (Improved Kilo Submarine) Sept to Nov 17

Krasnodar (Improved Kilo Submarine) May to June 17

Russian Northern Fleet Task Group

Admiral Kuznetsov (Kuznetsov class aircraft carrier) 15/10/2016 to 9/2/17

Pyotr Velikiy (Kirov class nuclear powered battlecruiser) 15/10/2016 to 9/2/17

Severomorsk (Udaloy-I class destroyer) 15/10/2016 to 9/2/17

Vice Admiral Kulakov (Udaloy-I class destroyer) 15/10/2016 to 2/12/16

Russian Naval Aviation (embarked Admiral Kuznetsov, Oct 2016 - Jan 2017)

MiG-29KR multi-role combat aircraft

•110th Independent Shipborne Fighter Aviation Regiment, Severo-morsk-3

Su-33 multi-role combat aircraft

•110th Independent Shipborne Fighter Aviation Regiment, Severomorsk-3

Ka-27PS&PL/KA-29TB naval helicopters

•830th Independent Shipborne Anti-Submarine Helicopter Regiment, Severo-morsk-3

Caspian Sea Flotilla warships engaged in Kalibr cruise missile strikes, Oct 2015

Dagestan (Gepard-class frigate)

Grad Sviyazhsk   (Buyan-M-class corvette)

Uglich   (Buyan-M-class corvette)

Veliky Ustyug   (Buyan-M-class corvette)

Syria Express - Logistic Shipping sailings from Black Sea ports to Tartus, Syria
Russian Navy Landing Ships
(Number of north/south bound transits through Bosphorous)

	2015	2016	2017	Total
Saratov (Black Sea Fleet)	7	6		13
Nikolay Filchenkov				
(Black Sea Fleet)	8	4	6	18
Aleksandr Otrakovskiy(Northern Fleet)	9	6	3	18
Minsk (Baltic Fleet)	1	11	2	14
Georgiy Pobedonosets (Northern Fleet)		10	2	12
Aleksandr Shabalin (Baltic Fleet)	5	6	1	12
Tsezar Kunikov (Black Sea Fleet)	10	9	9	28
Novocherkassk (Black Sea Fleet)	11	5		16
Yamal (Black Sea Fleet)	5	8	11	24
Azov (Black Sea Fleet)	9	5	3	17
Korolev (Black Sea Fleet)	10	1	4	15
Total				187

Merchant Vessels chartered by Russian MOD logistic company, Oboronlogistica (Number of north/south bound transits through Bosphorous)

	2015	2016	2017	Total
Dvinitsa50 (ex MV Alican Deval)	1	4	5	10
Yauza	2	3		5
Kyzyl-60	1	2	3	6
Aleksandr Tkachenko	3	5	8	16
Leo 1		1		1
Taya Y		2		2
Atlantic Prodigy	1			1
Kazan-60 (ex Georgiy Agafonov")	1	3		4
Transfair	1			1
Vologda-50 (ex MV Dadali)	2	3		5
Transmar	1			1
Total	13	23	16	52

Appendix 2
Russian Military Fatalities in Syria, from October 2015 to December 2017

These tables are a compilation from a variety of sources, including RuMOD announcements and Russian media reports. They give the date, location and cause of soldiers deaths, as well as their unit where known.

24/10/15 Private Vadim Kostenko, RuAF, suicide
19/11/15 Captain Fedor Zhuravlyov, Spetsnaz, enemy fire
24/11/15 Lieutenant Colonel Oleg Peshkov, RuAF SU-24 pilot, shootdown
24/11/15 Marine Alexander Pozynich, 810th Naval Infantry Brigade, shootdown
1/2/16   Lieutenant Colonel Ivan Cheremisin, Spetsnaz GRU mortar attack
17/3/16   Senior Lieutenant Alexander Prokhorenko, Spetsnaz, enemy fire
12/4/16   Andrey Okladnikov, RuAF Mi-28 crew, non combat helicopter crash
12/4/16   Viktor Pankov RuAF Mi-28 crew, non-combat helicopter crash
7/5/16   Sergeant Anton Yerygin, International Mine Action Centre, sniper fire
2/5/16   Asker Bizhoyev, Military Police, shelling
3/6/16   Captain Maret Akhmetshim, Palmyra, in firefight
7/6/16   Junior Sergeant, Mikhail Shirokopoyas, Aleppo, mine
16/6/16   Sergeant Andrey Timoshenkov, 35th Army, suicide car-bomb
8/7/16   Lieutenant Evgeny Dolgin, RuAF Mi-35 crew, shootdown
8/7/16   Colonel Ryafagat Khabibulin, RuAF Mi-35 crew, shootdown
22/7/16   Private Nikita Shevchenko, 810th Naval Infantry Brigade, Aleppo, IED
1/8/16   Captain Roman Pavlov, RuAF Mi-8 crew, shootdown
1/8/16   Oleg Shelamov, RuAF Mi-8 crew, shootdown
1/8/16   Captain Pavel Shorohov, RuAF Mi-8 crew, shootdown
1/8/16   ?? Officer, Russian Centre for Reconciliation, shootdown
1/8/16   ??, Russian Centre for Reconciliation, Hostile fire, shootdown
5/12/16   Sergeant Nadezhda Durachenko, RuMOD Special Medical Unit, shelling
5/12/16   Sergeant Galina Mikhaylova, RuMOD Special Medical Unit, shelling
7/12/16   Colonel Ruslan Galitsky, 5th Guard Tank Brigade, 36th Army, shelling
16/2/17   ??, improvised explosive device
16/2/17   ??, improvised explosive device
16/2/17   ??, improvised explosive device
16/2/17   ??, improvised explosive device
2/3/17   Pte Artyum Gorbynov, 96th Separate Intelligence Brigade, ambush
9/4/17   Igor Zavidniy, contract soldier, mortar fire

20/4/17 Major Sergei Bordov, advisor to SAA, enemy fire
3/5/17 Lieutenant Colonel Alexei Buchelnikov, advisor to SAA, sniper
11/7/17 Captain Nikolay Afanasov, advisor to SAA unit, Hama, mortar fire
4/917 ??, contract soldiers, mortar attack
4/917 ??, contract soldiers, mortar attack
23/9/17 Lieutenant General Valery Asapov, 5th Army, mortar attack or drone bomb?
30/9/17 Colonel Valery Fedyanin, 61st Naval Infantry Brigade, Hama, mortar attack
10/10/17 Captain Yuri Kopylov, RuAF Su-24 crew, non-combat accident
10/10/17 Captain Yuri Medvedkov, RuAF Su-24 crew, non-combat accident
31/12/17 Renet Oimadiyev, mortar attack
31/12/17 ?? mortar attack
31/12/17 Major Artem Nikolaevich Kulish, RuAF Mi-24 crew, non-combat accident
31/12/17 ?? Matveev, RuAF Mi-24 crew, non-combat accident

The following casualties have not been confirmed by the Russian Ministry of Defence
01/10/15 Sergeant Edward Sokurov, 346th Spetsnaz Brigade, enemy fire
19/12/15 Maxim Sorochenko, Spetsnaz GRU, enemy fire
6/6/16 Oleg Arhireev, Spetsnaz GRU, landmine
14/6/16 Senior lieutenant Sergei Pechalnov, Spetsnaz GRU, landmine
19/6/16 Colonel Vladimir Bekish, 5th Guards Tank Brigade, 36th Army, shelling
8/12/16 Major Sanal Sanchirov, 56th Guards Air Assault Brigade, mortar attack
5/2/17 Lieutenant Colonel Igor Vorona, enemy fire
?/2/17 to ?/ 3/17 Sergei Travin, enemy fire
8/4/17 Lieutenant Colonel Gennady Perfilyev, enemy fire
18/4/17 ?? Naval Infantry, enemy fire
3/5/17 Captain Evgeny Konstantinov, enemy fire
3/5/17 Major Alexander Skladan, enemy fire
6/17 Ensign ND Kalandarov, 3rd Guards Spetsnaz Brigade, enemy fire
2/8/17 Captain Kurban Kasumov, 3rd Guards Spetsnaz Brigade, mortar attack
3/8/17 Valery Emdyukov, 3rd Guards Spetsnaz Brigade, mortar attack
16/9/17 Colonel Rustem Abzalov, enemy fire
16/9/17 Vladimir Tarasyuk, enemy fire
18–23/9/17 Magomed Terbulatov, Chechen military police, enemy fire
?/9/17 Yuri Khabarov, enemy fire
?/10/17 Mark Neymark, Spetsnaz GRU, landmine

Appendix 3
Russian Aircraft Losses in Syria, 2015-2018

This is compilation from a variety of sources, including RuMOD announcements, Russian media reports and confirmed via social media imagery

24/11/2015	Su-24 (RuAF), northern Latakia, shot down by TUAF F-16, 1 crew killed, 1 rescued
24/11/2015	Mi-8 (RuAF), northern Latakia, hit by AAA during CSAR, crew rescued, 1 crew killed
12/04/2016	Mi-28N (RuAF), eastern Homs, accident, two killed
08/07/2016	Mi-35 (RuAF or SyAAF), east Palmyra, hit by AAA, two Russian aircrew killed. RuMOD claimed this was a Syrian Helicopter being flown by Russian crew
01/08/2016	Mi-8MTSHV (RuAF), Idlib province, crashed after technical fault, five crew and passengers killed
03/11/2016	Mi-24 (RuAF), east Palmyra, hit on ground fire, crew recovered
14/11/2016	MiG-29KUB (RuN), crashed in Mediterranean due to technical fault, crew recovered
03/12/2016	Su-33 (RuN), crashed in Mediterranean due to technical fault, crew recovered
10/10/2017	Su-24 (RuAF), crashed in Latakia province due to technical fault, two crew killed
31/12/2017	Mi-24 (RuAF), crashed in Hama province after technical fault or wire strike, two crew killed
12/1/2018	Forpost (RuAF), crashed in Hama province, cause unknown
3/2/2018	Su-25 (RuAF) shot down in Idlib province by MANPAD

References, Sources and Bibliography

In researching this book I have not stuck to the traditional path that is usually followed when writing military history. The nature of the conflict in Syria meant it was just not possible to gain access to documents, interview participants or visit many of the country's battlefields.

Often the only eye that can be opened on the Syrian conflict is through non-traditional sources – social-media feeds from all sides in the war, as well as analysis of news media and commercial satellite imagery. The internet has made it possible to access the view Syrian, Iranian and Russian military inolvment in the Syrian war to a degree that has not been possible in earlier conflicts.

This is also the era of real-time monitoring of aircraft and ship movements which opens up new perspectives for military analysis that has just not been available before.

Aircraft movements can tracked from their ADS-B transponder data, via:
https://www.flightradar24.com/

Ship movements can similarly be tracked through AIS transponder data, via:
https://www.vesselfinder.com/

The movement of ships through the Bosphorus is monitored by a network of ship spotters based in the Turkish city of Istanbul. Their work is posted on:
https://turkishnavy.net/foreign-warship-on-bosphorus/foreign-warship-on-bosphorus-in-2015/
https://turkishnavy.net/foreign-warship-on-bosphorus/foreign-warship-on-bosphorus-in-2016/
https://turkishnavy.net/foreign-warship-on-bosphorus/foreign-warship-on-bosphorus-in-2017/

There are a number of Twitter feeds where the ship spotters report naval activity, with one of the most informative being: https://twitter.com/yorukisik?lang=en

A key part of monitoring the Syrian war is accessing commercial satellite imagery that is now available to allow a level of ground truth geo-locating still or video imagery to confirm its veracity. I have made extensive use of the following sites:
http://wikimapia.org/country/Syria/
https://www.terraserver.com/
https://www.google.co.uk/intl/en_uk/earth/

There are several online communities and Twitter sites devoted to geo-locating locations and military activity in Syria. This has been one of the most effective:
https://twitter.com/obretix?lang=en

There are a number of online investigative organisations that monitor events in Syria and have provided much information about the conflict. The most famous is *https://www.bellingcat.com* which is run by Elliott Higgins.

The Ukrainian-based *https://informnapalm.org* specialises in investigations into the Russian military. The South African-based Oyrx Blog *http://spioenkop. blogspot.co.uk* has carved a niche analysing Islamic State online material for issues of military significance.

Over the past three years I have been monitoring the progress of the Syrian war through a variety of means, creating a series of Powerpoint briefings incorporating multiple sources of information. They combine still imagery from social media posts and screen grabs from video clips posted online by individuals or news media organisations. These extensive briefings are reproduced on my website and can be accessed via: *http:www.timripley.co.uk*

References

In several chapters I have referenced a number of specific secondary sources such as new and government websites as well as social-media posts, as follows:

Chapter 3: Intervention Putin Style

The high-level discussions that led to the Russian and Iranian intervention in Syria are described in the following articles:

https://thesaker.is/the-commander-of-the-russian-military-grouping-in-syria-gives-first-interview/

http://www.reuters.com/article/us-mideast-crisis-syria-soleimani-in-sigh-idUSKCN0S02BV20151006

https://www.nytimes.com/2015/09/28/world/middleeast/iraq-agrees-to-share-intelligence-on-isis-with-russia-syria-and-iran.html?_r=0

Chapter 4: The Execution

Further context to the Russian and Iranian deployment to Syria can be found in these articles:

http://www.newsweek.com/man-who-stares-boats-449088

http://www.newsweek.com/russian-votes-syria-hint-size-military-deployment-501515

http://www.euronews.com/2015/09/29/russian-navy-pours-south-through-bosphorus

https://theintercept.com/2016/01/28/israeli-drone-feeds-hacked-by-british-and-american-intelligence/

Chapter 5: The Holding Action: Hama and Homs

The details of the early phase of Russian deployments to Syria can be found in the following articles:

https://informnapalm.org/en/russian-solntsepyok-heavy-flamethrower-systems-were-noticed-in-syria/

https://informnapalm.org/en/russia-began-a-concealed-ground-operation-in-syria/

The following social-media posts and video uploads were sourced:

1.   Cluster bombs/MLRS/TOS-1A test firing in Idlib and Hama

https://www.youtube.com/watch?v=4WpqnzKmZ-I

https://www.youtube.com/watch?v=6IsOBGDU98w

https://www.youtube.com/watch?v=WfacUxfJbFI

https://twitter.com/galandecZP

2.   TOS-1 firing in Latakia filmed from drone

https://www.youtube.com/watch?v=R1crK-_FsKY
https://www.youtube.com/watch?v=U1RXJvpHNyU
https://www.youtube.com/watch?v=s00XnMVPuA0
https://www.youtube.com/watch?v=YegxUegrl_4
3.   Su-25 strike in Hama
https://www.youtube.com/watch?v=x21fA3U8uWI
4.   Fighting around Shal al Ghab
https://www.youtube.com/watch?v=bNvEg9v3S0g
5.   Mi-25s over Hama province
https://www.youtube.com/watch?v=Y5S17riFMgw
6.   Syrian tanks, MLRS and Sagger missiles in Hama
https://www.facebook.com/Military.Media.Syria.Central/videos/
vb.465271610346058/476140002592552/?type=2&theater
7.   Syrian infantry assault with 4 x Mi-24 in support
https://www.facebook.com/Military.Media.Syria.Central/videos/
vb.465271610346058/475895719283647/?type=2&theater
8.   Syrian MLRS strike and Mi-24s in support
https://www.youtube.com/watch?v=RgNqAP1dEvE
9.   *Several Mi-25s fly over town in Hama*
https://www.youtube.com/watch?v=MyqnrhmNOa0
10.   Compilation of Mi-24 over Hama footage
https://www.facebook.com/Military.Media.Syria.Central/videos/
vb.465271610346058/474510192755533/?type=2&theater
Chapter 6. Red Air
The Ukrainian online group Inform Napalm has produced a very detailed analysis of Russian air crew involved in operations over Syria, at:
https://informnapalm.org/en/russian-bombs-civilians/
Chapter 9. Battle of Palmyra, March 2016
Details of the activity of Russian army units in the Palmyra operation can be found in this article:
https://informnapalm.org/en/syrian-mission-russian-120th-artillery-brigade/
11. Aleppo: Attack and Counter Attack – The Final offensive
Details of how Russian Special Forces held off rebel attacks are included in the following post:
https://www.youtube.com/watch?v=4Mmxpx7B1vY
Chapter 15. Back to Palmyra
https://informnapalm.org/en/russian-gifts-isis-left-behind-abandoned-military-base-palmyra/
Chapter 14. Boots on the Ground
The deployment of Russian MPs to Syria is described in this article:
https://warontherocks.com/2017/10/not-so-soft-power-russias-military-police-in-syria/
Chapter 15 The New Enemy
This South African Oyrx Blog pulled together a really good analysis of Islamic

State armoured units and logistics in this post:
http://spioenkop.blogspot.co.uk/2017/08/armour-in-islamic-state-story-of.html
Chapter 19 Operation Dawn
The promotion of General Surovikin is described here
https://russiandefpolicy.blog/tag/sergey-surovikin/
Chapter 20. Lifting the Siege of Dier Ez Zor
Russian logistic operations in Syria are described in this webpage:
http://eng.mil.ru/en/news_page/country/more.htm?id=12151279@egNews
US operations after the fall of Raqqa are described in this transcript:
*https://www.defense.gov/News/Transcripts/Transcript-View/Article/1359137/
department-of-defense-press-briefing-by-general-jarrard-via-teleconfer-
ence-from/*

Bibliography
The following books were referenced during the writing of Operation Aleppo.
They mainly profile a baseline of reference material on the performance of Russian-sourced aircraft, helicopters, warships and military equipment.
The Middle East Military Balance 1999-2000, Shlomo Brom, Belfer Centre Studies in International Security, 2003
Sukhoi Su-25 Frogfoot: Close Air Support Aircraft, Yefim Gordon and Alan Dawes, Airlife, 2004
Sukhoi Su-24 Fencer: Soviet Swing-Wing Bomber, Yefim Gordon and Keith Dexter, Aerofax 2005
Flankers: The New Generation, Yefim Gordon, Midland, 2001
Ilyushin/Beriev A-50: The 'Soviet Sentry', Yefim Gordon, Casemate, 2015
Mikoyan Mig-29 Fulcrum: Multi-Role Fighter, Yefim Gordon, Airlife, 1999
Soviet/Russian Aircraft Weapons: Since World War Two, Yefim Gordon, Midland, 2004
Soviet/Russian Unmanned Aerial Vehicles, Yefim Gordon, Midland, 2005
Tupolev Tu-95 and Tu-142, Yefim Gordon, Crecy, 2017
Antonov's Turboprop Twins: An-24/An-26/An-30/An-32, Dmitriy Komissarov and Yefim Gordon, Midland, 2003
Ilyushin Il-76: Russia's Versatile Jet Freighter, Yefim Gordon and Dmitriy Kommissarov, Aerofax, 2006
Mil Mi-8 / Mi-17 Rotary-Wing Workhorse and Warhorse, Yefim Gordon and Dmitriy Komissarov, Midland, 2003
Mil Mi-24 Hind: Attack Helicopter, Yefim Gordon and Dmitriy Komissarov, Airlife, 2002
Soviet / Russian AWACS Aircraft, Yefim Gordon and Dmitriy Komissarov, Midland, 2005
OKB Ilyushin: A History of the Design Bureau and Its Aircraft, Sergey Komissarov and Yefim Gordon, Midland, 2004
Russian Tactical Aviation: Since 2001, Dmitriy Komissarov and Yefim Gordon, Hikoki, 2017

Sukhoi Su-24: Famous Russian Aircraft, Yefim Gordon and Dmitriy Komissarov, Crecy, 2015

Tupolev Tu-160: Soviet Strike Force Spearhead, Dmitriy Komissarov and Yefim Gordon, Schiffer Military History, 2016

The Syrian Jihad: The Evolution of an Insurgency, Charles Lister, Oxford University Press, 2017

Su-25 'Frogfoot' Units In Combat, by Alexander Mladenov, Rolando Ugolini and Gareth Hector, Osprey 2015

Israel's Lebanon War, by Ze'ev Schiff and Ehud Ya'ari, Conterpoint, 1985

Russia's New Ground Forces: Capabilities, Limitations and Implications for International Security, by Igor Sutyagin and Justin Bronk, RUSI, 2017

Soviet Air Defence Missiles, Steven Zaloga, Jane's 1985

Index
People
Americans and British

124th Brigade Republican Guard 173
555th Regiment 42, 77, 78,
800th Regiment Republican Guard 104, 144, 170, 173, 174, 175, 176
Tiger Force 13, 14, 15, 42, 56, 57, 60, 61, 66, 72, 74, 77, 101, 102, 103, 104, 110, 111, 119, 121, 123, 124, 125, 128, 129, 136, 157, 158, 159, 160, 164, 165, 166, 167, 172, 173, 174, 175, 176, 177, 181, 182, 183, 208

Syrian National Defence Force, Para-military and Militia Units
Syrian Marines Regiment (Fouj Al-Mughawayr Al-Bahar) 74
Desert Hawks 72, 111, 123, 1668
Euphrates Hawks 170
Palestinian Jerusalem Brigade (Liwa al-Quds) 104, 105, 111, 112, 123, 126, 128, 164
Syrian Social Nationalist Party Militia 80, 81
Ba'ath Party Militia 78
Gozarto Protection Force 41
ISIS Hunters 136, 145, 173
Lebanese Hizbullah 18, 24, 25, 55, 56, 57, 58, 59, 62, 66, 72, 176, 179, 183, 184, 185, 186, 187, 188, 193
Firqa Fatayyemoun (Iranian/Afghani paramilitary) 58, 72, 128, 183

Locations
Abu Kamal 169, 181, 182, 183, 184, 185, 186, 187
Hmeinyan air base 29, 30, 34, 37, 39, 41, 44, 45, 49, 52, 53, 55, 56, 62, 63, 65, 69, 70, 71, 84, 87, 88, 97, 102, 120, 135, 154, 161, 163, 164, 173, 178, 187, 188, 189, 190, 196, 197, 198, 199
Kweires air base 56, 60, 61, 66, 111, 141, 160, 197
Manbij 152, 160
Mayadeen 181, 182, 183, 186, 191
Mozdok air base 48, 50, 71, 79, 81, 145, 184, 199
Al Shafirah garrison 56, 57
Sukhnah 77, 142, 170, 173, 174, 175,
Tabqa air base 78, 139, 155, 166
T-4 air base 41, 42, 72, 143, 145, 147, 148, 149, 165, 173

Military Equipment
Russian Navy Warships
Admiral Kuznetsov (Kuznetsov class aircraft carrier) 93, 100, 115, 116, 117, 120, 121, 122, 134, 188, 189, 194, 200
Pyotr Velikiy (Kirov class nuclear powered battlecruiser) 116, 134, 200
Moskova (Sava class cruiser) 50, 63
Severomorsk (Udaloy-I class destroyer) 116, 200
Vice Admiral Kulakov (Udaloy-I class destroyer) 116, 200
Admiral Grigorovich (Admiral Grigorovich-class frigate) 120, 121, 134, 199
Admiral Essen (Admiral Grigorovich-class frigate) 175, 200
Aleksandr Otrakovskiy (Landing Ships) 27, 201
Merchant Vessels chatered by RuMOD, via Oboronlogistica
Dvinitsa50 (ex MV Alican Deval) 28, 201
Aleksandr Tkachenko (Ro-Ro) 132, 135, 201
Vologda-50 (ex MV Dadali) 28, 201
Russian Missiles and Weapons
Bastion-P anti-ship missile 121, 188, 199
Iskander ballistic missile, 70, 197
Kalibr cruise missile 38, 48, 50, 89, 104, 120, 121, 134, 165, 168, 184, 189
Kh-55 air launched cruise missile 47, 50, 51, 89, 189
Kh-101 50, 89, 121, 146, 163, 168
Pantsir S1 anti-aircraft system 69, 76, 189, 196, 197
S-300 surface-to-air missile 189, 196, 197
S-400 surface-to-air missile 63, 69, 188, 189, 196
Russian Tanks, Vehicles and Artillery
BTR-82 troop carrier 21, 29, 37, 40, 48, 76, 78, 178, 181, 197,
Lynx vehicle 88, 102

T-90 tank 29, 59, 60, 66, 78, 119, 126, 170, 183, 197
Tigr vehicle 31, 88, 89, 151, 181, 189,
Typhoon mine protected vehicle 89, 189
TOS-1A thermobaric rocket system 30, 36, 39, 72, 74, 105, 145, 150, 188, 197, 206
BM-30 Smerch rocket system 30, 72, 89, 197
2A56 MSTA 152mm artillery 30, 37, 43, 78, 110, 144, 173, 181, 188, 197
Russian Air Force (RuAF) Aircraft
A-50 radar aircraft 90, 165, 173, 188, 198
Forpost tactical drone 13, 52, 53, 54, 64, 89, 90, 110, 115, 121, 123, 129, 130, 143, 145, 161, 163, 188, 190, 194
Il-20M reconnaissance aircraft 199
Il-22PP reconnaissance aircraft 199
Il-76 transport aircraft 28, 29, 33, 41, 42, 56, 65, 71, 79, 84, 135, 146
Il-78 tanker 29, 121
Ka-52 attack helicopter 70, 76, 89, 117, 142, 147, 150, 172, 188, 189
Mi-8 transport helicopter 30, 56, 62, 71, 72, 76, 107, 202, 204
Mi-24/25 attack helicopter 30, 39, 42, 43, 44, 62, 70, 71, 72, 73, 74, 76, 84, 99, 144, 173, 188, 203, 204
Mi-28 attack helicopter 70, 74, 76, 89, 142, 147, 148, 149, 151, 173, 188, 189, 202, 204
Mi-35 attack helicopter 72, 79, 147, 202, 204
MiG-29SMT fighter aircraft 199
Orlan-10 mini drone 52, 197
Su-24M strike jet 29, 42, 45, 46, 62, 63, 70, 159, 182, 185, 188, 190, 198, 202, 204
Su-25SM ground aircraft 29, 39, 45, 46, 49, 50, 64, 69, 92, 159, 164, 173, 176, 188, 190, 198, 204, 207, 208
Su-30SM fighter aircraft 29, 44, 45, 71, 146, 147, 163, 169, 188, 189, 198
Su-34 strike jet 29, 45, 48, 49, 52, 70, 79, 84, 89, 92, 104, 125, 159, 164, 185, 188, 189, 190, 198, 202
Su-35S fighter aircraft 45, 46, 147, 168, 188, 189, 198
Tu-22M-3 bomber 46, 47, 50, 51, 71, 79, 142, 146, 184, 185, 186, 198
Tu-95 bomber 46, 47, 50, 89, 121, 146, 163, 168, 189, 199
Tu-160 bomber 22, 46, 47, 50, 89, 92, 189, 199
Tu-214R reconnaissance aircraft 89, 188, 199
Russian Naval Aviation Aircraft
MiG-29KR fighter jet 115, 116, 120, 121, 200, 204
Su-33 fighter jet 115, 116, 120, 121, 189, 200, 204
Ka-27PS&PL/KA-29TB naval helicopters 200
Syrian and Iranian Aircraft
Aerospatiale Gazelle light helicopter (SyAAF) 74, 150, 170, 174, 199
Avro RJ-85 (Iran) 32
Boeing 747 Jumbo Jet (Iran) 32
C-130E Hercules (Iran) 33, 55, 65, 71
Mi-17 146, 172
Shahed-129 armed drone (Iran) 169, 184
Coalition Aircraft & Weapons
AH-64D Apache attack helicopter (US) 156
F-16 Fighting Falcon (US, Danish, Jordan, Portugal, Turkey) 63, 108, 122, 155, 159, 188, 204
C-130J Hercules (US & UK) 116, 154
MQ-9 Reaper armed drone (US & UK) 108, 189
MQ-1 Predator armed drone (US) 189
Tomahawk Land Attack Missile (US) 48, 161
Tornado GR4 bomber (UK) 159
Typhoon fighter (UK) 116, 172
CV-22 Osprey tilt rotor (US) 152, 153

Operation Aleppo, (c) Tim Ripley, 2018

Printed in Great Britain
by Amazon

80283540R00129